REGES CHRISTIANISSIMI

REGES CHRISTIANISSIMI

*History and Interpretation
in Bede's Account of the
Early Kings of Northumbria*

Clive Tolley

GRACEWING

First published in England in 2018
by
Gracewing
2 Southern Avenue
Leominster
Herefordshire HR6 0QF
United Kingdom
www.gracewing.co.uk

ISBN 978 085244 930 1

Cover design by Clive Tolley

Typeset by Word and Page, Chester, UK

Contents

Illustrations

Front cover. Bede the Scholar, window by Roy Coomber, 2011

Preface

'Christ is the Morning Star, who when the night of this world is past brings to his saints the promise of the light of life and opens everlasting day.' These words, presented in striking graphic form in Durham Cathedral on the Alington memorial, designed by George Pace, derive from Bede's commentary on the Apocalypse. They may be said to epitomise Bede's mission: to fill the darkness of error with Christ's light, an inspiration which fills his whole approach to the world and its history.

Archaeology may tell us much, but the world of early Northumbria remains one that comes to us largely through the words of Bede, who spent his life within the confines of the Northumbrian monasteries of Monkwearmouth and Jarrow but who nonetheless presented us with a picture of the whole realm of the Northumbria, and England more widely, that he lived in. Bede wrote many works, many being concerned with biblical exegesis, but he is best known for his magisterial *Historia Ecclesiastica Gentis Anglorum* ('Ecclesiastical History of the English People'), which he completed around 731.[1] Bede had one overriding theme: to show the spiritual development of the English people up to his time, from being pagans to staunch members of the Catholic Church.

The essays in this volume, originally composed at different times for various occasions, are merely case studies: I pick some incidents from the reigns of three (almost) successive early Northumbrian monarchs, Æthelfrith, Eadwine and Oswald,[2] all of which concern the coming of Christianity or interaction with the British Christianity which already existed among the native Celtic-speaking population before the Anglo-Saxon conversion. I devote two essays to each king: the first is 'secular', the aim being

---

[1] I use the standard edition of Bede's *Historia Ecclesiastica*, edited by Bertram Colgrave and R. A. B. Mynors, but at times provide my own translations in order to convey more precisely my own readings of the meaning of the text.
[2] Forms of names cause difficulties: rather than following the semi-latinised versions Bede employs, I have standardised names to their Old English forms (so Eadwine rather than Edwin, for example).

to understand the history from a modern perspective. Yet history was not understood in a modern way in the past; while Bede's spiritual concerns would not have been shared by everyone, it is a truism that the aim of uncovering supposedly objective history reflects a modern epistemology (notwithstanding the subjectively oriented truth that each age surely gets the history it craves): for past ages, history was part of a tradition, shaped to represent what people understood their position in the world to be based on a religious understanding—first pagan within the period under consideration, then Christian—of the cosmos. The second essay of each pair therefore looks at some of the more 'spiritual' (but not always Christian) understanding of history that Bede and his sources, and related traditions, espoused. A certain amount of overlap and repetition has been unavoidable.

I hope that the essays presented here will prove of interest both to historians and to those with a more spiritually inspired interest in the early years of the kingdom of Northumbria. The title is based on Bede's description of Oswald, 'Christianissimus rex'; Eadwine is similarly lauded for his Christian faith, and even the pagan Æthelfrith is regarded as an instrument of God's wrath.

Acknowledgements

The essay on 'Æthelfrith and the Battle of Chester' is a slightly revised version of that published (but without notes) under the same title in the *Journal of the Chester Archaeological Society* 86 (2016), pp. 51–95.

The essay on 'Oswald's Victory at Denisesburna' was published in *Hexham Historian* 27 (2017), pp. 57–73.

The essay on 'Oswald's Tree' is based upon one published, under the same title, in a less developed form, in *Pagans and Christians. The Interplay between Christian Latin and Traditional Germanic Cultures in Early Medieval Europe* (Germania Latina II), ed. T. Hofstra, L. A. J. R. Houwen and A. A. MacDonald (Groningen: University of Groningen, 1995), pp. 149–73.

I thank the original publishers for permission to reissue my essays in the present collection.

I would like also to thank the various readers, both anonymous and known to me, who have commented on the essays, and the editors of the journals where publication originally took place for their various suggestions. I thank Prof. John Hines for pointing me to some archaeological reports on Northumbria as I was drawing the work to a close. I acknowledge the permission granted by the Digital Atlas of the Roman Empire project to use their maps covering central Britannia as the basis for my maps of this area around the year 600.

The front cover shows a window from St Bede's church, Rotherham, depicting Bede the scholar, designed by Roy Coomber, 2011, and produced by Pendle Stained Glass Ltd, Padiham, Lancashire, whom we thank for permission to reproduce the image.

I thank my wife, Patricia, for her support and for proofreading the articles—and, many years ago now, for the gift of the Colgrave and Mynors edition of Bede's *Historia Ecclesiastica Gentis Anglorum*.

Thinking about Typology

THERE IS LITTLE NEED, I think, to explain the basis of argument in the 'secular' chapters of this book, as it will be self-evident. Yet while history may, for most modern readers, be a series of objectifiable events, an interplay of interactions between actors—all human—with different motivations, Bede, of course, did not read the past in this way. History for him is a playing out of divine purpose, and the events that lead up to the conversion of the English act as a sort of *praeparatio evangelica*. He understood history as having a moral purpose: it offered a stage on which to arrange past events and characters to demonstrate the unfolding of a moral or political truth (Ray 1997, 11–13). Bede, however, more than most historians of his era, was above all a biblical exegete: as Markus (1975, 13) observes, 'Perhaps we fail to do justice to Bede the ecclesiastical historian if we fail to read his historical work as he would have wished it to be read: in the light of his reflections on the "sacred history" contained in his commentaries on the Bible. In the perspective of the scriptures the struggle between the holy and the wicked was endemic.' This struggle was epitomised most forcefully in the work of one of Bede's major models, St Augustine of Hippo, who characterised the citizens of heaven in the world as denizens of the City of God. Augustine's is essentially an eschatological view of history, looking forward to its fulfilment at the Parousia, and this is reflected in Bede's approach to history, which 'turns on the belief that the lives and actions of the heavenly citizens on earth could give a foretaste of the future life, and more than that, were the precious evidence of the chord which already joined them to their true homeland' (Mayr-Harting 1976, 1). Yet for Bede, unlike for earlier Church historians such as Eusebius or Orosius, history was no simple progression, an advance to a goal (such as the triumphant fusion of Church and Empire in the politeia of the fourth century) (Markus 1975, 13).

Most of Bede's works consist of biblical exegesis, and he followed patristic models, his approach deriving ultimately (although indirectly) in particular from Origen, his more immediate inspirations being the works of Gregory the Great and Augustine.[1] Much of this approach is typological—a way of thinking that is largely alien to the modern mind, but commonplace for the patristic and medieval thinker (as pointed out forcefully by Laistner 1957, 160): repeated patterns and symbolic links are found between historical events, which make manifest the divine purpose.[2] As Holder (1990, 407) points out, Bede was careful not to allegorise away the literal meaning of texts (as Gregory, but not Augustine, had tended to do: Thacker 2005, 15–16), but he saw texts as imbued with a higher sense as well.

How does typology work? In biblical terms, many of the events of the Old Testament act as *types* or prefigurations to the *antitypes* of the New: for example, the sojourn of Jonah in the whale's belly (Jonah 1:17) stands in typical symbolic relationship with the antitype of Christ's sojourn in Hades after the Crucifixion. The key text, often cited by Bede (Holder 1990, 409), upon which typology is based is I Corinthians 10:11, 'Now all these things happened to them in figure, and they are written for our correction'. To delve further into the relationship between type and antitype, and how far that relationship is ontological and how far interpretative, would require a much deeper treatment than can be offered here; patristic interpretations do not all agree in their approach beyond accepting that some relationship existed which manifested divine providence. Origen, for example, did not accept that a historical event could act as a type to another historical event (*Commentary on John* 10.110), and railed

---

[1] He was fond of saying he followed in the footsteps of the Fathers (see Holder 1990, 401; Thacker 2005, 5 n. 23, notes several instances with references, but also observes that Bede's attitude was distinctly unservile towards them). Bede's chief sources were Ambrose, Augustine, Jerome and Gregory the Great, along with Cyprian, Hilary of Poitiers, Isidore of Seville and Cassiodorus, with occasional use of Origen, Basil of Caesarea, Gregory of Nazianzus and John Chrysostom; the dominant influence was the Alexandrian tradition of allegorical exegesis stemming from Origen (Holder 1990, 404–5). For a general account of Bede as a Church historian, see Mayr-Harting (1991, ch. 2) and, more penetratingly, Thacker (2010).

[2] The standard work on typology is de Lubac (1959–64), but see also Simonetti (1994) for a much briefer and accessible introduction.

against those who thought in this way, so his interpretation of Christ as the fulfilment of the Passover, for example, rejected the idea that the sacrificed Lamb of God was the antitype to the type of the Passover lamb of Exodus 12; rather, the antitype had an allegorical sense, consuming the sacrifice being realised as 'inwardly digesting' the Word of God 'embodied' in Scripture and deriving spiritual sustenance from it (Dawson 2001, 72–4). On Bede's more immediate sources, Gregory the Great and Augustine, Thacker (2005, 18) notes that whereas for Gregory, the Old Testament was an inexhaustible reservoir of moral exemplars (and need not be interpreted literally), 'for Augustine it was a pregnant narrative of the history of the people of God; the theme of the two cities intertwined throughout time invested the text with concurrent literal and figurative significance'; it was Augustine, in Thacker's view, that exercised the more fundamental influence on Bede.

Typology was overwhelmingly applied to the narratives of the Bible, and its application in this context was all but universally accepted. What of non-biblical, and post-incarnation, history? Typology, if applied to history, would enforce an essentially figurative, rather than literal, approach, just as it does in reading the Bible—'a grand exercise in the use of the imagination', as Meyvaert (1976, 45–6) called it—and a 'true' understanding of history would involve grasping the figurative connection between events.

Yet can Bede's *Historia Ecclesiastica* be read typologically? The obvious answer is no. Bede makes reference to the Bible often enough, but only as a moral exemplar, never figuratively—and in this he differs from Augustine, whose whole *City of God* might be described as a typological history of Rome (Furry 2013, 51–9).[3] It seems that Bede 'did not think it appropriate to figurally exegete the signs of history which God can and certainly did use, since they lacked any theological significance apart from God's taking them up into his providential care' (*ibid.*, 88). Scholars often emphasise the need to consider Bede's exegetical work

---

[3] Furry (2013, 54) points out some examples that would easily have lent themselves to a figural interpretation, such as the case of the apostate king Eadbald, son of Æthelberht, who goes mad, to be compared with Saul with his fits of madness under the power of an evil spirit.

alongside his *Historia Ecclesiastica*; Furry (2013) goes further and offers a detailed and extended discussion of the problem of the dichotomy in approach between his exegetical and historical works. The arguments are complex, and can only be touched upon here. One important issue Furry raises is just how far Bede really understood Augustine's elevated theological thought; he takes the example of Augustine's commentaries on the Genesis account of creation to make his point (*ibid.*, 71–86).

For Augustine, as God is eternal, creation cannot take place in time, since that would mean that time and change already existed and there would be no true eternity; God's act of creation is thus not like our acts of making. 'In principio' and creation refer to the eternal utterance of the Word, who is Christ: it is not that God spoke (to create the world) and then ceased speaking; rather, the utterance is eternal, and creation is eternal, all things coming into being at once (with an eternal existence in the Word). The days of creation form a logical, but not temporal, progression, and the temporal form of narrative given in Genesis acts as a story, understood as a historical account only by those who are not able to comprehend that it is essentially a metaphor. The form given to creation through the Father's uttering of the Word comes to abide in creation through the Spirit. Creation thus reflects the nature and relationship of the Trinity. History, then, is creation seen through time, and it forever takes on the form that God assigns it.

Bede, not wishing to abandon the literal sense of biblical texts, envisages a tension between a supposedly 'literal' and an 'allegorical' reading of the creation story, whereas for Augustine no such dichotomy exists, as the literal sense of the story — creation in eternity — is that which can be derived from a metaphorical reading. Bede, in short, interprets creation as if he were beholding it unfold, whereas for Augustine it is a matter of logical discourse.

There are deep implications for what history means in these varying understandings of creation. For Augustine, creation is given form in the primal divine *rationes*, and it is not only creation that has form and structure, but the entire course of human history. All of creation and human history are, through the *rationes*, inchoately present in the act of creation (represented narratively as lasting six days), and all the happenings of history are realisations of these *rationes*. For Bede, creation is a mechanical act of making, and hence God can intervene in the world, but this is meaningless within Augustine's understanding: God is not externally related to creation, but is in everything in the cosmos, and every action in the world is thus an action of God, not because it is not an action of a creature, but because it is by God's action that the creature is itself and has its own activity. Creation does not need to be given extra revelatory significance through special intervention: it possesses it by virtue of its existence — all creation points to God and Christ the Word. Bede, not comprehending this, simply viewed Scripture as an account of special revelation, beyond which it was not necessary or meaningful to read history exegetically. For Augustine, history rather points beyond itself, educating humanity about its origin and destination; every historical event and person is intrinsically charged with revelatory significance, and is thus capable of figural exegesis. In contrast, for Bede, God must act and take up particular historical events to give them revelatory significance. Furry concludes (*ibid*. 86) that 'Bede attempted to integrate theology and history, but was unable to do so in a coherent way that made theological sense of Genesis 1, and this manifests itself in various ways throughout his *œuvre*'.

Furry makes a strong case (and only a small part of his argumentation has been mentioned here). Yet we may, I think, be allowed to entertain some nagging doubts, at least over whether matters are quite so simple. Perhaps, indeed, Bede's intellect was insufficient to grasp Augustine's meaning; but Bede may also have had in mind his audience, many of whom would not have been so gifted. Another factor that may have made Bede wary of spelling out potential figurations with historical characters, apart from the fact that Origen regarded such a practice as illegitimate, is the pressing heresy of the time, Monothelitism, which saw Christ as having only one will: to present a person as acting figurally in history could be seen to imply a diminution or absence of free will on their part; if a figural reading were offered, it might have been considered wise to do so no more firmly than through hints. Furry also raises, but then dismisses, the idea that Bede may have deliberately not made explicit any figural readings of history, allowing his readers to find the connections; I am not so sure this is at all beyond the bounds of possibility. If Bede did couch his history with implicit figurations, then they could only be uncovered by a thorough sifting of all his historical works to determine which narratives could reasonably be seen as hinting at such figural readings—I discuss just one in the present volume, the case of Eadwine. It is, at this point, worth at least mentioning a few points which may imply a more figural underlying apprehension of history, or some parts of history, than Furry perhaps allows for.

Furry comments (*ibid.* 125) on how Bede, in his commentary on the Temple, views the Temple as a type for the antitype of Christ and the Church, and in doing so recontextualises the Temple in terms of Christ and the Church, which then become the normative background or context where alone the Temple makes true sense. Surely the same can be said about many Christ-like kings and their actions: do not Eadwine, and his constructing of a church in York, only receive their true sense in terms of their being realisations of Christ and the Temple (the Church) that he constructed? Bede need hardly spell this out, and to him such *imitatio Christi*, encumbent on all Christians, would perhaps have seemed essentially an issue of moral theology rather than figuration, yet this is surely a matter of perspective: once figuration is accepted at all as a principle for reading parts of history, are we limited to seeing it only where Bede makes it explicit? Moreover, it is fairly clear that some of Bede's sources took a different view from Bede on figuration in history (in so far as we accept Furry's conclusions). For example, as Furry notes (*ibid.* 22–3), Bede's hagiographical source for his life of St Germanus presents the saint as onboard a ship when a storm arises, which he calms by sprinkling it with water in order to get to Britain to calm the Pelagian heresy: this is clearly drawn from, and can be said to be in figural relationship with, the account of Christ calming the sea in Matthew 8 and Mark 4, although Bede again makes no explicit connection. Yet we may go further. Lapidge (1993, 14–15) discusses a passage from Bede's own *Vita Metrica S. Cuthberti*, where he employs figurative imagery (lines 252–85); Cuthbert is stranded with two monks in a frozen Pictland, with no food, and says (lines 262–4, trans. Lapidge):

> Cernitis, aequoreo canescat ut aggere tellus,
> Aer aquas manet, glacies mare, nox tegat aethram;
> Corda fame tabent hominumque iuvamina desunt.

6

> Do you see that the earth is whitened by a covering of hoar-frost, the air drips water, ice covers the sea and pitch-darkness covers the sky? Our spirits are weak with hunger, and the sustenance which men need is lacking.

They resort to calling on God, who once opened the red portals of the sea for his people, created a residence in a cloud, and brought bread from a cloud and water from a rock. Thus Bede alludes to the dark cloud which protected the Israelites (Exodus 14:20), the cloud raining down manna (Exodus 16:13–14) and Moses striking a rock for water (Exodus 16:6). For the Israelites, manna lay on the ground like hoar frost; the dripping air evokes the water from the rock but also the promised land, dripping with milk and honey: hence

> the landscape in which Cuthbert and his companions find them-selves is a symbolic one: the very bleakness of the wintry scene, with hoar-frost covering the ground and the air dripping water, carries the symbolic promise of God feeding Cuthbert as he had fed his chosen people. Like Moses, Cuthbert is the prophet who reveals this promise to his followers. None of this is explicit in Bede's compressed diction; the symbolic meaning of the passage can only be recovered by meditation on its biblical resonances.

Questions may arise as to whether the connection between Cuthbert and Moses is truly figural (where there is some form of ontological connection) or merely allegorical, but it is obvious both that some form of powerful connection is present, and that Bede leaves it to the reader to perceive it.

If we do seek to find such typological connections of his-torical characters and events with biblical analogues — and it should be stressed that doing so in Bede's work is tentative and speculative — it is helpful both to clarify the terminology and consider the theology implicit in doing so (but, in the present context, only to a superficial degree which scarcely begins to do justice to the topic).

When dealing with non-biblical history, and in an effort to keep the approach essentially within the realm of typology rather than some less specific category of allegory,[4] it is useful

---

[4] How far it is useful to distinguish between allegory and typology in, for example, Origen, is debatable: Martens (2008) sees the distinction as only partially useful. DeGregorio (2010a, 133) notes that while Bede might expound

to add the nomenclature of what I will term the *metatype* (an after-type or trans-type): we might, for instance, regard Eadwine as a Christ-like king, and while we could say that Christ acts as a type to Eadwine as an antitype, it is clearer to retain Christ as categorically the *antitype*, and Eadwine as the *metatype*, a type occurring after (and dependent upon) rather than before the antitype, and of which it might be described as a figuration.

Traditionally, typological approaches were kept distinct from anagoge, which sees a presaging of the Parousia in events in the mundane world. Yet a similar symbolic interpretation underlies both. In the present context, for the sake of simplicity and to underline the unity in noetic approach, anagogical interpretations are brought within one terminological scheme: hence the fulfilment of a type in the Parousia may be termed an *anatype* ('ana-' corresponding to 're-'). An example would be Jerusalem (a metonym for the Chosen People), acting as a type for Rome (as a metonym for the Church) and for the anatype of the new Jerusalem (a metonym for the kingdom of heaven).

This terminology helps, I think, to maintain Christ at the centre of things—a matter of great importance to Bede, who was the first major historian to date history in relation, both before and after, to Christ's incarnation (*anno dominicae incarnationis*, i.e. AD) (Furry 2013, 41); the understanding implicit in the typological terms is, as I read it, consistent with Augustine's understanding of history as an unfolding, through the divine *rationes*, of the eternal act of creation. We might regard metatypes as primarily *imitationes Christi*, but if history is viewed from the perspective of eternity, then can there be said to be any essential difference between a type, coming temporally before, and a metatype or anatype, coming temporally after, an antitype? Creation takes place through the utterance of the Word, and here it may be helpful to consider typology in terms, for example, of St Irenaeus's notion of *recapitulatio* (or *anakephalaiosis*; e.g. *Against Heresies* v, ch. 21). This was a rhetorical term, meaning 'setting

various levels of meaning (literal, allegorical, tropological, anagogical), 'it is the basic twofold distinction between a literal/historical meaning on the one hand and some kind of spiritual meaning on the other—variously termed "allegorical", "figurative", "mystical" or "hidden"—that informs the hermeneutical procedure most often followed in his Old Testament commentaries'. I am defining this 'figurative' approach here largely in typological terms.

out the headings again', in other words 'summing up', whereby Christ 'sums up' all the stages of human life, but without sin, and thus acts as the means of atonement. The implication is also more literally one of 'putting the head back on', Christ being the sinless head of all human endeavour which the Fall removed from mankind's activity, making all things in the fallen world incomplete. Irenaeus may not have been a particular influence on Bede, but I would see a sacramental understanding of history, which could be viewed as essentially Irenaean, as implicit in his approach: when, for example, Bede stresses, repeatedly, that Eadwine's kingship depends on the kingship of the King of kings, he indicates that human kingship receives its meaning from coinhering in the kingship of Christ, who is *caput*, the head, or wellspring of meaning, for all human endeavours, much as the celebration of each eucharist coinheres in, and in my terminology is a metatype of, the breaking and sharing of the bread and wine at the Last Supper (a breaking and sharing which Christ himself makes into a type of the antitype of his Crucifixion).[5] The logic of this analysis is that, given the coin-

---

[5] The doctrine I am propounding here, implied I believe in Augustine's doctrine of divine *rationes* which are implicit in and direct creation, perhaps finds a closer parallel in the doctrine refined and developed by Maximus the Confessor, who saw creation as filled with *logoi*, meanings or principles (*rationes* in Latin), that inhered in the divine Logos, Christ; when divinised (through atonement), a person would become a portion of God, in so far as he exists through the *logos* of his being, which is in God (Ambiguum 7). It is unlikely that Bede would have known the works of Maximus, but Maximus himself was in the tradition of Gregory of Nazianzus, who had some influence on Bede. Moreover, Greek learning entered Anglo-Saxon England through Theodore of Tarsus, archbishop of Canterbury (668–90), who knew the work of Maximus well, and may well have met him at the Lateran Synod in 649 (see Behr, Louth and Conomos 2003, 144). This synod was called by Pope Martin to refute the Monothelite heresy, espoused by the emperor in Constantinople; the result was that the emperor sent his envoys, arrested Martin, deported him to Constantinople, then exiled him to the Crimea, where he died miserably. Along with Martin, Maximus was arrested and himself subjected to torture: for Maximus was best known for his stout condemnation of Monothelitism. At the very time of the arrests, in 653, Benedict Biscop, the founder of Bede's monastery, along with Wilfrith, the great churchman and founder of Hexham Abbey, were either already in Rome or about to arrive there, and can hardly have been unaware of these momentous events. Pope Vitalian (657–72), who sent Theodore to Canterbury, was instrumental in opposing Monothelitism, and Theodore called the Council of Hatfield in 679, which reaffirmed the

herence of Eadwine's kingship in Christ's, 'if we be dead with him, we shall also live with him: if we suffer, we shall also reign with him' (II Timothy 2:11–12); hence the death in battle of the Christian king Eadwine against a pagan and an apostate acts as a sort of martyrdom into life and reign eternal.

In addition to the sort of typological thinking so far discussed, derived from and exemplified already in the Bible, Christians in the classical world were confronted with what to do with their cultural heritage, with its origins in paganism. While attitudes varied, the mythographic approach became commonplace, whereby classical myths and legends were approached allegorically, as symbolising aspects of the Christian story. This approach may be encompassed within a definition of typology that does not demand the types be derived from the Old Testament. Bede lived in the early-medieval world, not the classical, and his access to classical sources (and culture in general) was much more limited; nonetheless, he knew Vergil well, and classical references are scattered throughout his work (Laistner 1935, 242).[6]

An area where both biblical and classical typology appears to be particularly significant in the *Historia Ecclesiastica* is what may be termed the *praeparatio evangelica* of the English people. The significance of typological exegesis to Bede's historical understanding is emphasised by McClure (1983, 76): 'Thus his exegesis of the Old Testament is particularly relevant to the study of his historical writing, because here he was dealing with the people of Israel at various stages in their history, in conditions which he readily perceived were analogous to those determining the development of the Anglo-Saxon kingdoms.'

In book I of his history, which covers the history of Britain before and up to the advent of the Anglo-Saxons, Bede presents five migrations to the island of Britain in succession, of the Britons, the Picts, the Irish/Scots, the Romans and the English. Only the last proves successful and final, the reason being that the Germanic tribes win the right to the island because the previous

canons of the Lateran Synod. Bede certainly knew the outlines of the history of what happened, and the issues involved, as he summarises them in his *Cronica Maiora* (see Ó Carragáin 1994, 15–17).

[6] Lapidge (2006, 106) notes that Bede 'had seemingly internalized every aspect of Vergil's poetic technique', which is particularly apparent in his *Vita Metrica S. Cuthberti*.

inhabitants, the Britons, fell into moral turpitude and failed to convert the newcomers to Christianity (*Historia Ecclesiastica* 1.22, pp. 68–9). The coming of the English was, indeed, divinely ordained to inflict evil upon the miscreant Britons (*Historia Ecclesiastica* 1.14, pp. 48–9); they were not 'noble savages', but savages acting as the instrument of God (1.xv 'the fire kindled by the hands of the heathen executed the just vengeance of God on the nation for its crimes'). It is a *leitmotif* of Bede's work that the Britons had forfeited their right to rule Britannia through their apostasy and failure to convert the English (interestingly, this only seems to have applied to the British within areas the English were settling: he contemns the Scots, for example, far less).[7] The crossing of the North Sea to a destined land acts implicitly as a metatype to the crossing of the Red Sea, and subsequent occupation of Canaan, by the Israelites; in typological biblical exegesis, the crossing of the Red Sea and then the Jordan into the Holy Land formed a type to the antitype of the baptism of Christ in the Jordan;[8] the Holy Land into which the neophyte (the metatype or anatype) crosses in baptism is the realm of heaven. Thus the English are rewarded with the promised land on the island of Britannia through their baptism, which proves them worthy of their possession.[9] This typology is reinforced

---

[7] Quite what Bede meant by the 'English' ('Angli'), and his terminology, are matters of discussion: see in particular Brooks (1999). It seems that a more widespread term for English speakers in Bede's time was 'Saxon', but papal sources referred to the Angli. The continental Saxons were very much in evidence in Bede's time, but were obdurately pagan, whereas the continental Angli had disappeared; Bede thus settled on a usage whereby 'Angli' referred primarily to the English after their conversion, but at the time of their settlement, when they were pagan, Bede tends to call them Saxons. There is, however, some doubt as to how far Bede conceived the inhabitants of specifically named Saxon areas (Essex, Wessex, Sussex) as being included in the overall 'race of the English'.

[8] It would be more accurate to say that the crossing of the Red Sea by Moses acted as a type to the antitype of the crossing of the Jordan by Joshua, but elements of both Old Testament events are combined in the understanding of Christ's baptism as an antitype with a two-fold type behind it.

[9] It is possible that further nuances underlay the concept: Bede was certainly aware of islands as monastic retreats, focused centres of spiritual power, from which missionary activity sprang (just as the English in general, from the island of Britannia, once converted, were expected to go forth and convert others): the obvious examples are Iona and Lindisfarne. Such an island is a

by a mythographic reading of Vergil's *Aeneid* (Howe 1989, 62): the mighty realm of Rome—which to Bede of course acted as a metonym of the Church, of which Jerusalem, the metonym of the Promised Land, was a type—was the result of a destined migration, by ship, from Troy; the English migration was a metatype to this (with the implicit understanding that 'Rome' stands for the *ecclesia anglicana* that is to be built). The spiritual state of the Britons and the English is contrasted through parallelism (not of a specifically typological sort): the mission of St Germanus, before the English advent, succeeded in eradicating the heresy of Pelagianism, but the recidivist Britons then slipped further from the path of truth, and hence were destined to failure in their land, whereas the mission of Augustine to the English was successful, and the English political success was a reflection of their spiritual standing (Howe 1989, 67).

Over all, it might be said that a figural approach to history, in my understanding, is closer to a modern approach to works of fiction than to history, and many of the tools of literary analysis, such as symbolism, parallelism, allegory and *figura* are relevant to an analysis of Bede's writing and that of others of his era.

Bede was keen to maintain the literal meaning of history, and eschewed giving it explicit figural interpretation, fearing, no doubt, this would undermine its reality in a Monothelite sort of way. I would, therefore, by no means venture to suggest that all the readings suggested here would have been in Bede's mind as he wrote, but I do suggest that a careful delving into the text he produced shows that it lends itself to this sort of interpretation, despite Bede's reticence in explicitly acknowledging the legitimacy of figural readings of history.

---

half-way house between earth and heaven, and Britain as a whole might be viewed in a similar light, as the refuge and reward of the English, who had left their pagan ways behind on the Continent, and who were now striving to attain the kingdom of heaven (this, incidentally, is a powerful motif in the early writings of the modern Catholic writer, J. R. R. Tolkien). Britain in turn might be seen as a microcosm of the whole world, viewed as an island on which our salvation is worked out, as is clear from later *mappae mundi*, where the world appears as a round collection of islands, an *orbis terrarum*. However, Bede does not, I think, develop this theme.

ÆTHELFRITH

✝

In his *Historia Ecclesiastica* ii.2 (pp. 140–3), Bede recounts a battle fought by the Northumbrian (Bernician) king, Æthelfrith, against the British near the city of Chester, as a conclusion to his presentation of a second meeting of St Augustine with the British bishops, at which Augustine was snubbed, resulting in the Britons suffering their due come-uppance (my translation).

Siquidem post haec ipse, de quo diximus, rex Anglorum fortissimus Aedilfrid collecto grandi exercitu ad Ciuitatem Legionum, quae a gente Anglorum Legacaestir, a Brettonibus autem rectius Carlegion appellatur, maximam gentis perfidae stragem dedit. Cumque bellum acturus uideret sacerdotes eorum, qui ad exorandum Deum pro milite bellum agente conuenerant, seorsum in tutiore loco consistere, sciscitabatur qui essent hi quidue acturi illo conuenissent. Erant autem plurimi eorum de monasterio Bancor, in quo tantus fertur fuisse numerus monachorum, ut cum in septem portiones esset cum praepositis sibi rectoribus monasterium diuisum, nulla harum portio minus quam trecentos homines haberet, qui omnes de labore manuum suarum uiuere solebant. Horum ergo plurimi ad memoratam aciem, peracto ieiunio triduano, cum aliis orandi causa conuenerant, habentes defensorem nomine Brocmailum, qui eos intentos precibus a barbarorum gladiis protegeret. Quorum causam aduentus cum intellexisset rex Aedilfrid, ait: 'Ergo si aduersum nos ad Deum suum clamant, profecto et ipsi, quamuis arma non ferant, contra nos pugnant, qui aduersis nos inprecationibus persequuntur.' Itaque in hos primum arma uerti iubet, et sic ceteras nefandae militiae copias non sine magno exercitus sui damno deleuit. Extinctos in ea pugna ferunt de his qui ad orandum uenerant uiros circiter mille ducentos, et solum l fuga esse lapsos. Brocmail ad primum hostium aduentum cum suis terga uertens, eos quos defendere debuerat inermes ac nudos ferientibus gladiis reliquit. Sicque conpletum est praesagium sancti pontificis Augustini, quamuis ipso iam multo ante tempore ad caelestia regna sublato, ut etiam temporalis interitus ultione sentirent perfidi, quod oblata sibi perpetuae salutis consilia spreuerant.

15

Thereafter, that most powerful king of the English, Æthelfrith, of whom we have spoken, presented his great army, gathered near the city of Chester, which is called *Legacæstir* by the English and more correctly *Caerlegion* (Chester) by the British, with a massive slaughter of that apostate race.[1] When he was about to launch into battle and saw their priests, who had assembled to pray to God for the forces waging war, and who had set themselves apart in a safer place, he enquired who they were and what they were going to do by gathering there. Most of them were from the monastery of Bangor, where there was said to be so great a number of monks that, when it was divided into seven parts with superiors over each, no division had less than 300 men, all of whom were accustomed to live by the labour of their hands. After a three-day fast, most of these had come to the battle in order to pray with the others. They had a defender named Brocmail, whose duty it was to protect them against the barbarians' swords while they were intent on their prayers. When Æthelfrith heard the reason for their coming he said, 'So, if they are calling out to their God against us, then, even if they do not bear arms, they are still fighting against us, assailing us with their prayers against us.' So he ordered weapons to be directed against them first, and then he destroyed the rest of the forces of their wicked host, though not without heavy losses to his own army. It is said that in this battle about twelve hundred men were slain who had come to pray and only fifty slipped away and fled. Brocmail and his men at the first enemy attack turned their backs, leaving those whom they should have defended unarmed and helpless before the savage swords. Thus the prophecy of the holy Bishop Augustine was fulfilled, although he had long been translated to the heavenly kingdom, namely that those heretics would also suffer the vengeance of worldly destruction because they had despised the counsels offered for everlasting salvation.

---

[1] I differ somewhat from Colgrave and Mynors on the interpretation of this sentence. The most natural reading is to take 'exercitu' as a dative, a grammatical flourish that displays a familiarity with classical rhetoric. I take the text to indicate that Chester is the city near which the battle took place, rather than the object of Æthelfrith's raid, as Colgrave and Mynors imply, 'ad' being rather too weak to indicate such a meaning clearly.

Æthelfrith and the Battle of Chester

Introduction

KING ÆTHELFRITH, who ruled over Northumbria in the late sixth to early seventh century, led a series of expansionist raids against the British kingdoms along the western seaboard, and was a fierce and successful leader. So relates the main historian of the period, the Northumbrian monk Bede, writing a century or so later. Among these expeditions far from Æthelfrith's homeland that Bede recounts was a victorious foray to Chester. The battle which took place is unusual for the period in the detail with which it is described, and unique in having left us archaeological remains in the form of a 'battle cemetery' at Heronbridge, just to the south of Chester. I do not engage here with the details of the excavation of the site but I raise some questions about their interpretation and consider the general historical situation in northern Britannia at the time; I also take up some points raised by the modern historiography of the battle, in particular the reliability of the ancient sources.

Written sources

Bede

While Bede is regarded as a good historian, the writing of history served different purposes from those of modern historians, and the rhetorical arrangement and presentation of the text reflect this.[1] In the present case, the account forms the last of a

---

[1] Although Bede regarded himself as a 'true historian' ('verax historicus'), this term does not designate an assembler of past facts; rather, the purpose of recounting history was moral, and it was the duty of the true historian to point

three-part section concerning the mission of St Augustine and his interaction with the native British Church. A thorough and penetrating analysis of the whole section, which largely supersedes earlier discussions within the areas covered, is offered by Stancliffe (1999, particularly 124–9 for the Chester portion).

The first part of Bede's account deals with Augustine's meeting with the British clerics at an oak tree on the border between the Hwicce and Wessex, the second concerns a second meeting (possibly at Chester; it involved representatives from Bangor, at least), and the third presents the battle of Chester as retribution for the behaviour of the British Church towards Augustine. Whilst it is clear that Augustine, directed by his master, Pope Gregory, took a high-handed approach towards the native Church, expecting it to submit without question to his authority, Bede is wholly on his side, and regards all that the British suffered, in particular at Chester, as their just deserts.

The three parts of the overall presentation must derive from different sources, a matter that Stancliffe discusses at some length. The first part is told directly, without reference to any sources, and contains nothing that could not derive solely from an English source (which includes Roman sources held, for example, in Canterbury); here, Augustine belittles the British representatives by performing a miracle, which they are unable to achieve themselves. The second and third parts, however, contain information that must have derived from a British source, and they are peppered with qualifying statements such as 'they say', indicating some reluctance to accept the full validity of the underlying source. Bede often uses such qualifying statements to indicate an oral source, but in this case a written source, containing the British names Brocmail and Dinoot (and probably Carlegion, the British name for Chester), must lie behind Bede's account; the qualifications do not here indicate orality but rather an origin among the British, whom Bede in general held in low regard. The positive depiction of Bangor and its learned inhabitants reflects an original British bias, which Bede preserves but somewhat besmirches with his own excoriations of the British *gens perfida*.

out what was good and what bad in the characters and events described; a good historian was an *exornator rerum*, 'adorner of matters' (Ray 1997, 11–13).

The source document, which I see as being British, was, Stan-cliffe argues, most probably in Latin; its ultimate origin must surely have lain with the monastery of Bangor or someone closely associated with it. It is highly unlikely to have come to Bede from Canterbury, whose archives Bede always esteemed (and quoted in an unqualified way, as with his description of Augustine's first meeting), but exactly how Bede came by it is open to some debate. Stancliffe (1999, 128) suggests that the monastery of Malmesbury, founded within a generation or so of the battle of Chester on the border between Wessex and the Hwicce and hence in the general area of Augustine's oak-tree meeting, may have held the document, whence it came, possibly with additional information relating to the whole interchange between Augustine and the British Church, to Bede.[2]

Stancliffe rightly dismisses the notion that any British oral traditions lie behind the account of the battle of Chester as reported by Bede (the details of the names, and of the organ-isation of the monastery of Bangor, effectively preclude this); this is not, however, to deny that such traditions may have existed, and may have influenced other, later British sources, which I consider below. On the other hand, the depiction of King Æthelfrith in general is quite likely to have its origins in oral heroic poetry among the English (though even here, the figure of Æthelfrith is made Saul-like, with Eadwine in exile as a David-figure, according to the biblically inspired rhetoric of Bede's understanding of history); the description is general in nature, and decidedly adulatory, which would reflect its origins in praise poetry addressed to a warrior prince, plenty of remnants of which are found in Old English verse (though of course in a Christianised form).[3] The battle of Chester might,

---

[2] Stancliffe's arguments, which are more detailed than can be entered into here, are more convincing than, and supersede, those of Chadwick (1963), who entertained notions of links with Canterbury and/or West Midland monasteries.
[3] Thus *Beowulf* sets its opening theme as 'the fame of the kings of the Spear-Danes in days gone by'; the Northumbrian Cædmon, our earliest recorded poet (from a couple of generations after Æthelfrith), begins his praise poem 'Now must we praise ...', before picking 'the guardian of heaven' as his subject, instead of an earthly prince as his predecessors would have; Bede describes Æthelfrith as 'gloriae cupidissimus' ('most eager for glory', *Historia Ecclesiastica* I.34, pp. 116–17), which is close to being a direct translation of the last word of *Beowulf*, praising its hero, 'lofgeornost', 'most eager for praise' —

of course, have featured in such praise poetry for Æthelfrith, if he survived long enough to hear it, but it is unlikely that it would have supplied any of the details Bede gives us, which surely derive from the written British source discussed above.[4] The implications of this are that the description of Æthelfrith as singling out the monks for slaughter—which makes no sense from a pagan king's perspective—is a projection of motive onto a pagan foe by the Christian-minded monks of Bangor, who we may surmise viewed him as a sort of devilish tormentor who brought about their martyrdom, a point picked up by Bede, who, while accepting the basis of the interpretation, turned the tables and viewed Æthelfrith as an instrument of divine retribution, a viewpoint that we may be confident was absent from the original British document derived from Bangor.

One difficult matter in Bede's account is the action of Brocmail. His treacherous betrayal of his helpless charges fits Bede's overall narrative of the perfidious British very well, but it is more difficult to explain how the event was recorded within a British context. It is possible that Bede has put his own slant on an event that in his source was not so negatively viewed, but there might also be something like a dynastic struggle implicit in the account, with Brocmail coming, for example, from a neighbouring clan rather than the royal family under whose protection the monastery lay. At this distance, and in the absence of any further evidence, this is of course mere speculation.

The *Anglo-Saxon Chronicle*

The entry for the battle in the *Anglo-Saxon Chronicle* may be dismissed as a worthless derivative of Bede (cf. Bu'Lock 1962, 47), which gives no further information other than assigning a date of 605, which is inferred, without a great deal of consideration, from Bede in that it follows on from the last previously mentioned dated event; the specification that two hundred priests prayed

Colgrave and Mynors (in Bede, *Historia Ecclesiastica*, p. 116 n.) note that 'most eager for glory' recalls the Old English *domgeorn* and kindred words in poems such as *The Wanderer* and *Judith* used to describe the typical heroic warrior.
[4] Higham's notion (1992, 6) that oral English poetry provided Bede with information about the battle is unconvincing, particularly in light of Stancliffe's perceptive analysis.

for victory on the British side, of whom fifty escaped, derives from Bede's account, with 'mcc' presumably misread as 'cc'.

The *Historia Brittonum*

The *Historia Brittonum*, traditionally but probably inaccurately ascribed to Nennius, was a work compiled in Gwynedd in 829–30 on the basis of earlier sources; the earliest manuscript (British Library, Harley 3859) dates from *c.* 1100 (Charles- Edwards 2013, 346). The work contains valuable information which, as it is derived largely from British traditions, supplements what is found in Bede. Nonetheless, although annals of an arguably extensive nature were used (*ibid.*, 358–9), much of what informs this 'history' was traditional poetry or stories, in which the presentation of events was adapted for rhetorical effect, including the adaptation of tradition to reflect the particular concerns current at the time of the work's composition; this includes the creation of an anachronistic version of history which opposes the Welsh to the English—Charles-Edwards (*ibid.*, 447) characterises it as an *apologia pro gente sua*. (For a survey of the *Historia Brittonum* as a historical document, and its sources, see *ibid.*, 437–52.)

The *Historia Brittonum* does not directly mention the battle of Chester, but chapters 61 and 63 include an interesting piece of information about Æthelfrith, which will have some relevance later in the discussion:

> Ida [. . .] junxit Dinguayrdi guurth Berneich. [ch. 61]

> Eadfered Flesaurs regnavit xii annis in Berneich et alios xii in Deur; xxiv annis inter duo regna regnavit, et dedit uxori suae Dinguoaroy, quae vocatur Bebbab, et de nomine suae uxoris suscepit nomen, id est Bebbanburth. [ch. 63]

> Ida [. . .] joined Din Guaire to Bernicia.

> Æthelfrith the Artful reigned 12 years in Bernicia and another 12 in Deira. He reigned 24 years in the two kingdoms, and gave Din Guaire to his wife, whose name was Bebba, and it was named Bamburgh from his wife's name.

The nickname given to Æthelfrith, in Welsh within a Latin text, suggests a vernacular, legendary source (presumably Welsh heroic poems), but the rest of the information could well derive from more annalistic material.

The Irish and Welsh Annals

The battle of Chester is mentioned in various Irish annals. They are somewhat complicated in terms of their history and survival (see Charles-Edwards 2006; 2013, 346–59). The Chronicle of Ireland was composed in the tenth century on the basis of earlier annals, and went up to the year 911, but it survives only in the form of daughter chronicles such as the *Annals of Ulster* and the *Annals of Tigernach*, whose manuscripts date from Tudor times (but nonetheless preserve, it is believed, much intact material from many centuries earlier) (Charles-Edwards 2006, 1). The source used by the Chronicle of Ireland for entries up to 642 was a chronicle of Iona, recording events of interest to the kingdom of Dál Riata, which included the battle of Chester (for the Iona chronicle's strata see Charles-Edwards 2006, 38). The *Annals of Ulster* entry for 613 reads:

> Bellum Caire Legion ubi sancti occisi sunt & cecidit Solon m. Conaen, rex Britanorum

and the Clonmacnois branch adds:

> Et Cetula rex cecidit. Etalfraidh victor erat, qui post statim obiit.

Charles-Edwards (2006, 128) gives the reconstructed form of the Chronicle of Ireland in English translation as follows; the second part, in italics, is from the Clonmacnois version (*Annals of Tigernach*) and cannot therefore be assigned with confidence to the Chronicle of Ireland:

> The battle of Caer Legion, where holy men were killed and Solon son of Conan, king of the Britons, fell, *and King Cetula fell. Æthelfrith was the victor, who died immediately afterwards.*

The *Annales Cambriae* (A text, MS Harley 3859) record the battle, and another event in the same year, 613:

> Gueith cair legion . et ibi cecidit selim filíí cinan . Et iacob filíí beli dormitatio .

> The battle of Chester. And Selim son of Cinan fell there. And the falling asleep of Iacob son of Beli.

The manuscript is, as noted, from *c.* 1100, and it also contains the Harleian genealogies; as annal entries stretch up to the time of

Owain ap Hywel, king of Dyfed, who died *c.* 970, and the opening Harleian genealogies converge on Owain, the original on which the manuscript is based is likely to be from the third quarter of the tenth century (Charles-Edwards 2013, 346–7). The *Annales Cambriae* appear to have been composed at St David's in Dyfed.

The analysis of the development of the Irish and Welsh annals in more detail is highly complex, and has been subject to a good deal of controversy.[5] It is sufficient here to note that, according to the most recent research, the *Annales Cambriae* in fact appear to be, in large part, a tenth-century abbreviation derived from the Chronicle of Ireland in its Clonmacnois version (Charles-Edwards 2013, 349), and are thus to a degree a secondary source in comparison to the Chronicle of Ireland — though the matter is complicated by the fact that the Chronicle of Ireland no longer exists as such, and also not everything in the *Annales Cambriae* is derived from the Chronicle of Ireland.[6] The derivative nature of the *Annales Cambriae* and their complex later history need to be borne in mind when assessing their content, but we are still left with a good deal of uncertainty about their early history. Ultimately, if — and I would regard this as a big if — the information in the Chronicle of Ireland and the *Annales Cambriae* about the battle is not in essence derived from Bede with some

---

[5] Nora Chadwick attempted such an analysis, including a discussion of the battle of Chester (e.g. Chadwick 1963), but her rather loose arguments (cf. the animadversions of Gelling 1992, 77, on these) are superseded by the most recent analyses, particularly those of Charles-Edwards; earlier works on the battle of Chester that rely on Chadwick's arguments (e.g. Bu'Lock 1962) are similarly compromised. There seems little point here in rehearsing the details of this earlier scholarship, but a few points need to be made. Chadwick (1963, 175) argued that the Irish and Welsh annals for the period covered by the battle all derive from a lost collection of Northern Annals from northern Britain, and this notion was pursued by other historians; cf. the related perspective of Kathleen Hughes (discussed and refuted in detail by Charles-Edwards 2013, 347–59). However, Charles-Edwards (2013, 352) argues that the British element in the Chronicle of Ireland is probably independent of any northern British chronicle used by the *Annales Cambriae* — and furthermore the suggestion that such a chronicle underlies both the *Annales Cambriae* and the *Historia Brittonum* is open to question, as is the existence of any very close textual connection between these two works (2013, 355–7).

[6] The early Welsh forms of the names Selim and Cinan would not appear to lend themselves easily to derivation from the recorded Irish forms Solon and Conan, perhaps suggesting an independent origin.

additions from legendary tradition, then it must derive from a Welsh source (or oral informant) known to the monks of Iona (the chronicle of which fed into the Chronicle of Ireland); note, for example, the Welsh form Cair Legion for Chester (which, however, also occurs in Bede as Carlegion, whence it may have been taken). It has already been argued that Bede's account of the battle must go back to a document that derived ultimately from Bangor; the simplest supposition would be that the same monastery recorded the event in its annals, from which the *Annales Cambriae* derived the information, though through how many intervening stages is difficult to say. There is, of course, no direct evidence for such a supposition; it is merely the result of applying Occam's razor.

Whatever their precise development, the Irish and Welsh annals, through the many recensions and revisions they underwent over many centuries, had plenty of opportunity to make use of sources such as Bede, and to incorporate allusions to legendary tradition; it is clear, for example, that Bede's *Chronica Maiora* (which do not mention the battle of Chester) were used as a basis for some aspects of the Chronicle of Ireland (Charles-Edwards 2006, 3, 52). Annals, like chronicles, inscriptions, chronicles or poetry, could and did serve political ends, and it would be a mistake to accept whatever they say as being historically accurate.

A number of observations may be made on the basis of the critical approach just espoused. Firstly, the dates in the Chronicle of Ireland and the *Annales Cambriae* are almost certainly wrong for the period under discussion. It has long been recognised that a mistake has been made with the dating of entries as a result of the Iona chronicler splicing two separate sources relating to the period up to the year 642, and they should be revised in such a way that the date of the battle is actually intended to be not 613, but 616, or possibly 615 (Charles-Edwards 2006, 128; 2013, 352; the observation had also already been made long ago by Plummer 1896, II, 77).

The entry in the *Annales Cambriae* for Iacob (Iago) is on a separate line and is not connected with the battle; a 'falling asleep' suggests death from old age or illness, not falling in battle.[7] Iacob

---

[7] He is mentioned in the Welsh Triad 34 (Bromwich 2014, 79) as having suffered one of the three unfortunate hatchet-blows of Britain, but this is

may be connected with Welsh royal dynasties, and be identified as the Iacob, great-grandson of Mailcun (the Maglocunus of Gildas) and grandfather of Catgollaun (Cadwallon) of Harleian Genealogy 1 (Bartrum 1966, 9); Cadwallon, king of Gwynedd, overthrew Eadwine of Northumbria in 633/634 and ravaged his realm for a year (Bede, *Historia Ecclesiastica* ii.20, pp. 202–5). However, there is no reason on the basis of this annal to associate either Iacob or the house of Gwynedd with the battle, despite many historians having done so.

The Cetula of the *Annals of Tigernach* has been identified with Cadwal Crysban (Bartrum 1993, *s.v.*), who appears as Catgual crisban in the Harleian Genealogy 3 pedigree of the princes of Rhos (Bartrum 1966, 10). He was a great-grandson of Cinglas (the Cuneglasus of Gildas). It is possible that he did take part in the battle, but again his name may have been attracted into association with the battle as a result of legendary fame; more-over, the identification of Cetula as this Cadwal is supposition, and may reflect the desire of modern scholars to carry on what their predecessors in the Middle Ages no doubt did, which is to look for connections between events and characters known elsewhere from tradition, even when there is no particular jus-tification for doing so.

Similarly, the association of Selim (Selyf in more modern form) with the battle may be the result of a desire to link events with legendary heroes, and could have been made long after the event, given the contorted history of the annals, although, as noted below, there are reasons to think the annal entry is in essence correct. Selyf is a major figure who appears in a number of sources, both saints' lives and poetry; his father Cynan is similarly well represented, and in one genealogy appears as the maternal grandfather of the great king Cadwallon (Bartrum 1993, *s.v.* 'Selyf Sarffgadau'; 'Cynan Garwyn'). Selyf appears as one of the three battle-leaders of Britain in Triad 25 (Bromwich 2014, 48), and elsewhere has the epithet *sarffgadeu*, 'serpent of

---

out of keeping with the annal's 'falling asleep' and may represent confusion with the later Iago ab Idwal, who died in 1039 (*ibid.*, 403). There was a poem dedicated to Iago son of Beli, the *Marwnad Iago ap Beli*, but this has been lost (Bartrum 1993, *s.v.* 'Iago ap Beli'); his appearance in the annals is likely to be a reflection of either his renown in poetic tradition, or his sponsoring of religious foundations.

battles', a title which Bromwich (*ibid.*, 498) views as originating in bardic encomium: a prestige built up in poetic tradition is likely to have its origins in the activities of a successful king, even if it is not strictly historical in itself.

Selyf's grandfather in genealogical tradition was Brochfael/ Brochwel (later forms of Bede's Brocmail). It has been supposed that Brochwel might have retired to the monastery and could have been called upon to act as an aged warrior when needed. As Bartrum notes (1993, *s.v.* 'Brochwel, captain at the Battle of Chester'), this is unwarranted; Brochwel was a particularly common name, borne by many kings and heroes (cf. entries in Bartrum 1993). There is no reason to associate Bede's Brocmail with any such hero kings, particularly in view of his reprehensible behaviour. It is notable that this Brocmail makes no appearances in any other recorded traditions, understandably so.

The entries in annals are not, then, particularly reliable, and could be explained as the imposition of legendary figures on events that were derived from elsewhere, for example from Bede. This does not on itself make the entries untrue, but they can in no way be relied on to give authoritative information.

The Harleian genealogies

The main source of early genealogies, the Harley 3859 manuscript, was composed under Hywel (950–c. 970); some other genealogies appear to date from a similar time (Charles-Edwards 2013, 359). The analysis of Charles-Edwards (*ibid.*, 359–64) makes abundantly clear that the genealogies were arranged as political propaganda for the ruling houses, primarily of Gwynedd, and reflect the *realpolitik* of the time of Hywel. For example, Hywel belonged to a dynasty which had ruled Gwynedd for little more than a century, but links were made to the previous dynasty, the descendants of Cunedda, through his mother, and a similar tactic was used to justify his rule over the kingdom of Dyfed. Genealogies represented the political situation of the time of their composition through the imposition of a diachronic interpretation of that situation; they can therefore scarcely be relied on to represent the realities of several centuries earlier, as viewed from different centres of power, though they may contain fragments of such realities (*ibid.*, 447–51).

Welsh poems and related bardic materials

Welsh (or British) bards, supposedly from the time of Ida, first English king of Bernicia (mid-sixth century), are known by name in the *Historia Brittonum*. However, the manuscripts of Welsh poems supposedly composed from the sixth century onwards date almost exclusively only from the thirteenth to fourteenth centuries, and even if the texts reproduce earlier versions, they bear little resemblance to what could have existed in the sixth or seventh centuries (Charles-Edwards 2013, 364; also his survey of verse more widely, *ibid.*, 651–79). In addition, the dating of the composition of many Welsh texts has recently been brought later, closer to the dates of the manuscripts (Charles-Edwards 2013, 653–5). Before they reached their extant forms, poems were passed down in a mixture of oral and written versions, and were subject to considerable revision on the basis of the wider bardic heroic tradition. Moreover, from its inception a poem is a literary, not a historical, work: its purpose is not to relate events, but, for example, to praise a ruler or to evoke the pathos of loss; events are therefore incidental, and motives of the protagonists subject to the literary whims of the poet.

Poems may sometimes preserve information about genuine events or people, but this needs to be extracted and interpreted cautiously.[8] Thus Rowland (1990, 120–41; cf. Gelling 1992, 72–6) shows that the *Canu Heledd*, depicting the ravaging and loss of Shropshire to the English in the seventh century, is wholly unhistorical, and represents the concerns of a later time (illustrated for example by the poet's having to fabricate historically inaccurate Welsh names on the basis of existing English ones);[9]

---

[8] It is indeed possible to construct a picture, a detailed one even, of the political context of the battle of Chester on the basis of sources derived from bardic tradition; this is essentially the line followed by both Mason (2007) and Davies (2010). Yet the historian's approach to works of literary fiction—which is what all such poems are—should always be one of distrust; it is not sufficient to simply state, as both Mason and Davies tend to do, that some source is unreliable, and then in fact rely on it to formulate a historical scenario.

[9] Rowland (1990, 139) notes that place-names are anachronistic and indicate the poet's lack of real knowledge: Bassa is an English name, the Eglwysau Basa being a translation of Baschurch, Ercal is English in form (the Welsh should be Erchal), Dinlle Vreconn is influenced by Wreocen (it should be Dinlleu Gwrygon), Y Drefwen, the 'White City', is probably a mistranslation of Whittington (cf. Charles-Edwards 2013, 674).

violent incursion into Powys from Mercia began only in the mid-eighth century. In the case of the *Canu Heledd*, Gelling (1992, 73) warns how 'the powerful poetry of the verses can still seduce scholars into accepting their message': but verisimilitude is not veracity. We would be unwise, therefore, to accept uncritically the picture of Mercian–British relations at the time of the battle of Chester that is evoked here. On the other hand, the elegy for Cynddylan, prince of Powys, the *Marwnad Cynddylan*, which is set at the same time, presents no such Mercian conquest, and appears to envisage the hero Cynddylan working alongside the Mercians in some of the battles mentioned by Bede; it is most probably essentially a seventh-century work (Rowland 1990, 122–3). The conclusion drawn by Rowland (*ibid.*, 120–41) in her extensive critical investigation of the early Welsh poems is that the genuinely early ones show a consistent picture of collaboration between the forces of Powys and Gwynedd with Mercia against Northumbria throughout the first half of the seventh century.

Another ancient poem, the *Trawsganu Kynan Garwyn*, features Cynan, the father of Selyf of the *Annales Cambriae* entry. Cynan is praised for his victories over neighbouring British peoples, without mentioning the English: this would reflect the reality of the situation in the north Wales area before Æthelfrith's incursion, which appears to have been the first penetration by the English this far west (Charles-Edwards 2013, 16).[10]

The most directly relevant fragment of Welsh poetic lore for the battle of Chester is found in the triads, the *Trioedd Ynys Prydain*. The triads represent a distillation of bardic tradition, in the form of snippets of information topically arranged into groups of three; many of the ancient poems from which the information originally derived are now lost. Triad 60 (Bromwich 2014, 171) mentions the *gweith*, the action or battle, of Perllan Fangor, the Orchard of Bangor. The fifteenth-century BL Cotton Cleopatra B.v version of the *Brut y Brenhinedd*, a Welsh rendering of Geoffrey of Monmouth's *History*, is the only authority

---

[10] One of Cynan's victories stands out, over Cernyw; this later meant 'Cornwall', which is highly unlikely within the context of the local Welsh regions otherwise mentioned. It has been suggested this may be a last memory of the name of the Cornovii (see Rivet and Smith 1979, *s.v.*), the tribe that inhabited the lowland marches of Shropshire and Cheshire.

for identifying the battle of Perllan Fangor with the battle of Chester, but Bromwich (*ibid.*, 172) regards this as representing a genuine tradition (it would be difficult, indeed, to relate it to any other battle). There is no reason to posit a separate battle of the Orchard of Bangor in addition to the battle of Chester: they are one and the same event (cf. Bartrum 1993, *s.v.* 'Caerlleon (Chester), Battles of').[11] The Orchard of Bangor may relate to the historical battle of Chester, but the triad represents what was remembered in poetic tradition, which, as noted, may not form a historically reliable source of information; I give the triad the benefit of doubt in the arguments that follow, but in a separate article I note some of the probable poetic allusion, interwoven with historic reference, implicit in its imagery: in short, the image of an orchard may relate both to the Celtic Otherworld (seen most obviously in the isle of Avalon, or apples), and to the orchard of the Song of Solomon 4:13, which in patristic understanding stood for martyrdom; hence the Orchard of Bangor may point to the monks' passage to the heavenly Otherworld through martyrdom at the battle.

Geoffrey of Monmouth

Various post-Norman Conquest sources mention the battle; these are largely derived from Bede, and it is highly questionable whether they contain anything of independent value derived from ancient sources. Geoffrey of Monmouth is the most significant of these post-Conquest sources; he wrote in the earlier twelfth century. Geoffrey claimed to have used an ancient book in the British tongue, given to him by Archdeacon Walter of Oxford, as his source, but in fact he used—or, to put it more accurately, manipulatively misused (cf. Wright 1986)—primarily Bede, Gildas and the *Historia Brittonum* for his accounts of British history, with his own imagination as the source for much of the fantastical material; his near-contemporary, William of Newburgh, already regarded him as having invented most of what he recounted: 'It is quite clear that everything this man wrote about Arthur and his successors, or indeed about his

---

[11] Davies (2010, 146) posits two conflicts, but his argument relies on affording Geoffrey of Monmouth some undeserved historical credibility.

predecessors from Vortigern onwards, was made up, partly by himself and partly by others, either from an inordinate love of lying, or for the sake of pleasing the Britons' (cited from the introduction to Thorpe's translation of Geoffrey, 1968, 17); the view of a modern, critical historian, Karen Jankulak (2010, 17), is scarcely less damning: 'Geoffrey combined invention with well-known and named sources, and mixed them, seeming to disregard truth and perhaps even the appearance of truth'. Whether Geoffrey's ancient British book ever existed has always been doubtful, and Geoffrey can be shown to have deliberately lied about his sources (for example, five of his seven attributions of stories to Gildas are made up: *ibid.*, 15), but he did have access to sources of Welsh history (*ibid.*, 14), possibly compiled into one book, parallels to which are still extant (such as the lists of names in Harleian manuscript 3859: Jankulak 2010, 15; see §3 of Thorpe's Introduction, and Jankulak 2010, ch. 2, for surveys of Geoffrey's sources). Yet the existence of such sources does not justify the assumption that Geoffrey is relaying ancient information whenever his account of an event differs from or supplements other, earlier accounts: a comparison between such extant sources as Geoffrey may have used and his own history reveals a wholly different character to the two types of account, and the only reasonable approach is to assume that the source of Geoffrey's 'information', when it cannot be traced to extant sources, is his own imagination, until specific arguments to the contrary are made in individual cases.[12] There is nothing to indicate any such lost source in the case of the battle of Chester. Yet the two most significant modern discussions of the battle of Chester, by David Mason and Sean Davies, both—to my mind rather surprisingly—afford a degree of credibility to Geoffrey; it is hence worth quoting what Geoffrey says and considering its reliability (*The History of the Kings of Britain*, bk xi, ch. 189; ed. Reeve, p. 261; trans. Thorpe, pp. 266–8):

> Edelbertus ergo rex Cantiorum, ut uidit Britones dedignantes subiectionem Augustino facere et eosdem praedicationem suam spernere, hoc grauissime ferens Edelfridum regem Northam-himbrorum et ceteros regulos Saxonum instimulauit ut collecto

---

[12] Pace (2012) shows that some such source is likely to underlie Geoffrey's accounts of Penda of Mercia, for example.

grandi exercitu in ciuitatem Bangor abbatem Dinoot et ceteros
clericos qui eos despexerant perditum irent. Adquiescentes
igitur consilio eius, collegerunt mirabilem exercitum et prouin-
ciam Britonum petentes uenerunt Legecestriam, ubi Brochmail
consul urbis aduentum eorum expectabat. Venerant autem ad
eandem ciuitatem ex diversis Britonum prouinciis innumerabiles
monachi et heremitae, et maxime de ciuitate Bangor, ut pro
salute populi sui orarent. Collectis igitur undique exercitibus,
Edelfridus rex Northamhimbrorum proelium iniuit cum Brochmail, qui pauciori numero militum resistens ad ultimum relicta
ciuitate sed prius maxima strage hostibus illata diffugit. At
Edelfridus ciuitate capta, cum intellexisset causam aduentus
praedictorum monachorum, iussit in eos primum arma uerti,
et sic mille ducenti eorum in ipsa die martirio decorati regni
caelestis adepti sunt sedem. Deinde, cum praedictus Saxonum
tyrannus Bangornensium urbem peteret, audita ipsius insania
uenerunt undique obuiam illi duces Britonum, Bledericus uidelicet dux Cornubiae et Margadud rex Demetarum, Caduanus
Venedotorum, et conserto proelio ipsum uulneratum in fugam
propulerunt, sed et tantum numerum exercitus eius peremerunt
ita quod decem milia circiter et sexaginta sex corruerunt. In
parte etiam Britonum cecidit Bledericus dux Cornubiae, qui
ducatum in eisdem proeliis ceteris praestabat.

When Ethelbert, the King of the men of Kent, saw that the Britons
were refusing to accept the authority of Augustine and were
scorning his preaching, he bore it very ill. He stirred up Ethelfrid, King of the Northumbrians, and a number of other petty
kings of the Saxons. A huge army was assembled and ordered
to march to the city of Bangor[-is-Coed] and destroy Abbot
Dinoot and the other churchmen who had scorned Augustine.
They accepted Ethelbert's orders, collected an enormous army
together and set out for the land of the Britons. They came to
Chester, where Brocmail, who was in command of that city,
awaited their coming. A great number of monks and hermits
from the city of Bangor had sought refuge in Chester, so that
they could pray there for the people's safety. Armies were drawn
upon both sides and Ethelfrid, King of the Northumbrians,
joined battle with Brocmail. Brocmail stood firm against him,
although his force was smaller. In the end, however, Brocmail
abandoned the city and fled, but only after inflicting enormous
losses on the enemy. When Ethelfrid occupied the city and
discovered the reason why these monks whom I have mentioned
had come there, he immediately let his soldiery loose against
them. That same day 1,200 monks won the crown of martyrdom
and assured themselves of a seat in heaven. After this the Saxon
tyrant marched to the town of Bangor. When they heard of this

mad frenzy, the leaders of the Britons came from all directions to oppose him: Blederic, Duke of Cornwall; Margadud, King of the Demetae, and Cadvan of the Venedoti. Battle was joined. They wounded Ethelfrid and forced him to flee. They killed so many of his army that some 10,066 died that day. On the side of the Britons there died Blederic, Duke of Cornwall, who commanded the others in these wars.

There is practically nothing here that calls for any other explanation than a biased misreading of Bede — the little that cannot be so explained is a random series of names of Welsh princes, culled from other sources known to Geoffrey (no other source indicates any association between these characters and the battle of Chester). Let us look at just a few of the features of Geoffrey's account.

a. Although Geoffrey relies on Bede, he lends a distinctive flavour to his account, typical of his overt bias in favour of the British (on this, see Jankulak 2010, ch. 4), in which he distinguishes himself markedly from Bede in his adulation of the British monks and the demonisation of the English (particularly Æthelfrith, the 'Saxon tyrant' full of 'mad frenzy' pursuing the monks even after their defeat back to their monastery, and after affording many of them a glorious martyrdom — notwithstanding the sturdy resistance of the British in massacring so many of their foes).

b. Geoffrey is adept at lending an air of verisimilitude (at least for his contemporaries) by ascribing motives to his actors, but ones which can be grounded in nothing but his own surmise. The notion that Æthelberht of Kent could 'stir up' Æthelfrith to attack the monks of Bangor as a vendetta for their mistreatment of Augustine is preposterous, but it reflects a particular way of reading between the lines in Bede's rather more subtle (and credible) account; the idea that Æthelfrith was especially motivated to attack the monks in Chester because they had gone there to pray for the people's safety is almost as incredible, though again it derives from an overzealous reading of the more nuanced account that Bede gives (which itself is not very believable at this point).

c. Equally preposterous is the notion that over ten thousand of Æthelfrith's troops perished — but the precise number of 10,066 of course acts as a deliberate premonition of 1066, the year when the Normans—who, in the eyes of Geoffrey and other writers, saw themselves as restitutors of their lost *imperium* to the Britons—defeated the English, the successors of Æthelfrith, at Hastings.

d. Geoffrey's siting of the battle within the city of Chester is an overreading of Bede's 'ad Ciuitatem Legionum', where 'ad' means 'at, near', not 'in'; Geoffrey has a notion of the storming of cities, such as took place in his own day indeed, whereas Chester around 600 can scarcely have consisted of much more than a series of derelict Roman buildings, which certainly did not offer a suitable site for battle as conducted at this time. Bangor similarly appears anachronistically as a city.

e. Æthelfrith's vindictive religious reasons for marching on Bangor are a clear invention of a Christian of a later age and mentality.

f. The notion that two battles took place, one at Chester and a second at Bangor, derives from Bede's mention of both Chester and Bangor in his account: Geoffrey's reading is nothing more than a crude *reductio ad absurdum* of the idea of vengeance being wrought against the monks of Bangor, which the overcoming of Chester, as opposed to Bangor, the dragon's head itself, did not suffice to bring to a satisfactory conclusion, in Geoffrey's reckoning. As archaeological investigation has shown, Geoffrey was wrong in both respects, as the battle took place neither at Chester nor at Bangor but, as Bede indicated, 'ad Ciuitatem Legionum', *at* but not *in* Chester.

It is possible that in some details Geoffrey may by chance have hit upon the truth, but it is not acceptable to use his account as *evidence* for anything to do with the battle; any possible truths in Geoffrey's account must be independently argued. I therefore now set aside Geoffrey as not warranting further consideration; moreover, I refrain from engaging with arguments, such as those involving, for example, pincer-movement tactics between Heronbridge and Chester (Davies 2010, 157, developing an idea put forward by Mason 2007, 51), which, although arguable in theory from a tactical point of view, are nonetheless based primarily on accepting Geoffrey's account of the battle. Historians are bound to use the materials available to them, but relying on Geoffrey of Monmouth is tantamount to building a house of cards upon a quicksand foundation of late-medieval fantasy.

The battle cemetery

The site of the battle of Chester has now been established with a fair degree of precision. Heronbridge is an open-field site lying somewhat over two kilometres south of the centre of Chester on a main Roman road and close to the River Dee (Fig. 1). A fairly extensive Roman settlement flanked the road at this point, on the lower ground between the Heronbridge rise to the north and the slope up to the village of Eccleston to the south; it was abandoned by around 400, and nothing is now visible above ground. Excavations undertaken from 1929 to 1931 revealed that a series of burials in north–south rows, with their heads to the west, had been laid into the Roman remains; all the skeletons were male, aged mainly 20 to 45, many showing signs of a violent death. The skeletons excavated are held in Manchester University Museum. Excavations continued intermittently after the war, up until 1967; the suggestion that the burials related to the battle of Chester was made in 1951 by Graham Webster, but technology was not sufficiently advanced to prove or disprove this (Mason 2007, 48).

Any doubt over the dating of the skeletons was removed by the latest excavations, undertaken by David Mason and the Chester Archaeological Society in 2002–5 (see, provisionally, Mason 2002; 2003; 2004; 2007, particularly ch. 3; the final report is still awaited). Further skeletons were uncovered, and these have been radiocarbon-dated and the region of the upbringing of two of them investigated by radio-isotope analysis: a date of around 600 has been confirmed (one was dated 430–640 at 95.4% confidence, and at 530–620 with 58.4% confidence; a second was dated 530–660 at 95.4% confidence and 595–645 at 51.5% confidence: Mason 2004, 42), and they were not local, but from an area stretching from the Peaks up to the Grampians (one of them being from a coal-bearing region), suggesting a Northumbrian origin (Mason 2004, 51).[13] Mason calculated that at least 120

---

[13] For the sake of argument, I follow Mason's opinion that the skeletons are those of Northumbrian warriors. However, the radio-isotope tests, as summarised by Mason (a fuller report on them is very much needed), leaves a great deal of uncertainty. The area of definite overlap between the two analysed is the area of the Peaks; if this could encompass the southern Peaks, then the thought immediately arises that these may be Mercian soldiers, as

Fig. 1. The Heronbridge site, looking south-east over the rampart towards the Dee and beyond. The picture is taken from somewhat to the south of the excavated battle cemetery.

bodies were interred, though of course only a relatively small portion of the overall cemetery has been excavated. Detailed pathological reports indicated an array of violent injuries, as well as indications of earlier, healed injuries, suggesting protracted military service. As Mason notes, the most reasonable conclusion is that the burials represent fighters from Æthelfrith's army. The British dead would presumably have been afforded obsequies locally, taken care of by the native population. Early Anglo-Saxon burial involved both interment and cremation. Cremation occurred in Deira, but not in Bernicia (O'Brien 1999, 75), so the burials are consistent with Bernician practice.

this area has a number of pagan Anglo-Saxon burials, and must have been within the ambit of nearby Mercia. This would corroborate the argument that it was a joint Mercian–British alliance that opposed Æthelfrith, and the cemetery would have been laid out by the local population, which almost certainly means the monks of Bangor. As the cemetery is within the rampart at Heronbridge, this in turn raises the likelihood that the rampart demarcates an ecclesiastical compound; the east–west alignment of the bodies, although explicable in terms of local topography, might also suggest the obsequies were carried out by Christians, even if the victims were not themselves Christian. There is clearly a need to undertake radio-isotope analysis of further skeletons, and possibly DNA tests too, given that radio-isotope analysis is unlikely, for example, to be able to distinguish between someone from Chester and someone from York.

The rampart

Still visible at Heronbridge is an earth rampart surrounding a large area of around six hectares of ground, one side of which runs alongside the course of Eaton Road (effectively, the Roman road), while at north and south it curves towards the river (see the plan in Mason 2007, 45); it overlies the Roman settlement. Excavation has also revealed that the rampart, now much diminished, was once much more impressive, with a ditch some 5.5m wide and 3m deep, with the rampart around 2.5m high and 4.5m wide (*ibid.* 46). As far as the limited excavations have gone, the burial pit and the rampart respect each other spatially, neither underlying or cutting into the other; there is therefore nothing that explicitly links the results of the battle with the rampart.

Radiocarbon dating of flax stems from the rampart ditch to the late seventh to mid-ninth century indicates secondary usage as a flax-retting tank (Mason 2004, 53; 2007, 54). This gives a wide date range of *c.* 400 to *c.* 700 for the construction of the rampart. Excavation in its interior has been insufficient (especially given the evanescent nature of post-Roman remains) to determine what type of use the enclosure marked out by the rampart was put to. The battle of Chester, which took place at the very same site, to judge from the skeletal remains, falls within this period, but it seems irresponsible to yield, without further evidence, to the temptation to assume the rampart demarcated a fort intimately connected with Æthelfrith's campaign.

The topography of the fort needs some comment:

a. The fort is certainly defensible: it is protected by the River Dee along one side to the east, a steep-sided stream (now largely filled in) to the north, and another to the south, with a Roman road (useful for swift movement) along the west.

b. On the other hand, the site can be quaggy, and is moreover overlooked slightly on three sides; thus it does not follow the normal pattern of an elevated hillfort.

c. The fort is fully open on one side; this may not preclude a defensive purpose, as this side is closed off by a substantial river, but it may suggest that access to the river was as important as defence. Access to the Roman road appears less important than to the river: the rampart seems to have been unbroken, meaning access from the road must have been over it.

d. It has good visibility in some directions, but not others; it seems to be geared to viewing especially towards the north-east to south-east, rather than towards the Welsh hills or to the south beyond Eccleston towards Bangor (*pace* Davies 2010, 155–6, following Mason). A better site for visibility towards Wales would be afforded by an area just to the west of Eccleston, which is moreover more elevated and defensible.

e. It could defend against attacks equally from any direction, if we allow that the river served a defensive purpose (*pace* Mason 2007, 54, who sees it as clearly laid out to fend off attacks from the south or west); essentially, it guards the lower Dee valley.

The provenance of the fort also calls for comment; Mason (*ibid.*, 55) aptly draws a comparison with Æthelfrith's stronghold of Bamburgh, but the inference that this favours a Northumbrian origin for the earthwork seems misplaced:

a. Comparable fortifications, constructed in post-Roman times or Iron Age examples reused, are characteristic of British areas of the west; several examples are found in north Wales (see the useful survey, with a map of some examples, in Snyder 1998, 176–202), such as Dinas Emrys, Deganwy, Dinorben and Dinerth (Din Eirth, now Bryn Euryn) at Colwyn Bay (which may have been held by the small principality of Rhos).

b. Heronbridge's large size is notable, something it shares, if not on quite such a scale, with South Cadbury, for example; the reuse of Roman building rubble for the revetment at South Cadbury (Snyder 1998, 182) also matches that of Heronbridge (Mason 2004, 51).

c. The purpose of such defended sites varied, but, apart from military uses, one was undoubtedly seasonal trading, as was the case with Tintagel (Snyder 1998, 185). Another was to act as ecclesiastical compounds; examples in western Britain were often huge (see the summary and references in Mason 2004, 56–7). Mason dismisses the possibility that Heronbridge could be an example of such an enclosure, but his arguments are weak. The idea that the compound would duplicate Bangor, and that two such religious establishments existed so close together is unlikely, seems of little weight: the fact that the battle was remembered as the Orchard of Bangor indicates (probably) that Bangor had a subsidiary foundation somewhere around Eccleston, whose very name points to the existence of such an establishment; the 'church' (or 'church estate') in question could just as well have been at Heronbridge as at Eccleston itself. The very numbers of monks remembered as being attached to Bangor suggests they could well have been dispersed among various daughter-establishments in the area. If the attack was on a monastic compound, presumably being used also to house an army, then the decided focus on the battle as an attack on monks receives an explanation. The situation of the enclosure directly on both the Roman road and the river would allow access from Bangor by both routes (it is some way from the main Roman road, but directly on the river; on the other hand, the river meanders exceedingly). The openness to the river may imply a desire to access it, rather than the compound serving purely military purposes; hence either a trading post or ecclesiastical compound seems feasible.

d. When examples are found in English areas, most notably Bamburgh and Yeavering, it is clear from documentary or archaeological evidence that they were pre-existing British structures (Snyder 1998, 195; O'Brien 1999, 63; cf. *Historia Brittonum*, ch. 61).[14] A British origin for Heronbridge is therefore more likely, but an English reuse is quite possible.

What historical context during this period, therefore, would favour the construction of a large fort, requiring considerable man-power, with river (and road) access apparently determining its siting in a somewhat less than optimal defensive position, close to a Roman city which also acted as a port?

a. It could be a British construction, in effect a continuation of the legionary fortress of Deva, acting as a bulwark against

---

[14] Mason (2004, 55) admits that these Northumbrian forts date from pre-Anglo-Saxon times, and were therefore not early Northumbrian creations, but nonetheless does not draw the inference I do, that therefore the Heronbridge fort could also be a British product, taken over by the English in the way Yeavering and Bamburgh were. For a survey of erstwhile northern British fortified centres, later taken over by Northumbrians, see Alcock (1988); some such centres were on the annual royal circuit, and probably had minimal year-round occupation (by a royal reeve). Most habitation, of a temporary nature, would have been in tents: hence archaeological excavation, for example at Doon Hill, may reveal apparently scant signs of dwellings.

attack primarily from local tribes.[15] The battle would represent the Northumbrians taking out a local centre of power,
as it seems they had done with Bamburgh half a century
or so earlier. The fort would also function as a mustering
point for an army from surrounding realms, such as Higham
postulated as preceding the battle. This view of the rampart
links it with comparable known fortifications in the area,
and explains the proximity of the burials to the rampart: the
warriors were buried where they fell, storming the fort. Yet it
is scarcely a classic hillfort such as Din Eirth, which suggests
that its original primary purpose was not purely defensive; a
seasonal trading emporium or ecclesiastical enclosure, which
might take on other uses as required, would suit better as an
interpretation. In this scenario, the British forces would be
mustering in the fort, with the monks of Bangor assisting their
campaign with prayers and fasting; the intention was either, if
this was an offensive strike aimed at Northumbria, to proceed
over the Dee and march towards Deira, only for Æthelfrith to
storm them before they were able to, or, if it was essentially a
defensive move aimed at preventing Æthelfrith proceeding
into Powys, to wait at Heronbridge and draw Æthelfrith on
into some semblance of an ambush. Two features of early
Anglo-Saxon funerary practices may also hint at the fort's
existence at the time of the battle. Burials often took place
in pre-existing monuments such as barrows: this appears to
have been an act of symbolic appropriation of the ancestral
lands of the subjugated local populace; northern Bernicia has
a number of such burials (O'Brien 1999, 70, 186). Departed
warriors could also act as sentinels, buried on the edge of
territory held and overlooking enemy areas as a guard against
them; such burials are particularly common in the Midlands.
If the Heronbridge rampart already existed, burial within it
could be seen as fitting into both these types: sovereignty of

[15] I do not find the dismissal by Mason (2004, 53) of the notion the fort could
have been a British construction, on the basis that it defended primarily
against incursion from the west, particularly convincing. The fort guards the
lower Dee valley, without any obvious bias in which direction it is primarily
defending against. Even if it were guarding against attacks from the south
and west (which is doubtful), this would be as relevant to British rulers of
Chester as to English ones.

the land is marked by burial within a secured local monument associated with power, and the departed warriors look out from the rampart over the still-British lands around.

b. It could have been constructed by Æthelfrith. The rampart was far more substantial than that of Roman marching camps; the labour required in my view precludes its having been built before the battle, particularly as it could have held about ten times the numbers of troops he is likely to have led.[16] Æthelfrith could perhaps have constructed it afterwards as a defensive measure aimed at securing the local area, and thus access to the sea and the other facilities of the Chester environs already noted. His heavy losses, however, point to his having withdrawn sooner rather than later. And if he built it afterwards, why pick precisely the site of the battle, when there are other sites nearby that afford better visibility towards the highlands (and would offer the opportunity for a more classic type of hillfort)? The proximity of the burials and the rampart is either (more or less) coincidence, or there is a direct connection; yet, if there is a connection, it makes better sense to see the rampart as already in existence, the burials being situated at it because the warriors were killed in storming it.

c. When we turn to Æthelfrith's successor, Eadwine, a quite different situation emerges. Eadwine is recorded by Bede as having overcome Anglesey and Man (*Historia Ecclesiastica* II.5, pp. 148–9): Chester is a likely port for the navy that this clearly implies, continuing the function it had in Roman times. The battle at Heronbridge was the only recorded suppression of British power around Chester before Eadwine, so the territory would still have been hostile and not securely in Northumbrian hands in his reign. The rampart could thus have been a defensive measure carried out in connection with Eadwine's campaigns in the

---

[16] Davies (2010, 156) notes that 'for an army on campaign to build an entirely new fortification on this scale was, as far as the evidence can reveal, unprecedented'; I draw the inference from this that it is wiser to seek another solution, but Davies presses ahead with the notion regardless, and adds the further inference that its construction implies Æthelfrith was unable to take the city, which would have provided an easier option.

Irish Sea.[17] It guards against attack by land both from the south and from the area of Clwyd, but is open to the river without steep slopes; this enabled those posted inside both to attack any enemy ships proceeding along the river, and also to control and guard any trade along the river (such as supplies for Eadwine's navy) or the nearby Roman road; possibly, the Huntington basin (currently a silted-up marshy area) could also have acted as a sort of ships' depot (for shallow vessels, at least). It is at a safe distance from Chester to guard passage (whether hostile or not) towards the city and port, but not too far to put itself beyond usefulness. Its position immediately on the site of the battle the Northumbrians had recently won would essentially be fortuitous in terms of its purpose, though not as regards its symbolic significance. The lack of any link between cemetery and rampart beyond the symbolic is a weakness in this proposal, but the battle would have taken place just a few years earlier, and the construction here could potentially have acted as a reaffirmation of English control, placed directly on the site of the battle they had recently won. We might ask why Eadwine would not simply use the walled *castra* of Chester itself, instead of expending the effort of constructing a fort at Heronbridge. We may, however, question how far the Northumbrians would have wished to make use, for defensive purposes, of a ruinous collection of Roman buildings, which they were not used to living in and probably regarded as useful primarily for ceremonial purposes, as Eadwine did at York in establishing his new church there; more importantly, the Heronbridge site, on the Welsh side of the Dee and on the Roman road south, was arguably better placed to guard against ingression, and might stymie incursions over the Dee to Chester and beyond. (Obviously, the same arguments apply if the fort was established in connection with Æthelfrith's occupation of the Chester environs.)

---

[17] Mason (2007, 42) notes that Eadwine may have established Chester as a base for his exploits in this region, without considering the Heronbridge fort in this light.

The topography of the area

Bede's account implies that whoever originated the traditions behind it was aware that the English king could indeed have picked the monks out from his vantage point before the battle — which is not to say that he actually did so, but that he could be imagined to have done so. This is, I think, likely to reflect the actual topography of the site, known to the original writers of the accounts Bede used (Fig. 2).

Proceeding south from Chester, the Roman road crossed the Dee, then after around a hundred yards dog-legged up a fairly steep slope; from here, the main road proceeded south towards Heronbridge, and on to Viroconium (Wroxeter). Another route split off towards Ffrith and the Welsh highlands, but this too later divided south-west (or possibly west) of Chester, with a branch going roughly along the north Wales coast. The interpretation of the aims of the battle is made more difficult in that it is not clear where the road into Wales (Margary road 66a; see for example the *Digital Atlas of the Roman Empire*) branched off south of Chester. The Lache Eye marshes had to be causewayed or avoided; the most direct dry route would follow roughly the current main road through Lache in a south-westerly direction. Even if a fully constructed military road did not exist along this route (because, for example, it existed further south), or had fallen out of use, almost certainly some form of path did, serving anyone coming from north Wales wishing to cross the Dee at Chester, or travelling in the opposite direction; there is no need to proceed as far south as Heronbridge to do this.[18]

---

[18] I therefore differ from Mason here. On his plan of the area (Mason 2007, 44), he marks the Roman road to the south-west (and then north-east to the Welsh coast) as diverging from the main road southwards just at the northern end of the Heronbridge site, which would mean that Heronbridge was next to the route into north Wales; this route is extrapolated from a short stretch of Roman road marked to the west of Heronbridge on the plan (evidence for the excavation of which is not cited, but it was discovered during excavations of the Chester Business Park in 2002). The Heronbridge settlement may well have been served by a road from the south-west, but this is just as likely to have been supplementary to a more direct road coming into Handbridge (i.e. roughly the road through Lache). The local Chester antiquary, Tom Welsh, who has carried out extensive survey work on Roman roads and ancient earthworks around Chester, emphasises to me, on the basis of an investigation of records

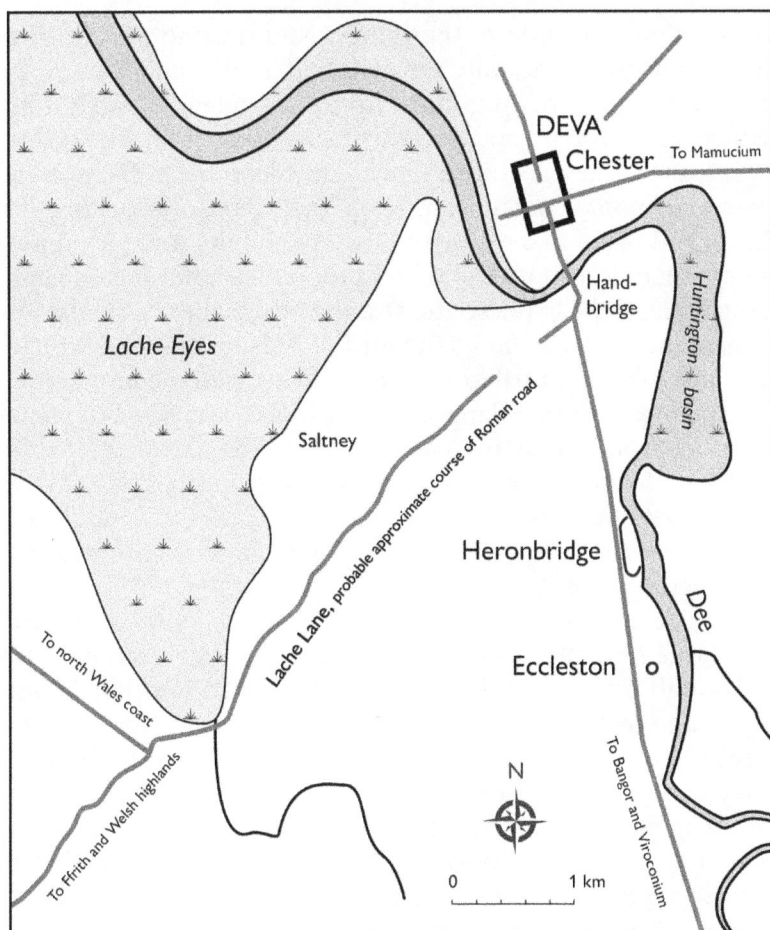

Fig. 2. Topography of the Heronbridge area, as envisaged for the time of the battle. It should be noted that the course of Roman roads is conjectural for much of their length.

After a flat stretch of around a mile, the Roman road south from Chester dipped slightly at Heronbridge for about a hundred yards; the ground again rises slightly to the northern end of the rampart just to the east of the road, and is a little up and

of archaeological excavations and land surveys, just how fragmentary our knowledge of the road system actually is: it is possible, for instance, that the Roman road to Viroconium crossed the Dee just south of Eccleston, rather than at Aldford, and that the road into north Wales crossed the Lache Eyes on a causeway.

down along the side of the rampart for around a third of a mile, then rises gradually for over half a mile, and is cut into by several fairly deep gullies, up to the village of Eccleston, which stands on a good defensive site: apart from the incline to its north, there is quite a steep slope down to the Dee on its east, and another, not quite as steep, to its west, overlooking flat land (and some marshland) to the Welsh hills some six miles away; there is a shorter and less pronounced, but nonetheless noticeable, slope to the south, and the land is then fairly flat for a mile and a half as far as the ford at Aldford, beyond which, at a distance of a further nine miles over varied countryside, lay the monastery of Bangor, which was on the Dee but some distance from the main Wroxeter road. The site of the battle therefore forms a shallow dip in the landscape, beside the Dee to the east and overlooked to both north and south (and to a lesser degree to the west) by slopes which, while not excessively steep, are quite noticeable.

The Heronbridge site is marked, as noted, by the presence of a large rampart immediately next to the excavated burials. Although technically in a hollow, the large rampart is not at a huge tactical disadvantage, as the slopes towards it are gentle, and the rampart itself would both have prevented easy access, and increased visibility for those upon it. Visibility from here is an important factor, and encompasses a wider band of the horizon than many surrounding sites which might seem on other grounds preferable for a defensive position: northwards towards Chester—limited (unless a watchtower were raised quite high, to be able to see along the flat road into the city); north-eastwards—good; it is possible, in particular, to see the Roman road entering the city from the east, along which Æthelfrith probably came; eastwards— very good up to the rise immediately east of the Dee, but no further; south-eastwards—very good, with views right over to the mid-Cheshire ridge; southwards—good as far as Eccleston, but no further; south-westwards—limited, only as far as rise to the west of Eccleston; westwards—limited to a few hundred metres, but a raised platform would afford visibility to the Welsh hills, but not the plain in between, across which incursions towards Chester would take place; north-westwards—very limited, as there is a rise in the ground here, unless a high tower existed, from which the Saltney area might to an extent be viewed. The best views, therefore, are afforded towards the quadrant from north-east to south-east.

The portion of the ridge on which Eccleston stands might seem to offer a force approaching from the south a good vantage point from which to launch an attack downhill towards Heronbridge; in reality, and considering the size of forces at this period, the distance is too great for a charge, and is hampered by gullies. In contrast, for a force approaching from the north, it is but a short distance from the rise just to the north of Heronbridge down to the rampart and the site of the battle; moreover, it would be possible to view anyone contained within the rampart quite clearly (as Æthelfrith is supposed to have done with the monks). An attack could easily be launched from here, but would face a ditch and a rise in the ground just before the rampart itself; a more likely tactic would be to swing slightly to the west and tackle the rampart from the slightly higher ground in that direction, without a ditch in the way (it is also along the western rampart that the excavated battle cemetery was found). Tactically, the site of the battle makes better sense if the rampart was in place: the defenders would have a strong defensive wall and good visibility in several directions (and more so if they had watchtowers), but attackers would have some advantage in being able to descend a slight slope to reach the fort: a battle between equal forces could go either way here. If the rampart was not there at the time of the battle, we have to imagine the British forces descending over a mile from Eccleston to approximately where the cemetery lies to meet the English, who would have launched an attack from the Heronbridge rise, covering a much shorter distance, much to their advantage. If the British forces were at Eccleston, as they must have been before the battle, it is difficult to conceive why they would set out to confront the English in this way to their own disadvantage, instead of drawing the English on to attack at Eccleston.

Place-names

Chester

That Chester is the site near which the battle took place is scarcely in doubt: the Old English *Legacæstir* (along with slight variants), first recorded by Bede in the context of this battle, occurs as the city's name up until the eleventh century, when the *Lega-* was dropped, giving 'Chester'; the Old English form derives from Old Welsh *Cair Legion* (Dodgson 1981, 2–7). The Roman form Deva (see Rivet and Smith 1979, *s.v.*) does not survive as the name of the city, only the river, but in any case probably always meant '(the fortress) on the Dee'. The English form *Dee* must have been borrowed from Old Welsh *Dēw* before *ē* > *ui* in the seventh century (Dodgson 1970, 21).

Eccleston

The name *Eccleston*, although English, includes as its first element a British word derived from Latin *ecclesia*, 'church'. As far as records indicate, the only word for 'church' ever used in Old English was *cirice* (derived ultimately from Greek *kyriake*). Several place-names in *Eccles-* exist, particularly in northern England and south-eastern Scotland; there is a concentration in Lancashire, and Eccleston south of Chester could be regarded as an outlier of this group, which would put it within a contiguous area west of the Pennines overrun by Northumbria mainly in the early seventh century, even though it came to fall later within the kingdom of Mercia. Some important work on *Eccles*-place-names has been carried out in recent years, for example by Hough (2009) and James (2009). From this it emerges that places containing the element *Eccles-* were probably designated as such by British speakers as a sort of pseudo-place-name indicating 'the church' or 'church estate', and that the term was adopted by English speakers, who took it as a place-name proper (without necessarily understanding its commonplace meaning, and without borrowing it into English as a word for 'church'). Elements such as *-ton* were added by the English to indicate a settlement.[19] The name clearly indicates the presence

---

[19] Hough argues (2009, 116–17) that compound names with Celtic elements that occur only in Scotland, such as Ecclefechan, are later formations, and

of both English and British speakers in the vicinity for a time, the English learning from the British that the place was designated (an) *eglēs* and then using this as a proper noun in English. The English name would have been given either by neighbouring English-speakers to a British settlement, or by the English inhabitants of such a settlement after the British-speaking inhabitants had departed or gone over to speaking English, but while its particular status as an *eglēs* was remembered (it is possible that, using a form adapted to the phonology of English, *eclēs* was retained as a substrate item from their earlier language by new speakers of English): in the case of Eccleston, this must be the early to mid-seventh century; a similar date is arrived at independently for the Dee (see above).

The *eglēs* nomenclature need not necessarily indicate the presence of an actual church, however. James (2009, 126–7) points out that the primary meaning of *ecclesia*, the Church as an institution rather than a building for worship, was most probably current in the post-Roman period in Britain, the primarily concrete sense only taking over in succeeding centuries, probably only after the tenth century in British areas. In the sixth century, the physical presence of the Church would have been manifested mainly in rather lowly oratories and the buildings of proto-monastic communities; *eglēs* would have referred to the location of a Christian community, encompassing both the homestead, along with a place of worship, and its accompanying land. The pagan English would have regarded *eglēs* as the name for a particular type of land-holding, subject to the jurisdiction

notes, for example, that the saints commemorated in such names appear to have lived around 700; the earliest forms of the names would have consisted of the simplex *Eccles* (in the earlier form *Eglēs*). This is what is encountered in England, where compound Celtic forms are not found. A date well before 700, such as Hough considers likely for the simplex *Eccles* names, is entirely consistent with Eccleston having gained its name shortly after the battle of Chester in the early seventh century (though the *-ton* may perhaps have been added slightly later: Gelling notes (2009, 8) that this element is common from *c.* 700, and with the loss of long unstressed vowels in English in the early eighth century, *Eccles* might be perceived as a genitive of a name, calling for an additional element to give a folk-etymological meaning like 'settlement of Eccle'; cf. James 2009, 129). It is fairly clear that Eccleston must have received its name after the battle of Chester at a point when English settlement was becoming established here, i.e. roughly the mid-seventh century.

of the Church institution; they are unlikely to have been interested in the Christian religious dimension as such (*ibid.*, 141). (As James points out, this differs from earlier interpretations, which took *eclēs* to be a term used by the early, pagan English to designate a Celtic church building.)

James (*ibid.*, 131–3) argues that *Eccles* place-names in Northumbria may indicate church estates, originally British, which were taken over by the English as useful, cohesive landholdings (whether or not any ecclesiastical presence was maintained by the English), with a system of administration, command of which would have facilitated the rapid expansion of Northumbrian power in the late sixth and early seventh centuries. West of the Pennines, *Eccles* place-names between the Fylde and the Mersey correspond to later hundreds, for example, indicating the likelihood of administrative continuity from British to English authority. Such a connection cannot be shown so clearly in the case of Eccleston, but it may be noted that both Eccleston and Bangor-is-coed, whose connections are considered below, are included within the Domesday Cheshire hundred of 'Dudestan' (Broxton), despite being on opposite sides of the river. At the least, the place-name Eccleston may point to a link with the Northumbrian adoption of pre-existing British estates evidenced elsewhere, and hence indicate Northumbrian presence here, whether under Æthelfrith or his successor Eadwine.

Bede's account of the monks of Bangor at the battle, combined with the archaeological evidence that the battle took place close to Eccleston, suggests that the ecclesiastical estate or *eglēs* from which Eccleston took its name belonged to the monastery of Bangor. Triad 60's link between the battle and the Orchard of Bangor points in the same direction, and the orchard in question may be identified with the *eglēs*, a sort of 'grange' (to use a term applicable to a later period). The *eglēs* need not, of course, have been precisely in modern Eccleston; the place-name merely indicates that the *tūn*, settlement, was somewhere near an *eglēs*. This fact, and the acknowledgement that an *eglēs* was not a church building but an estate, may, unfortunately, render recent archaeological attempts to pinpoint a British church in Eccleston fruitless (see Fig. 3 for a picture of the supposed site of such a church or monastic foundation).

Fig. 3. Eccleston old churchyard, with Eccleston church tower in the background. The 'old church' is in fact probably a folly. The site, enclosed by a curved wall, as seen in the photograph, is tantalisingly reminiscent of ancient circular church sites, and is strategically situated, a raised area overlooking the Dee valley; however, recent excavations by the Chester Archaeological Society have not revealed any sixth-century materials.

Bangor

Bangor is the name of at least three early ecclesiastical foundations in Wales (Bangor on the Menai, Bangor-is-Coed on the Dee, and Bangor Teifi). The name indicates a stockaded enclosure (a cloister, as it were), *bangor* still being a word in agricultural use for an enclosure protected by a wattled fence strengthened by a plaited top (Owen and Morgan 2007, *s.v.* 'Bangor'). Bede's form, 'Bancornaburg', is partially anglicised: 'burg' means a defensible enclosure, and 'Bancorna' is probably the genitive plural of an ethnonym, so 'the protected enclosure of the people of Bangor' (*ibid., s.v.* 'Bangor-is-Coed'). There is little doubt that the site of Bangor on the Dee is intended, though the generality of the name's meaning could leave open the possibility that some other early ecclesiastical site was intended. The precise site of the monastery (assuming it was close to Bangor-is-Coed) cannot be determined: if, as is likely, it was on the actual river, its remains have almost certainly been swept away by the many changes in the course of the Dee over the centuries in this area.

The local context

The fact that the battle took place south of Chester hints at the city's relative unimportance, in that the British chose not to make a stand to its north-east, the direction from which the English forces almost certainly proceeded. It could therefore not have been a major focus of population or power at the time, though it could presumably still function as a port (though even here, it may have been superseded by Meols, on the north Wirral coast, at least as a trading entrepôt).[20]

Quite what Chester's status was is difficult to determine. Much of the evidence that has survived at Wroxeter that has enabled us to see this city flourishing into the early seventh century (White and Barker 1998, ch. 7) would not have survived at Chester owing to later urbanisation, but the evidence reviewed by Mason (2007), scant though it may be, tends to suggest a rather lower level of post-Roman occupancy.

Mason (*ibid.*, 30) notes the probability that the city where a council of British ecclesiastics met Augustine in 601 was Chester, though Bede does not specify the location—the *Annales Cambriae*, at least, say it took place in the *urbs legionis* (which is in fact a rendering of the Old Welsh name of the city, *Cair Legion*). The *Annales* may not be independent of Bede here; the identification of the location could easily have been surmised from the general contextual mention of Chester and Bangor in the *Historia Ecclesiastica*. Yet the surmise is probably correct: Bede's narrative shows the deep involvement of the monks of Bangor, with the implication that the council must have been held close to their monastery, juxtaposed with their later destruction at the battle of Chester, explicitly close to the monastery. Augustine's prophecy of calamity visited upon the British heretics appears to be directed not so much at the British Church in general as at hosts at the 601 council, namely the monks of Bangor, who now met a grisly end, close to where, it is implied, the council

---

[20] See the survey by Griffiths, Philpott and Egan (2007), which details an array of finds from pre-Roman times up to the Viking period; Higham (1993a, 63) also notes that a small number of finds indicates some activity at Meols from the fifth to seventh centuries; there is some indication from finds at 1 Abbey Green of the importation of mediterranean wares into the city in the post-Roman period (Snyder 1998, 167; Thomas 1981, 25).

had been held. Chester then emerges as a city with symbolic significance, suited to host a Church council; it is also likely to have had its own bishop. However, as Mason indicates, it also probably had the practical advantage of being able to accommodate the parties concerned, particularly if, as seems likely, the *principia* buildings were still in a state of repair to offer facilities such as a large hall (we might compare the survival of the *principia* at York, which Eadwine used as a palace, setting up the predecessor of York Minster in its grounds: Bede, *Historia Ecclesiastica* ii.14, pp. 186–7 and n. 3). The city may well have been regarded as neutral ground, as opposed to the monastery itself, and as offering the sort of Roman urban setting that Augustine would be used to from the Continent as a venue for a council—the hosts are keeping up appearances, in other words, and this illustrates an essential difference between the sub-Roman British still seeking to maintain some semblance of Roman culture while the pagan English, to judge from what can be seen of Æthelfrith's action, had no regard for it whatever (and only acquired it upon their adoption of a form of Roman culture in the form of Christianity). Yet the population of the city was probably very small, despite its possible symbolic status.

If Chester was not the local centre of population, what was (in so far as a 'centre' existed at all)? The clue may lie in what Bede tells of Bangor: although his account of over 2100 monks living and working there is surely exaggeration, we are presented with the picture of a substantial community, and centre of politico-ecclesiastical power. It would be a mistake to think in terms of an urban centre, but if Bangor was anything like as substantial as Bede hints, it must have been the most significant focus of population and power in the immediate area. The site of the battle could be interpreted as indicating a desire to make a stand to defend (for the British) or take (for the English) this more important centre, rather than the largely symbolic city of Chester itself (though its port may have been of interest). It is even possible that Heronbridge itself was part of the monastery dispersed among 'daughter-houses'.[21]

---

[21] We can, at present, approach such questions only in the crudest terms. A pressing need exists to assess the whole landscape around Chester: there are, for example, many earthworks in the Eccleston area apart from the

The wider political context

Establishing the wider political situation around the time of the battle is highly problematic (cf. Higham 1993a, esp. 30–6). The development of the early Welsh (British) kingdoms is discussed by Charles-Edwards (2013, 14–21). Around 600, there was an array of smaller subkingdoms, whose allegiances would have shifted,[22] in addition to the large realms that are better known, such as Gwynedd (this situation is also supported by the historical memories reflected in the earliest Welsh poetry, with Powys in particular being a fluid entity: Rowland 1990, 125). Whatever the details, any overarching kingdom such as Gwynedd or Powys must have been composed of a number of smaller subkingdoms, the names of which may survive in later commotes such as Tegeingl or Dogfeiling. In the face of an onslaught from Æthelfrith, the smaller realms in the area would have formed an alliance: hence Æthelfrith's strike was in effect against Powys, conceived as a union of lesser sub-kingdoms.

A similar situation almost certainly obtained in English areas. The Midlands probably had a multiplicity of smaller kingdoms (Brooks 1989, 163); the smaller examples would have been little more than ancestral clan holdings, but, as the Tribal Hidage indicates, these small realms such as the Pencersæte or Tomsæte were gradually becoming tributary districts of more powerful kingdoms (Bassett 1989a, 18–23). The actual origins of the English kingdoms are matters of debate (*ibid.*, 3–5), but,

---

Heronbridge rampart, almost none of which have been subjected to any archaeological assessment (many are no doubt later, but we simply do not know). It is probable that in the sixth century a complex network of church estates, military sites, farms and so forth existed, with varying levels of defence, but at present nothing can be discerned about this system, and concentrating solely on sites such as Eccleston church or the Heronbridge rampart is likely to skew our understanding.

[22] Some memory of this situation may be preserved in poetry. Rowland (1990, 135) argues, for example, that this is discernible in the dedication of the poem *Marwnad Cynddylan* to the king of Gwynedd. It was probably composed shortly after the death of the Powys prince Cynddylan's death, which may have taken place at the battle against Northumbria at Winwæd in Yorkshire in 655, where the Mercian king Penda fell, along with his Welsh allies. The Cyndrwynyn (the family of Cynddylan) seem to be hinting in the poem that should Gwynedd wish to claim an area of Powys, Dogfeiling, which was under the rule of a rival clan, the Cadelling, they would not object.

apart from initially small-scale settlement of possibly already functioning estates, at least one element was the take-over, whether by clan-based settlement groups or erstwhile mercenaries posted by the British authorities to guard strategic sites, of pre-existing British administrative areas (*ibid.*, 24–5);[23] this might give rise to larger realms almost from the outset, and it would also allow for some continuity in large-scale administration, which could be relevant to the development of the Cornovian territory into Mercia, for example. The geopolitical situation in central Britannia around the year 600 is presented, in tentative form and in broad strokes, in Fig. 4.

Gwynedd

North-west Wales—essentially Snowdonia and Anglesey, extending south and east to an undetermined distance—was in Roman times the region of the Ordovices (see Rivet and Smith 1979, *s.v.*). They are last mentioned in a fifth-century inscription, which is followed fairly soon by the first mention of Gwynedd, which was clearly essentially the same realm renamed, most probably representing an alliance over the Irish Sea with the Féni (whose name gave rise to 'Gwynedd')— the Irish settlement in this area being substantial, with Irish speakers probably surviving until *c.* 600, by when they had become assimilated (Charles-Edwards 2013, 178–9, 190). The story found in the *Historia Brittonum* (ch. 14 and 62) by which Gwynedd was established by a British force from the north, and expelled the Irish, has no historical basis and represents the propaganda of a later century (*ibid.*, 190: 'the legend tells the opposite of the truth').

---

[23] Bassett (1989*a*, 25) notes the example of the Romano-British town of Great Chesterford in Essex being taken over by the inhabitants of nearby Bonhunt; the importance of Lichfield within the realm of Mercia might suggest something similar, by way of a take-over of Wall, the nearby British Letocetum (whose name Lichfield perpetuates). Brooks (1989, 169) argues that 'it is at Wall rather than at Lichfield that archaeologists should seek the sub-Roman and early Christian roots of the Mercian kingdom'.

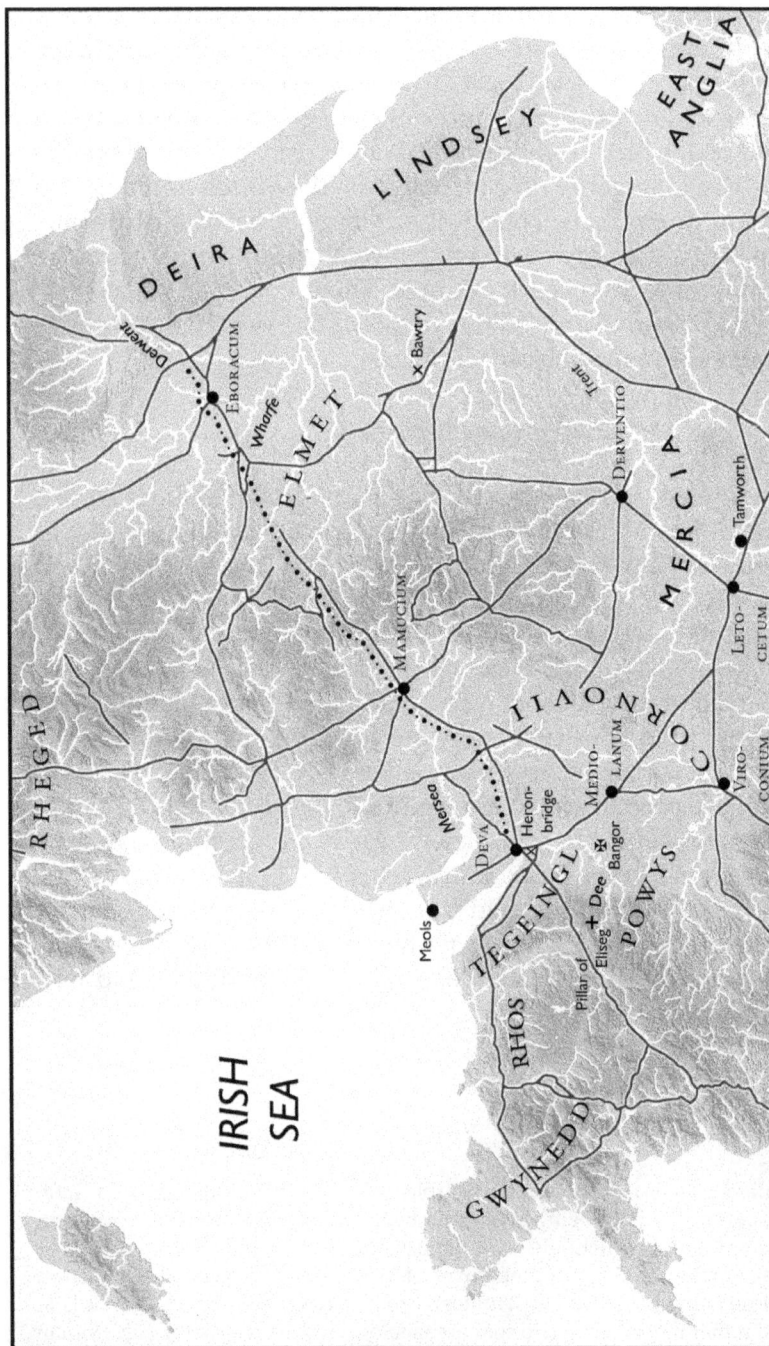

Fig. 4. British and English kingdoms, Roman roads, places mentioned, and Æthelfrith's probable route (dotted).

Powys

The origins of the later realm of Powys are debatable; the name does not occur before the ninth century but in origin must be much older, from Latin *pagenses*, 'country folk'. Charles-Edwards (2013, 16, 389) tends to favour the *pagenses* being a break-away group from western Cornovian territory (characterised by town-dwellers, presumably, as at Wroxeter), but there is little indication the Cornovii ever extended far into what is now Wales, where the heartland of Powys lay from the time it was first recorded; note, for example, the siting of the Pillar of Eliseg (an early monument of Powys) in the Valle Crucis. As noted, the notion of Powys having lost the lands of Shropshire is a later poetic fabrication, even if it retains the basic truth that British lands became English. If the Cornovii 'became' Powys, then only the region's westernmost fringe eventually ended up in the new polity, which must have absorbed a series of smaller entities to the west.

The fall of Selyf, king of Powys, at the battle of Chester may be the result of annalistic attribution of legendary figures to recorded events, but even if it is, a king of Powys, in the sense of a possibly loose amalgamation of smaller realms,[24] is likely, whatever his name may have been, to have led a contingent against Æthelfrith, and, given Æthelfrith's victory, to have fallen.

Tegeingl

In the north-east of Wales in Roman times lived the tribe of the Deceangli (see Rivet and Smith 1979, *s.v.*), whose name survives in that of the area of Tegeingl, along the western Dee estuary. They had no *civitas* capital, as far as is known, and may have been under direct Roman governmental control, as lead was derived from their territory. It is probable that their eastern border was the Dee.

[24] It is interesting that in the *Life of St Beuno*, the saint cursed Selyf's sons never to pass on their kingdom; Harleian Genealogy 27 indeed indicates the kings of Powys bypassed Selyf in terms of descent, going through what must be his brother, Eliud, instead (Bartrum 1966, 12; Bartrum 1993, *s.v.* 'Selyf Sarffgadau'); Harleian Genealogy 22 (Bartrum 1966, 12) has the ancestry of Selim, identical with that of genealogy 27 from his father upwards, but concludes with no descendants for Selim. There may be a hint that he has been absorbed into the genealogy from another line, possibly of a sub-kingdom.

Higham (1993*a*, 72) views the origins of Powys as lying in north-east Wales, hence roughly the area of the former Deceangli, though surprisingly he does not mention Tegeingl in this connection.[25] However, the north-east corner of Wales does not correspond to the heartland of the later kingdom of Powys, so the proposal is rather questionable. Where Higham's postulated proto-Powys would have been ruled from is also not clear; we might think of Rhos, but this sub-kingdom when recorded later was very much a secondary part of Gwynedd.[26] It is arguable that the influence of Gwynedd is likely to have extended even at an early period into north-east Wales.

Despite some weaknesses in Higham's proposals, we may, for the sake of argument, postulate a realm in the north-east of Wales that we may term Tegeingl (covering a larger area than the later-recorded district of Tegeingl); the reason for doing so, apart from the likelihood of some tribal continuity from Roman times, is to ward off the assumption that around the year 600 the political situation was the same as a few centuries later, with a few large kingdoms in operation; if Powys existed, it would have had a much looser organisation, and areas such as Tegeingl would have been subject to varying allegiances.

The Cornovii

In Roman times, the northern Marches were the territory of the Cornovii. Their *civitas* capital was Viroconium (Wroxeter). They appear to have occupied all the lowlands south of the Mersey between the Welsh highlands and the Peak District, and southwards a little distance from Wroxeter, bordering on

[25] Higham altered his views; he had previously (e.g. 1992) viewed Powys as descended from the realm of the Cornovii. The idea that the people were *pagenses* because they had no cities of their own, unlike their neighbours to the east, is not specially convincing.

[26] This is illustrated in the genealogies of Gwynedd, where the peripheral territories were assigned to the sons of Cunedda other than Einion Yrth, who was the ancestor of the kings of Gwynedd and also of Rhos, with the core territory of the realm, along with Rhos, thus being marked out as distinct (Charles-Edwards 2013, 361–2; cf. 316, where the independent dynasty of Rhos is noted). Mason (2007, *passim*) frequently uses 'Din Eirth', a fortress almost certainly associated with the Rhos dynasty, as a metonym for the kingdom (proto-Powys) that controlled the Chester area, a usage which hides many unargued assumptions.

the Dobunni; towards the east they bordered the Corieltavi of Lincolnshire and Leicestershire, perhaps a little to the east of Tamworth. In subsequent discussion I refer to the Cornovii in reference to the post-Roman situation; the successor realm to the Roman *civitas* of the Cornovii was probably actually known by the name of its 'capital', Viroconium (compare how the realm of the Silures became Gwent, from the city Venta: Charles-Edwards 2013, 17), and this is perpetuated in the English term, Wreo-censæte, 'inhabitants of Viroconium' (rather than 'of the Wrekin': Higham 1993a, 69), who appear as tributaries of Mercia in the Tribal Hidage. According to Higham's analysis, they occupied Shropshire and Cheshire and some of Staffordshire; in 600, these would certainly still have been British, not English. Viroconium, the destination of the Roman road southwards from Chester, was still a place of significance at this time, and possibly still the administrative heart of a realm that included Chester. If, as Higham argues, the Wreocensæte were a continuation of the Cornovii, their territory had clearly shrunk: the eastern part of the Cornovian realm was taken up by English Mercia.

There is some incongruity in seeing small realms in many areas, both Welsh and English, alongside large units, the successors of the *civitates*, but such may have been the case; in reality, the local lords within such large units are likely to have increasingly lent their allegiance to more powerful, warrior-based kingdoms nearby, whether British or English, which suggests that by 600, the *civitas* of the Cornovii as a functioning administrative unit may have been somewhat superficial in its authority, a moribund entity that was soon to be displaced by Mercia and Powys.

Mercia

Our understanding of the battle of Chester depends in no small part on the status of Mercia. Mercia proper appears, on the basis of the earliest pagan burials, to have been based around the middle Trent valley, in the area just upstream of Burton (see O'Brien 1999, map 21; Gelling 1992, 29; Brooks 1989, 162),[27] and

---

[27] The separate conglomeration of fairly early, pagan, finds in the southern Peak District indicated on O'Brien's map represents the Pecsæte, listed as tributary to Mercia in the Tribal Hidage.

extending to Repton, where a Mercian royal monastery was situated at least from the late seventh century (Brooks 1989, 162); the origins of Mercia probably lie in the sixth rather than fifth century. It cannot have taken long to expand beyond the heartland, for example the six miles or so south to encompass Lichfield and Tamworth, where the later archbishopric and royal hall were situated. Yet around the year 600, English settlements in the West Midlands were still limited (Higham notes, 1993*a*, 77, 90, that pagan English burials did not extend much beyond the upper Trent valley and the Peak District or into Cheshire), and the British *civitas* capital of Wroxeter was still an entity to be reckoned with. Brooks (1989, 163) argues that it was only later, under Penda in the mid-seventh century, that a powerful kingdom of Mercia emerged. The battle of Chester falls in the middle of a century or so during which Mercia grew from a small English enclave on the eastern edge of the Cornovian territory to the major political power of the Midlands, but just what its status was around 600 is debatable.

Higham seeks to push back the rise of Mercian hegemony. He argues (1995, 75–7) that around the time of the Anglo-Saxon Tribal Hidage, which he views as having been undertaken for Æthelfrith's successor Eadwine but which uses an earlier Mercian tribute list, Mercia was a significant English realm, with a number of tributary tribes under it. In another important article (1992) that revises the whole context of the battle of Chester, he argues that it was already significant under Æthelfrith's contemporary, Cearl.[28] Eadwine clearly regarded him as a powerful ally, able to protect him from Æthelfrith, as he not only spent a considerable portion of his exile under Cearl, but also married his daughter, Cwœnburh, who bore two sons to him there (Bede, *Historia Ecclesiastica* ii.14, pp. 186–7). The marriage alliance indicates Cearl entertained the hope of ousting Æthelfrith from the

---

[28] Some additional points to note are that the Church council held at Chester in 601 between the British and Augustine must have involved passage through Mercian lands controlled by Cearl, and he may even have sponsored the council as a riposte against the interference in his affairs implicit in Æthelberht's support for a bishop, Augustine, who was intent upon subjugating all the British bishops to him (and hence to political control from Kent); Cearl may not have been Christian, but the British population who lived on and within his borders were (Higham 1993*a*, 86).

throne of Northumbria; yet Eadwine's long sojourn in Mercia, while it indicates that Cearl regarded Northumbria as an ongoing threat, also points to protracted insecurity on Cearl's part in effecting the usurpation of Æthelfrith. The battle of Chester may represent an attempt at it, however. Cearl needed greater forces to undertake the foray, which meant forming an alliance with British forces. These would have been unwilling to support him until they saw some benefit to themselves. Æthelfrith's continued raiding of British areas, as reported by Bede, would have inclined the British realms towards forming the alliance Cearl was seeking.

It is interesting that Eadwine is regarded in Welsh tradition as a great traitor. This may derive simply from his attacks on north Wales when he was king, but such actions do not amount to treachery as such; however, if he had been the beneficiary of Welsh support in an abortive attempt to take the throne (which in the end he achieved with East Anglian assistance), only later to exploit the weakening of Welsh forces that his rival Æthelfrith had achieved in defeating the army gathered for the very purpose of putting Eadwine on the throne, the derision with which Welsh tradition regarded Eadwine would be explicable.

Bede does not hint at Mercian involvement—but he also gives no indication of who was leading the British forces either, his focus being solely on the monks. Higham (1992, 7) suggests that just as Chester had formed a suitable central venue for churchmen travelling from the British areas of Wales and the western seaboard of Britain, and was on the hub of the Roman road system, so too it might have functioned as a mustering point for a force drawn from the Marches, north Wales and Mercia, as it set out to harry Northumbria, and perhaps attempt to put Eadwine on the throne. The reason for Æthelfrith fighting as far west as Chester would be that he swooped down on this force and destroyed it. If Mercia was indeed involved and was defeated, Northumbria would have imposed a friendly ruler on it after Cearl (who may have been killed in the battle); Eadwine's subsequent ability to operate freely around the Irish Sea, unhindered by Mercian aggression as far as we know, would thus be explained.[29]

---

[29] In this scenario, Eadwine either escaped the battle or was not in it; if Cearl

Mercia's relations with the British appear to have been collaborative, a reflection, no doubt, of the origins of Mercia. The British would initially have regarded Mercia as an area of English settlement within their own Cornovian realm and under its control, but in time any real power would have become focused on the warrior-based nascent English kingdom; this had certainly taken place by 600, but Mercian expansion had so far been minimal, and the British may well have maintained the delusion of authority resting in their hands. Thus, instead of thinking of two opposed realms, of the British Cornovii and the English Mercians, we should envisage two co-existent world-views: the British regarded themselves as the legitimate controllers of the region, including its English populace, while the English saw themselves as heirs to the local administration of the Cornovian region, including Chester, even though as yet they occupied only a small part of it. The succeeding period of English expansion in the seventh century was in all likelihood to a large degree a switching of allegiance of local lords away from the increasingly ineffective British authorities (other than those in the highlands) to the powerful king of Mercia, accompanied by an English acculturation (Higham 1993*a*, 90, 99; he thinks the British Cornovii, the Wreocensæte, may have survived until 642, when direct rule was imposed by Mercia). Æthelfrith's incursion deep into Cornovian territory without meeting any noted resistance suggests a weakness of political control in the area, with the British authorities ineffective but with strong Mercian power still not extending much beyond its heartland in this direction.

The political relations between Mercia and the British realms at the time of the battle of Chester are uncertain, but Mercian aggression towards Powys can be discerned only from the time of Æthelbald (716–57) onwards (Rowland 1990, 138); before this, all evidence, both English and Welsh, points to Powys and Gwynedd working alongside Mercia in conflict with Northumbria (Rowland 1990, 125–38). The earliest clear instance is the

fell in it, or died at this time, Eadwine would have been forced to flee rapidly to Rædwald. The ruler arguably imposed on Mercia by Æthelfrith was either Pybba or Eowa; Penda, the details of whose reign are not wholly clear, later rebelled and established Mercia as a power hostile to Northumbria (Higham 1992, 10; Charles-Edwards 2013, 391).

defeat by Cadwallon and Penda of Eadwine at Hatfield Chase in 633/634. The death of Oswald in the Marches at Maserfelth (Oswestry) in 642 almost certainly reflects a Northumbrian attempt to defeat Powys as an ally of Mercia, splitting the Welsh from their Mercian allies; the battle of Cogwy (as it is known in Welsh tradition) was celebrated for example by Cynddelw in the late eleventh century as a clash between Powys and Oswald (Rowland 1990, 124). The natural conclusion, particularly if Mercia was already as significant as Higham reckons, would be that Æthelfrith's incursion was a prototype of what his son Oswald attempted a little later, an effort to defeat Powys and thus stymie Mercian–British collaboration against Northumbria.[30]

Northumbria

Æthelfrith's kingdom of Northumbria was formed of two realms, Bernicia and Deira;[31] Æthelfrith was from the royal house of Bernicia, but, as king of Bernicia, took over Deira around 604, and exiled the males of its royal house, including Eadwine.[32]

---

[30]   The details of the battle in which Oswald perished are unknown, but, if we accept that it took place at Oswestry, it is notable that a substantial Iron Age fort lay nearby (Fig. 17), and the course of battle could possibly have been similar to that at Heronbridge, with the Northumbrians attempting to storm a British stronghold (though evidence for occupation of the fort at this stage does not appear to have been found).

[31]   Both names are of British origin, and hint at take-overs of pre-existing political entities, or of the earlier existence of English subrealms within predominantly British political structures. The name 'Bernicia' relates to a gap, which Charles-Edwards (2013, 384) suggests may have been the Solway–Tyne corridor, which the earliest English here may be envisaged as guarding (whether placed there by themselves or originally by the local British authorities), around the Corbridge area. The name 'Deira' probably means the people of the Derwent valley; Eadwine is recorded as having a royal hall here, and the pagan temple was at Goodmanham, near Market Weighton, in the hills above the valley—it probably marks an ancestral focus, and is close to one of the earliest Anglo-Saxon cemeteries at Sancton (see the discussion in Chapter 2). By Æthelfrith's day, Deira encompassed pretty much the East Riding of Yorkshire.

[32]   Æthelfrith married the Deiran princess Acha (who bore St Oswald to him), either before or after taking Deira, and exiled the male members of the dynasty, namely Hereric (father of St Hild of Whitby: Bede, *Historia Ecclesiastica* IV.23, pp. 406–7) and his younger uncle Eadwine. Hereric fled to the protection of King Cerdic (Ceretic), it seems in Elmet, and was poisoned there (Bede, *Historia*

Bede makes it clear that Æthelfrith was an expansionist ruler (he defeated the Scots of Dál Riata, for example), but fairly rapid expansion began much earlier; for example, the *Historia Brittonum* (ch. 61) indicates that the Northumbrian royal fort of Bamburgh was taken by Ida, founder of the Bernician dynasty, from the British in the mid-sixth century (Charles-Edwards 2013, 383). The areas controlled by the English were, however, small at this time: burial evidence indicates that Anglo-Saxon physical presence in Bernicia, including Yeavering, and Elmet in the fifth, sixth and early seventh centuries was minimal (O'Brien 1999, 185). Æthelfrith's successor Eadwine continued the expansionist policy, subjugating the isles of the Irish Sea, and destroying the subject kingdom of Elmet, very near to Deira (its boundary was probably the River Wharfe), as well, in all likelihood, as other areas such as Rheged around the Solway Firth (Higham 1993*b*, 99; 1995, 80, 83). Thus Æthelfrith's incursion as far as Chester was part of a much longer-term expansion of the realm of Northumbria.[33]

Ecclesiastica IV.23, pp. 410–11), no doubt at the instigation of Æthelfrith, but Eadwine escaped. It cannot be determined when their exile began, but it is unlikely to have been long after 604. Eadwine would not have been a claimant to the throne of Deira while Hereric was alive, so his marriage to the daughter of the king of Mercia most probably took place after this. Eadwine therefore spent a decade or so in exile before he was able to take Northumbria.

[33] One difficulty in making assessments of the politics of this remote period of Northumbrian history is that there is something of a watershed between Æthelfrith and Eadwine. The one was a pagan, the other Christian. It is not, in this case, that Bede was prejudiced against the one and adulatory towards the other—he is remarkably positive towards Æthelfrith. But the reign of Eadwine is considerably more fully, and precisely, described than Æthelfrith's: this is a reflection not only of the beginning of written records, but also of Eadwine's implicit adoption of *romanitas*, and hence the norms of political motivation that characterised the 'civilised' world. Whereas Æthelfrith appears to have acted essentially as a Germanic warlord, a king of an originally very small realm (which expanded as a result of his activities), raiding and defeating his enemies but with not much more than local horizons, Eadwine moved in a wider world: his baptism and establishment of a church in York was a statement of his arrogation of the power of Rome, in the city which proclaimed the first Christian emperor, Constantine—a symbolic act, not a mundanely practical one in a city which can scarcely by this stage have been much more than a pile of semi-ruinous buildings, but an act which marked the aggrandisement of Eadwine's kingship from the level of a warlord based in the Derwent valley and Yorkshire Wolds to one who was part of the Roman Christian empire.

East Anglia

The other main central Anglo-Saxon kingdom was East Anglia, under Rædwald. Rædwald was under the protection of Æthelberht of Kent: he would not have been in a position to start wars without Æthelberht's approval (Higham 1992, 5) and would thus have been contained as a threat to Northumbria. When Æthelberht died in 616, Rædwald became free either to appease the powerful Æthelfrith or to confront him. He chose confrontation: for now he had Æthelfrith's rival, the exiled Eadwine, in his court, a situation which gave him the opportunity to put a friendly ally on the throne of Northumbria. However, before this Rædwald, under pressure from the Northumbrian king, had come very close to betraying Eadwine to Æthelfrith—Bede shows a king vacillating.[34] His reasons were no doubt twofold: the risk of the undertaking (in the event, he lost his son in the battle which toppled Æthelfrith), and his impotence to act while Æthelberht was alive. What can be deduced about the likely course of events? Æthelfrith's campaign away from East Anglia, culminating in the battle at Chester, implies that Rædwald was not yet a threat, or he would have focused his efforts there, and also that Eadwine was not yet at Rædwald's court, which might have had a similar effect.[35] It is probable, therefore, that Eadwine came to Rædwald after the battle of Chester, possibly indeed as a result of it if it is seen as having undermined the power of Mercia, where he had previously been in exile. Rædwald, in

(Higham, 1995, 30, notes that Bede downplays Constantine, probably because he was an upstart; Eadwine is likely to have exploited the imperial connections with York, though of course this is surmise based on what can be deduced from his other actions.)

[34] Bede lays the credit for dissuading Rædwald from betraying Eadwine on his queen (*Historia Ecclesiastica* II.12, pp. 180–1), who regarded such behaviour as dishonourable. This is a typical example of how women are presented as exercising political influence, if not direct power, in Germanic tradition, and, stereotypical as it may be, it is not necessarily untrue.

[35] Davies (2010, 155) assumes that Eadwine could already have been at Rædwald's court at the time of the battle; he concludes that from Æthelfrith's perspective 'A decisive victory could have persuaded Rædwald to throw his weight behind the Northumbrian king and to dispose of his rival, Edwin'. This seems a little contorted to me: if Æthelfrith was willing to engage in battle to get at Eadwine, why not just attack Rædwald, instead of campaigning on the other side of the country?

taking the exiled prince in, may have calculated Æthelfrith to have been seriously weakened after his losses at Chester, offering him the opportunity to use Eadwine to extend his power-base into Northumbria at some point. Yet Æthelberht would have been alive, meaning that Rædwald could not put Eadwine to immediate use, but he must have expected to be able to do so soon, since harbouring him made him a target of Æthelfrith, as Bede makes clear, and in the meantime Eadwine may have been regarded as more of a liability than an asset; hence a date late in Æthelberht's reign is likely. The several attempts to persuade Rædwald to yield Eadwine up that Bede records suggest a sojourn of some time, but not a long time, given how precarious the situation of harbouring him was. Some such length of time is consistent with the fact that no direct connection between the battle and Æthelfrith's final demise in 616 is suggested by Bede's narrative. Rædwald in fact surprised Æthelfrith (*Historia Ecclesiastica* II.12, pp. 180–1), suggesting a period of peace when he had no little time to muster an army. Bawtry, the probable site of Æthelfrith's final defeat on the Idle, is a likely site for a battle between Northumbria and East Anglia, but it is less convincing as a place of passage back to Northumbria from Chester, so a more natural inference would be to dissociate the Chester campaign from it altogether. Hence a date of 615 or slightly earlier is preferable for the battle of Chester.

The Dee valley

Chester (along with Heronbridge) and Bangor emerge as being in a marchland area between realms. As Bangor is east of the Dee, it could technically have been in Cornovian territory, but it is today, and has long been, in the Maelor Saesneg, an extension of Wales between Cheshire and Shropshire; such meandering boundaries could have existed around 600 as well.[36] The lower

---

[36] Higham (1993*a*, 30) notes that Ptolemy records that Mediolanum (Whitchurch, in Shropshire) was in Ordovician territory, which makes better sense if the Ordovices are thought of as an umbrella tribe that stretched across north Wales into what is now England. Higham sees continuity between the Ordovician situation of Mediolanum and the Maelor Saesneg, but his suggestions are open to serious questioning. Ptolemy's ascription of Mediolanum to the Ordovices is highly doubtful, and it is dismissed in the discussion of

Dee valley, with Bangor at the southern end as the river came down from the highlands, and Chester at the river mouth to the north, lies on a boundary between the highlands of Wales and the plains of Cheshire and Shropshire, and, in 600, was situated on the edge of areas under Mercian influence and those which were falling under Northumbrian control as Æthelfrith harried the British west of the Pennines. It was a nexus not only of the Roman road system, but also of the political interests of the day. It was at this nexus, possibly guarded already by the fort at Heronbridge, that Æthelfrith was striking.

The battle

The date of the battle

Bede, our primary source, does not date the battle, merely setting it between the death of Augustine in 604 and Æthelfrith's demise at the hands of Rædwald of East Anglia in 616, and indicating it was closer to the latter but without making any link between the battle and Æthelfrith's defeat. A date of 615/616 for the battle is clearly what the now lost source chronicle underlying the Chronicle of Ireland and *Annales Cambriae* intended, which implies that such a dating is fairly ancient, but this does not make it historically reliable. The date is more than likely to derive from an over-reading of Bede: the narrative of Æthelfrith's death in 616 follows on immediately after the description of the battle of Chester. Indeed, the *Annals of Tigernach* (and probably the Chronicle of Ireland before it) record it as taking place 'immediately' after the battle; this need be no more than an over-zealous reading of Bede. From this, it was inferred that the battle of Chester also took place in 616 (or possibly 615).

Rivet and Smith (1979, 121), who note that Ptolemy's account is full of errors of this sort; they regard Mediolanum as being in Cornovian territory. The notion that the Maelor Saesneg represents the continuation of on obtrusion of Ordovician (Deceanglian) territory across the Dee also stretches the bounds of likelihood, given the turbulent history of the Marches over many centuries, and notably, for the Anglo-Saxon period, the construction of Wat's Dyke and Offa's Dyke, which include the Maelor Saesneg in Mercia. Nonetheless, the general observation that boundaries between areas of control around 600 could allow for territorial obtrusions of the Maelor Saesneg type remains valid.

Why did Bede not date the battle himself? Almost certainly he was unable to do so, because his source consisted of an account derived ultimately from Bangor that dealt with the battle from a religious perspective, not a chronological one, and Bede did not venture to supply information he did not have. The annalists appear to have had no such compunction—and there is no reason to believe they had any more information than Bede. In assessing the course of events that actually took place, therefore, we do not need to feel compelled to accept that the battle took place in 615 or 616 if there should be compelling reasons to date it somewhat earlier (though not so much earlier that it would encroach on Augustine's death in 604). As noted, one likely, but not certain, scenario would see Eadwine seeking refuge with Rædwald after the battle, and staying there long enough for several attempts to be made on his life, but briefly enough to escape Rædwald's inclination to yield him up, which would suggest a date of 615 or perhaps 614 for the battle.

Æthelfrith's aims and targets

The chief difficulty in ascertaining Æthelfrith's aims, and hence the targets of his campaign, is that we cannot determine whether he was acting offensively, or responding to an offensive launched against Northumbria. Bede gives no indication of an attack planned against Northumbria in connection with the battle, but his information was extremely limited; even so, it highlights the position of Eadwine as an exiled prince intent on reclaiming his throne at some point.

From Northumbria, Chester is on the route to the realms of north Wales. The most straightforward interpretation of the battle is that it took place where the Welsh forces mustered to oppose an invading army; Æthelfrith was simply extending his conquests of British territories west of the Pennines, without singling out any specific Welsh kingdom as his target. In practice, it was Tegeingl/Powys/the northern Cornovii that he confronted. By placing the fall of Selyf, king of Powys, at the battle, Welsh tradition recognises that defeat of Powys was Æthelfrith's aim, without indicating any wider forces being involved. We may discount Gwynedd as being directly involved (although Tegeingl could conceivably have been under its protection)—its heartland was too far from Chester—unless it was part of a wider alliance. As Gwynedd has often appeared in the historiography of the battle, however, a few further remarks are called for. Gwynedd, it is true, was the most powerful realm in north Wales, and within a generation its king, Cadwallon, was able to lead a successful campaign against Northumbria and overthrow its king, Eadwine (Bede, *Historia Ecclesiastica* ii.20, pp. 202–5). Mason (2004, 52, following Plummer's proposal, 1896, II, 93) suggests that part of the reason for attacking Gwynedd was that Æthelfrith's enemy Eadwine was trying to forge an alliance there; in reality we have no reliable evidence that he was seeking such an alliance:[37] it is only much later Welsh sources, and Reginald of Durham's twelfth-century *Vita Sancti Oswaldi*,[38] that indicate Eadwine ever took shelter in Gwynedd—and Reginald puts the exile *after* the battle, which makes better sense.[39] If Æthelfrith

[37] It may also be to overestimate rather Æthelfrith's specific concern about Eadwine: Bede makes it clear that Eadwine had no power while in exile, and Æthelfrith's actions against him appear to have amounted to trying to persuade hosts to poison him, rather than engaging in the perilous endeavour of leading armies against those who sheltered him.

[38] See Tudor (1995) on this text; fanciful and unreliable as it is, it nonetheless appears to have made use of some local legends, which, even if scarcely of obvious merit, were at least independent of the mainstream of literary tradition.

[39] Moreover, as Colgrave and Mynors note, had Eadwine been reared in Gwynedd, it is surprising that he did not become Christian—although this causes some difficulties of interpretation of Bede: if Eadwine did become Christian there, a mockery is made of the stories of his later conversion in Deira, but if he did not, why did Bede not rail against the perfidious British for not converting him? The truth is probably that even if Eadwine did become familiar with Christianity in Gwynedd, he chose to wait to align himself with the Roman form of the faith with all the political advantages it brought in terms of alliance with Kent and the wider connections with Christian Europe. The simplest, and most likely, reading is, however, that he did not spend time in exile in Gwynedd (other than possibly for a while after the battle), and that this is an invention of later medieval writers (cf. Gelling 1992, 77). As it is presented by Bede, the tale of Eadwine, the righteous heir persecuted in exile, smacks of derivation from a folk epic: the exile and his relationship to his erstwhile lord are a stock theme of much Old English heroic verse, such as *The Wanderer*, and exile combined with contention with a relative or rival also forms a mainstay of this verse, as in the tale of Finn and Hengest (summarised in *Beowulf* and told at greater length in *The Finnsburh Fragment*; we might also compare the Old High German *Hildebrandslied*). This is not to say it is a complete fiction, but the focus reflects the thematic concerns of saga rather than history.

intended to establish a presence in Cheshire, he would at some point have needed to confront Gwynedd, but to aim to push so far on an initial strike seems unconvincing; it would mean penetrating difficult terrain held by a warlike society, far from Northumbria.[40] Moreover, Heronbridge is situated on the road south, not directly on the route to Gwynedd.

It cannot have been Æthelfrith's intention to defeat Mercia, unless Mercia was in an alliance with northern Welsh realms, since Chester is nowhere near the heart of Mercia on the middle Trent and not on the route to it.[41] Such an alliance would be consistent with later joint Mercian–British attacks on Northumbria, though the first of these we know of was that between Cadwallon and Penda, who defeated Eadwine at Hatfield Chase on 12 October 633 (Bede, *Historia Ecclesiastica* II.20, pp. 202–3). Bede gives no hint of Mercian involvement at the battle of Chester, but if Mercia took part it would imply the involvement of Cearl's protégé Eadwine with British forces, and in particular with the perfidious British clergy singled out for retribution at the battle: so, even if Bede knew of such supposed involvement, he would avoid mentioning it. If Mercia was indeed involved in the battle, it implies that Æthelfrith was acting in a pre-emptively defensive manner, striking out against a Mercian–British joint force before it reached Northumbria, since it is unlikely that the

---

[40] Iago, the king of Gwynedd, is recorded in the *Annales Cambriae* as dying in the year of the battle; it has been suggested this might have acted as an impetus for Æthelfrith to launch an attack (Higham 1995, 132), but this is highly speculative. For Æthelfrith to have come as far west as Chester might suggest he may have been *en route* to Gwynedd, however (although I think not). Yet while Cadwallon's later expedition in reverse, from Gwynedd to Northumbria (indeed, to Bernicia), might suggest such an exploit was feasible also for Æthelfrith, it was quite different, in that Æthelfrith would be very deep into enemy territory, and he would have to have dealt with the difficult terrain of north Wales to reach the heartland of Gwynedd, whereas Cadwallon was moving through areas to the west (and even in some areas to the east) of the Pennines which were British, having been conquered by the English only a matter of years earlier.

[41] Chester is too far west for Mercia, around the middle Trent valley, and probably for the Cornovian territory, centred on Wroxeter, to have been Æthelfrith's likely target—the natural route from west of the Pennines would take Æthelfrith down through Middlewich (Salinae) and Whitchurch (Mediolanum); alternatively, east of the Pennines there is a route from York along direct Roman roads without crossing the uplands.

Welsh and Mercians would have had time to form an alliance and assemble at Chester in response to the swift sort of attack Æthelfrith appears to have been wont to launch.

Whether Æthelfrith's attack was essentially offensive or defensive, his overriding purpose may have been to split Mercia from its Welsh allies, and prevent either from launching incursions on Northumbria, by obtaining control over the northern Marches; Higham (1992, 7; 1995, 78), for example, argues that it may have been Æthelfrith's intention to confront the wider regional powers from the outset. The later engagement (Bede, *Historia Ecclesiastica* III.9, pp. 242–3) on 5 August 642 of Æthelfrith's son Oswald at Maserfelth (Oswestry: on the identification as such see Stancliffe 1995), just a few miles from Chester, could be seen as modelled on that of Æthelfrith. The position of Maserfelth between the areas controlled by Mercia and the Welsh kingdoms suggests that an objective for Oswald was to interpose himself between the allied Mercian and Welsh forces; Higham (1993*a*, 87) suggests a similar reasoning behind the geography of the battle at Chester. Whether Mercia's rule extended very firmly into the Marches, however, is rather less certain for 615 than it is for 642. Oswald was killed in the attempt; Æthelfrith was not, but nonetheless suffered serious losses. Both, therefore, met concerted opposition, which hints at a mighty alliance of regional powers in both cases.

We need also to consider the local target of the campaign, which can be defined as the lower Dee, from Chester through Heronbridge to Bangor. The ruinous Roman city of Chester itself would have been of little interest, and Æthelfrith appears to have passed through or round it, suggesting it was of great interest in itself neither to him nor to the British, but control of Chester at the hub of the Roman road network, and its port, would give access to the Irish Sea and trade there; it would also prevent Mercian expansion northwards, and incursions from Gwynedd towards Northumbria. Taking control of the local area of Chester, rather than the city *per se*, was thus almost certainly among Æthelfrith's aims. The battle took place at Heronbridge, however. While this may be more or less coincidental, as the place where Northumbrians coming from the north-east met British forces coming from the south-west, a different picture emerges if the fort was already in existence: Heronbridge itself may have represented a focus of local power, which Æthelfrith stormed. However, the local power that Bede represents Æthelfrith as confronting is specified only as the monks of Bangor (the presence of local secular powers being touched upon only lightly). If the monks were embroiled in the politics of the region, as their presence at the battle suggests, then Bangor emerges as a focus of power to be defeated. The battle took place at Heronbridge as this was an outlier of the monastery. The words placed in Æthelfrith's mouth in Bede's account, exhorting his men to put effort first into destroying the monks of Bangor, may, surprisingly, conceal a real objective of his, although of course he would scarcely have been motivated by religious persecution in the way the account intimates.

The battle strategy

Depending on Æthelfrith's aims, the strategy would have been either to defeat local or regional forces at one of their centres of power (such as a fort) and take control of the surrounding area, or to strike out to meet half-way a large opposing force moving against him.

In the latter case, it may be illuminating to compare what happened at the battle on the Idle, close to Bawtry, in which Æthelfrith was slain:

a. Æthelfrith attempted to subject Rædwald to his will in yielding up Eadwine, and was willing to contemplate military action;

b. Rædwald, however, struck out directly along the main Roman road from East Anglia into Northumbria, and surprised Æthelfrith;

c. Æthelfrith nonetheless managed to muster an army and set off towards East Anglia;

d. Battle was joined along the route between East Anglia and Northumbria at a major junction of Roman roads at a crossing of the Idle, in a debatable border district between areas controlled by Northumbria, Mercia and East Anglia;

e. The attacking army of Rædwald was victorious, and Æthelfrith was slain;

f. Rædwald nonetheless suffered serious losses.

This may be reduced to the following elements:

a. King A threatens king B [to yield up prince C/to desist from encroaching on his sphere of influence];

b. King B [with prince C] launches surprise attack on king A;

c. King A musters his army but is ill-prepared;

d. Battle takes place at place D, on the border between spheres of influence of king A and king B, on a Roman road near a river crossing;

e. King A is defeated [and prince C takes king A's throne];

f. King B suffers heavy losses.

It may at first appear that at Bawtry Æthelfrith was attempting (and failing) to reprise his role at Chester, striking out swiftly against an enemy who threatened him, but the parallel is more illuminating if at Chester Æthelfrith is thought of as king B, with Cearl (probably along with Selyf or other Welsh kings) as king A. We do not have a precise parallel to prince C, who at Bawtry was Eadwine, but this role was filled in retrospect by the shadowy Pybba or his son Eowa, one of whom succeeded Cearl and appears to have been subject to Æthelfrith. Place D is clearly Heronbridge, with its similarities to Bawtry. Thus Cearl, almost certainly strengthened by an alliance with the British, threatened Æthelfrith (or was perceived by Æthelfrith as a threat), who was encroaching on the spheres of influence of Mercia and the Welsh realms through his constant raids, probably with the prospect of replacing him with Eadwine. Æthelfrith responded by launching a surprise attack, and reached as far as Heronbridge, where, although the British and Mercians were preparing for battle, he essentially surprised them and defeated them, albeit with heavy losses, killing Selyf (and possibly Cearl). He then went on to replace Cearl with a vassal prince, Pybba/Eowa.

No two campaigns would have been identical, of course. Nonetheless, the arenas of action were necessarily of a limited scope within the sorts of society of the time, and such similarities in overall strategy appear unsurprising. Of course, if we were to push matters and take the postulated similarity as evidence of what took place, we would end up with a circular argument. Yet the suggested course of events offers a meaningful interpretation in its own terms of the few facts we have.

The element of surprise implies speed. Although Chester is a good distance from the Northumbria of the time, Æthelfrith would have been on his own territory (including the vassal realm of Elmet) well up into the Pennines, and after his descent from the hills above Manchester, it could take him as little as a couple of days to reach Chester, while news might precede him only if there were fast horsemen to take it.

Æthelfrith's route

Being able to move quickly, as Æthelfrith almost certainly did, suggests keeping to good routes, and it is notable that this battle took place on a Roman road (as did many battles of the time: Æthelfrith's subsequent defeat at Bawtry, for example, took place where the Roman road from the south-east, followed by Rædwald from East Anglia, crosses the Idle close to the boundary of Elmet).

If Æthelfrith came directly from Northumbria, as is most likely, the Bernician centre of Bamburgh is an improbable point of departure (*pace* Davies 2010, 148); the much closer southern realm of Northumbria, Deira, which Æthelfrith had ruled since 604, is far more likely, although he could have come down into Deira from Bernicia shortly beforehand. York itself, which was probably only seriously occupied later, by Eadwine, is less likely to have acted as a point of departure than somewhere in the Derwent valley, the centre of Deira, where Eadwine is said to have had a hall later (Bede, *Historia Ecclesiastica* ii.9, pp. 164–5). This would have brought him across the Pennines through Mamucium (Manchester, a minor settlement in Roman times) and westwards across to Chester. This route would have involved crossing the British kingdom of Elmet, east of the Pennines and abutting Deira (Higham 1993*b*, 84–7), but Elmet was probably little more than a client kingdom by this stage.[42] If he came from campaigns further north on the western side of the Pennines, then the postulated Roman route into Chester from Warrington would be a possibility.[43] It is unlikely that he approached from further south, and then up through Mediolanum (Whitchurch):

[42] The likelihood that Æthelfrith arranged the assassination of Hereric there indicates this, though harbouring Hereric also shows Elmet maintained a degree of independence still.
[43] This approximately follows the Hoole Road into Chester, or more precisely the earlier, pre-turnpike, route marked by Newton Hollows.

this would imply his crossing vast swathes of territory to the south of the Pennines that were not in Northumbrian hands, and would also imply an encounter with the British or Mercian forces to the south or east, not north, of Bangor.

At Chester itself, Mason (2007, 51) suggests Æthelfrith may have avoided the city and diverted on a minor Roman road which appears to have forded the Dee just north of Heron-bridge, though, as Mason admits, the ford has not actually been uncovered. This is possible, but there is no reason to suppose that anything other than the main Roman road through Chester was used; taking a large body of armed men over a substantial river would, moreover, scarcely be the option of choice when a functioning Roman bridge almost certainly existed at Chester itself. Æthelfrith would also need to have gained knowledge of the ford, which required local informants — an unlikely scenario on this strike deep into enemy territory. If Æthelfrith went through the town itself, it implies that there was little resistance; alternatively, he may simply have skirted the walls and proceeded over the bridge. There is nothing to suggest that the fabric of the city itself was anything of significance to him.

The type of encounter

Æthelfrith was a warrior king who harried widely, following an expansionist policy that had already been established by his predecessors; in the *Historia Ecclesiastica* (1.34, pp. 116–17) Bede compares Æthelfrith to Saul, and notes that he ravaged the British more widely than any other ruler. Æthelfrith's attacks were probably comparable with the initial Viking raids of later centuries, fairly random and followed by swift withdrawal, rather than aimed at immediate subduing and settlement of the land. To caricature in a nutshell, a Germanic warlord's aims would have been in the first place to gain glory and booty by defeating his foes, and only thereafter to grant land to his followers. The objective of the campaign, then, would have been to secure a decisive victory over the local lords, with a possible view to subjugation.

Yet the Chester campaign may not merely have been one of Æthelfrith's raids against the British. The conflict was no mere skirmish, but a confrontation between major powers, as is shown by the level of casualties, and by the general geo-political situation outlined above. Æthelfrith would then either have been making a defensive strike against other kingdoms rising up against him, or himself launching an offensive against other kingdoms.

The size of the forces

Mason (2004, 42) estimates there must be at least 112 warriors buried on the site, and probably rather more than this; these probably represent Northumbrian casualties. Bede states that Æthelfrith had a *grandis exercitus* and suffered heavy losses, but while this indicates its strength relative to the norms of the time, it says little about its actual size, and must, in any case, be based on oral memory. He also states that twelve hundred monks of Bangor fell on the opposing side, but his figures are unreliable here too; they are most probably motivated by biblical numerological concerns. Nonetheless, the fundamental fact of substantial forces being involved is probably true. Davies (2010, 153) presents a useful survey of information about troop numbers in this period: other attempts at taking whole realms sometimes involved forces of under a hundred, and a couple of hundred warriors could be reckoned as substantial. However, as the Heronbridge battle cemetery is unique we have nothing to compare it with directly: it may not be specially exceptional, as the numbers of troops given in written sources are not nec-essarily reliable. Balancing the size of force needed to achieve decisive victories deep in enemy territory with the problems of maintaining such a force, somewhere between five hundred and a thousand men seems the best estimate.

How did Æthelfrith muster such a powerful army? The basis of his power would certainly have been the *comitatus*, his per-sonal band of warriors, which would have consisted of more experienced, landed lords, and younger, unlanded fighters, who were seeking glory in battle and the reward of land and wealth (see Evans 1997 for a detailed discussion of the *comitatus*). The members of his warband would themselves presumably have had their own followers. The whole system relied not on the notion of an army raised to defend the land (the *fyrd* of later centuries), but on personal loyalty and patronage (Abels 1988,

185; Davies 2010, 152) — the lordless exile is a standard figure of misery in Old English poetry — and the main source of wealth was victory in war, so the *comitatus* system was essentially expansionist by definition. There was a limit to the numbers of followers that could be kept in check in such a system, and the size of Æthelfrith's forces is likely to have been at the upper limit in these terms. Loyalty depended on success, and the size of Æthelfrith's forces is a function of their success, which we may surmise them to have enjoyed in previous campaigns: Æthelfrith was a king who commanded loyalty because he defeated so many foes and overran their lands.

A limit, particularly in terms of loyalty, would also be set by the rapid expansion of the Northumbrian realm (which itself was a result of loyalty): those who regarded themselves as 'truly' English would rapidly be spread thin on the ground, ruling over large numbers of the native population, who may not have been so willing to serve their new masters. This would limit both the number of loyal followers a lord could muster to follow him into battle, and incline him not to depart from estates that might not be under full control. Æthelfrith appears to have been exceptional in how far he was able to go with a system that at a certain point was bound to implode.

The site and course of the battle

Within the Chester area, several sites might have been chosen for the battle. During the Civil War, a great battle took place in 1645 on Rowton Moor to the east of Chester. The British might be expected to have made a stand against Æthelfrith in this area before he could reach Chester. The fact that the battle did not take place here is revealing. The city itself was presumably unable to raise forces for its defence, suggesting it was relatively unimportant; and other local lords did not regard it as sufficiently significant to try to defend it either. The force which did confront Æthelfrith had at least in part come up from, and been heavily supported by, the monastery of Bangor-is-Coed, some miles to the south, and evidently they did not envisage proceeding too far from their base. The Dee may have formed some sort of boundary which the forces of Powys/Tegeingl did not wish to cross, at least initially.

The British forces could have swept down on Æthelfrith as he crossed the Dee at Chester, or indeed tried to prevent him crossing. Yet the site is not really suited to battle: the space of a few hundred yards between the slope and the river was (and still is) strewn with the remains of Roman quarries, and in places is almost precipitous. Faced with an opposing force, the English are unlikely to have risked crossing over here at all, and neither would the British be likely to want to risk battle here.

The battle in fact took place at Heronbridge. Why? If the fort was in existence, the British would have taken up position in it, with the aim of preventing English advance into Powys/ Tegeingl, and the English would have attacked, sweeping down from the plateau just to the north of Heronbridge, with each side calculating they had an equal advantage. The specific site of battle thus makes best sense if the fort was in existence, but in more general terms, Heronbridge, with its gentle slopes, is the first site on the Roman road south of the Dee to offer a potentially good field for combat. The English would want to stop on the plateau just north of Heronbridge and urge the British to attack them uphill; the British would try to do the same in reverse, stopping at Eccleston. The skeletons are buried much closer to Heronbridge, suggesting, if this overall scenario is correct, that the English lured the British on, or that the British were so intent upon attack as to ignore their disadvantage; the apparent site of the battle is quite a distance on foot from Eccleston.

The distance from Bangor, and the fact that many of the monks from there decided to go to the battle site, fasting for three days beforehand, indicates either that the community must have received news of the English force some days in advance, and were thus not precisely surprised, or that these preparations marked the launch of an intended campaign against Northumbria, which was indeed surprised and thwarted by Æthelfrith's sudden arrival. Bede's account relates that the contingent of monks from Bangor joined others who seem already to have been on site, which fits with the idea of the *eglēs* of Eccleston having been a daughter-house to Bangor itself, with its topography thus familiar to the Bangor community. This implies that the choice of where to make their stand lay in the hands of the British, who knew the area, even if the decision to launch into battle there was taken by Æthelfrith.

The monks would have been in an ecclesiastical compound whose existence is commemorated in the name Eccleston. This could have been in the fort, which may indeed have been constructed as an ecclesiastical compound, or somewhere in the area of present-day Eccleston. However, in the latter case they would not have been visible to Æthelfrith, if he stopped on the plateau just north of Heronbridge, as is likely, so the presence of the fort at the time of battle again makes better sense, assuming we accept Æthelfrith's glimpse of the monks as having some factual basis.

If Æthelfrith's foes were stormed within their fort at Heronbridge, it might be inferred that they were at a disadvantage and were adopting a defensive position. However, the fort would have been reckoned both strong enough to resist attack and able to contain considerable numbers of troops who could easily sally forth to lead an attack, so occupying it may not have seemed markedly defensive to its garrison. Nonetheless, viewed over a shorter time-span of a couple of days or so, Æthelfrith may still have surprised his enemy, even though they were possibly expecting him imminently.

Consequences of the battle

In the longer term, the battle may have had little impact from a Northumbrian perspective. Cadwallon, the king of Gwynedd, was able to overrun Northumbria in 633/634, and it was not until his defeat in 634/635 by Æthelfrith's son Oswald that Northumbrian, as opposed to Welsh, control of much of northern England can be described as secure. From the mid-seventh century, it is clear that the Chester area fell under Mercian control, and was never again ruled by Northumbria.

The shorter-term consequences are less clear. Æthelfrith must have stayed long enough to perform obsequies for the fallen warriors, but he may then have departed in view of his heavy losses. Alternatively, he may have left a Northumbrian presence, possibly constructing the Heronbridge fort on the site of the battle for this purpose. How great the Northumbrian control was cannot be ascertained, but it is probable that the battle at least destabilised the region: Cearl, Eadwine's patron, seems to have died at the battle or at about the same time, and Mercia was unable to exert any influence for some decades, either on the Chester area or against Northumbria, and may have had a king friendly to Æthelfrith forced upon it. It is probable that the region's instability forced Eadwine to flee to Rædwald, who, after the death of Æthelberht, helped him onto the throne of Northumbria (Higham 1995, 78–9).

Eadwine's subjugation of the area around the Irish Sea may not have been a direct result of Æthelfrith's campaign—Bede after all seems to regard Eadwine's success as his own. Yet it would at the least have built on Æthelfrith's victory indirectly, as a response to the instability that followed the battle.

The context of the battle: a summary

The summary that follows sets out the most likely-seeming interpretations of the battle and its context. Yet, in reality, there is too little firm evidence to be able to draw satisfactory conclusions on any aspect of the events and their causes, so every interpretation is contentious. Some of the chief issues that have a major bearing on our interpretations, but which cannot be answered as yet, are:

a. Was the fort at Heronbridge in existence at the time of the battle? This alters both our interpretation of what the battle itself involved, and the reason for it taking place precisely at Heronbridge.

b. Was Æthelfrith's victory the result of a spontaneous attack aimed at securing Northumbrian control of the area, or was he responding to forces already ranged against him?

c. Were Æthelfrith's opponents local British forces (Tegeingl/ Powys/Cornovii), or did they represent a wider Mercian–British alliance, which was intent on toppling him (and perhaps placing Eadwine on the throne)?

d. Did the battle achieve anything more than a temporary victory for the Northumbrians; in particular, was Eadwine's later subjugation of the area, including the Irish Sea, the result of a sustained (if superficial) Northumbrian presence in the region?

The date of the battle. The battle took place between *c.* 610 and 615, with 614 or 615 being perhaps the most probable date.

The fort. The fort could have been a fairly recent construction by the British, and it could equally well have been an ecclesiastical enclosure under the control of Bangor. It would have represented a centre of power, and possibly a mustering ground for warriors, which would have made it a direct focus of Æthelfrith's campaign. Almost as likely is that it was a later construction undertaken by Eadwine in his subjugation of the region. Less likely is that it was constructed by Æthelfrith, unless we assume he occupied the area for some time after the battle.

The aims. Æthelfrith's objective was to establish a Northumbrian bridge-head in the Chester area by defeating local chieftains (though not, initially, more distant powers such as Gwynedd and Mercia). The purpose was similar to that of his son Oswald a few decades later: to defeat Powys/Tegeingl and thus undermine the Mercian–British alliance that could threaten Northumbria; this would be achieved by extending Northumbrian power into the Marches. A secondary aim was to control the port and access to the Irish Sea, an objective that Æthelfrith's successor Eadwine achieved. Possibly, a more direct aim may have been to defeat an already existing Mercian–British allied force that was intent on overthrowing Æthelfrith, and perhaps putting Eadwine on the throne.

Æthelfrith's route and destination. Æthelfrith set out from Deira (Yorkshire), taking the shortest route to Chester through Elmet, over the Pennines to Manchester and then on to Chester. At Chester, he passed through the city (the Roman fortress), or else skirted it, then crossed the Dee over the extant Roman bridge, and proceeded down the Roman road towards Wroxeter. His destination was Powys/Tegeingl, perhaps crystallised as the fort at Heronbridge itself, a local centre of power which may in some way also have been closely connected with the monastery of Bangor.

The foes. Æthelfrith was intent on destroying the local bases of power, and his opponents need not have been drawn from a wider area than Tegeingl and Powys, including the monastery of Bangor and its holdings. They may well have been drawn from a wider field, however, including Mercia under Cearl; this would be consistent with later joint Mercian–British attacks on Northumbria.

The type of encounter. Æthelfrith led a swift but nonetheless mighty army by the standards of the time, with upwards of five hundred troops. The opponents must have had similar numbers. The battle therefore represented a conflict between major powers.

The site of the battle. There is nothing to indicate that any defence was made of Chester itself. The choice of Heronbridge at the monks' behest indicates a desire to stop the pagan forces proceeding any further towards Bangor or into Powys/Tegeingl. If it was in existence, the fort would have controlled access to these along the Dee valley, and it would have acted as a focus both for local forces to put up a stand at and for Æthelfrith to vanquish. Yet the site of battle may perhaps reflect a mustering point for British (and perhaps Mercian) armies, whence they intended to march on Northumbria, but where their progress was stymied by the sudden incursion of Æthelfrith.

The strategy and course of the battle. The battle site either represents the storming of the fort by English forces sweeping down on it from the Heronbridge ridge, or else it marks the site of the clash between English warriors descending from the north (the plateau north of Heronbridge), and British opponents from the south (the rise of Eccleston). The three-day fast of the monks implies that the British forces were expecting Æthelfrith, or else that they were preparing to set out for Northumbria with the expectation of meeting Æthelfrith on the way. The battle strategy may have been broadly similar to that of Rædwald's attack against Æthelfrith in 616: the attacker makes a swift incursion into enemy territory, his opponents rally and move to counter the attack, but are rather unprepared, and essentially they are surprised, leading to their defeat, but not without their inflicting heavy losses on the attacking forces.

The aftermath. Æthelfrith probably stayed long enough to perform obsequies for the fallen warriors, but his heavy losses, and the lack of evidence for immediate Northumbrian subjugation of the region, suggest that he soon withdrew; in this case, Eadwine's subjugation of the area and the Irish Sea reflects a separate campaign, but it is just possible that Æthelfrith established a presence sufficient to continue into Eadwine's reign.

Political consequences. Cearl of Mercia, Eadwine's patron, died at the battle or at about this time, and Æthelfrith's incursion enabled him to place a friendly leader on the throne of Mercia, forcing Eadwine to flee to Rædwald, who eventually (after the death of Æthelberht) supported his venture to depose Æthelfrith. The whole region was destabilised by Æthelfrith's incursion (Higham 1995, 78–9) and placed under the threat of Northumbrian domination, which in itself would have induced Eadwine to move elsewhere. Mercian overlordship of regions close to the Irish Sea must have been prevented long enough for Eadwine to exercise control over them, though in the long run Cheshire fell under Mercian suzerainty.

Conclusion

I have had three chief aims. The first has been to pursue a more nuanced approach to evaluating the written medieval sources on the battle of Chester. We have one account, by Bede, that could be termed 'reliable' — though even this is biased to serve his particular ecclesiastical purposes, and highly selective in what it tells; all other mentions or descriptions of the battle are, to varying degrees, untrustworthy as sources of historical fact, and could go back to Bede, along with a peppering of inference from Welsh heroic tradition. The second aim has been to consider the historical background and likely motivations behind Æthelfrith's expedition to Chester. While a general picture can be drawn, there are huge uncertainties, given our lack of information about the balances of power at the time. I have tried to outline some alternatives, but many possibilities remain. The third aim has been to highlight a few areas where there is still scope for further archaeological investigation. We await the final report on the most recent Heronbridge excavations, but it is already clear that this will open as many questions as it will answer. In particular, the rampart and its enclosure will need further excavation in the future: in principle, it should be possible to assign a more precise date to it, and to distinguish between its possible origins and uses, which include a protected seasonal trading-emporium site, a British 'hillfort', a British ecclesiastical compound, a fort built by Æthelfrith (a pagan) or one built by Eadwine (a Christian)—none of these can reasonably be excluded on the basis of current research or the archaeological investigation so far carried out. The skeletons also need further research at some point: a radio-isotope analysis of just two of them does not lead to conclusive proof of where the army came from; as reported at present, a non-local origin is indicated, but this might include Mercian as well as Northumbrian areas, which would put a very different light on the interpretation of the battle.

✠ B ✠

St Germanus and the Orchard of Bangor

Bede's account of the battle of Chester

EDE'S ACCOUNT OF THE BATTLE OF CHESTER forms the last of
a three-part section concerning the mission of St Augustine and his interaction with the native British Church
(see Stancliffe 1999 for analysis).

The first part of Bede's account deals with Augustine's meeting
with the British clerics at an oak tree on the border between
the Hwicce and Wessex, the second concerns a second meeting
(possibly at Chester; it involved representatives from Bangor, at
least), and the third presents the battle of Chester as retribution
for the behaviour of the British Church towards Augustine.
Stancliffe demonstrates that the first part derives from official
sources, probably held at Canterbury, but the second and third
betray a probable origin among the British, whom Bede in general held in low regard. The positive depiction of Bangor and
its learned inhabitants, framed within Bede's generally negative
account, reflects an original British bias. The source document
was therefore surely British; its ultimate origin must have lain
with the monastery of Bangor, though it remains unclear just
how it came into Bede's hands; it probably passed through
monasteries such as Malmesbury.

The implications of these observations are that the description
of Æthelfrith as singling out the monks for slaughter—which
makes no sense from a pagan king's perspective[1]—is a projection

---

[1] It might be argued, however, that Æthelfrith viewed the monks as magicians
working evil against him, in the way Æthelberht is reported to have feared
Augustine and his monastic band should he meet them inside (Bede, *Historia
Ecclesiastica* 1.25, pp. 74–5). I suggest that, while Bede, manipulating features

of motive onto a pagan foe by the Christian-minded monks of Bangor, who, we may surmise, viewed him as a sort of devilish tormentor who brought about their martyrdom. Bede, with little effort, turns this perspective on its head, and makes of Æthelfrith an instrument of divine retribution, a viewpoint that we may be confident was absent from the original British document derived from Bangor.

A difficult matter to explain in Bede's account is the action of Brocmail. His treacherous cowardice fits Bede's characterisation of the perfidious British very well, but how did the event come to be recorded within a British text? It is possible that some now-opaque dynastic struggle between local British lords lies hidden in the action, but I consider another possibility below, which entails seeing Bede's account, or rather the British document that lies behind it, as more than just a relaying of information about a battle.

The monks in battle

Bede's focus is on the monks. Even if he has recast its bias, his source, ultimately from Bangor itself, must have had the same focus. Ascribing to the English king a desire to make a special point of attacking the monks first must therefore have been surmise on the part of the brethren who escaped slaughter, a reflection upon the failure of the English forces to recognise their non-combatant role and the consequent massacre of their peers.

It may well be that the 'monks' included lay workers loosely associated with the monastery, but the purpose of the account is to evoke the extreme savagery directed at a group of undifferentiated 'innocent' religious (regardless of whether some may have been warrior lay brothers). There is no interest in non-monastics, other than in their treacherous guardian Brocmail and their pagan tormentor.

present in the original British document, may possibly have intended such a link to be drawn, this is actually part of his historical rhetoric, and even the Æthelberht story may well be part of this (the notion that magic is more effective within a building, for example, is surely invented): it highlights the power of the Church, even to the deluded minds of pagans (who interpret divine glory as threatening magical power).

The 'monks in battle' motif may reflect a general notion of the victory of the cross over pagan enemies, epitomised in the emperor Constantine's victory over Maxentius at the Milvian Bridge in 312, after his vision that he would conquer with the sign of the cross, yet a more specific tradition may underlie the account of the battle of Chester: the Alleluia victory of St Germanus of Auxerre, who came to Britain around 429 to preach against the Pelagian heresy; his Life was composed in Gaul around 480 by Constantius. It was well known to Bede, who quotes large portions of it, but it was almost certainly also known in monasteries such as Bangor; events from St Germanus's life featured centrally in the ninth-century Gwynedd composition, the *Historia Brittonum*. The Life's account of the Alleluia victory, as recorded by Bede (*Historia Ecclesiastica* 1.20, pp. 62–5), reads:

> Madidus baptismate procedit exercitus, fides feruet in populo, et conterrito [*recte* contempto *from Life of St Germanus*] armorum praesidio diuinitatis exspectatur auxilium. Instituto uel forma castitatis [*recte* castrorum] hostibus nuntiatur, qui uictoriam quasi de inermi exercitu praesumentes adsumta alacritate festinant; quorum tamen aduentus exploratione cognoscitur. [. . .] Germanus ducem se proelii profitetur, eligit expeditos, circumiecta percurrit, et e regione qua hostium sperabatur aduentus uallem circumdatam mediis montibus intuetur. Quo in loco nouum conponit exercitum ipse dux agminis. Et iam aderat ferox hostium multitudo, quam adpropinquare intuebantur in insidiis constituti. Tum subito Germanus signifer uniuersos admonet, et praedicat ut uoci suae uno clamore respondeant; securisque hostibus, qui se insperatos adesse confiderent, alleluiam tertio repetitam sacerdotes exclamabant. Sequitur una uox omnium, et elatum clamorem repercusso aere montium conclusa multiplicant; hostile agmen terrore prosternitur, et super se non solum rupes circumdatas sed etiam ipsam caeli machinam contremescunt, trepidationique iniectae uix sufficere pedum pernicitas credebatur. Passim fugiunt, arma proiciunt, gaudentes uel nuda corpora eripuisse discrimini; plures etiam timore praecipites flumen quod transierant deuorauit. Vltionem suam innocens exercitus intuetur, et uictoriae concessae otiosus spectator efficitur. [. . .] triumphant uictoria fide obtenta non uiribus.

So, still soaked in the waters of baptism, the army set out. The people's faith was fervent and putting no trust in their arms they expectantly awaited the help of God. The disposition and arrangement of the army was reported to the enemy; they were as sure of victory as though they were attacking an unarmed foe and hastened forward with renewed eagerness; but their approach was observed by the British scouts. [...] Germanus himself offered to be their leader. He picked out the most active and, having explored the surrounding country, he saw a valley surrounded by hills of moderate height lying in the direction from which the enemy was expected to approach. In this place he stationed his untried army and himself took command. The fierce enemy forces approached, plainly visible as they drew near to the army which was lying in ambush. Germanus, who was bearing the standard, thereupon ordered his men to repeat his call in one great shout; as the enemy approached confidently, believing that their coming was unexpected, the bishops shouted 'Alleluia' three times. A universal shout of 'Alleluia' followed, and the echoes from the surrounding hills multiplied and increased the sound. The enemy forces were smitten with dread, fearing that not only the surrounding rocks but even the very frame of heaven itself would fall upon them. They were so filled with terror that they could not run fast enough. They fled hither and thither casting away their weapons and glad even to escape naked from the danger. Many of them rushed headlong back in panic and were drowned in the river which they had just crossed. The army, without striking a blow, saw themselves avenged and became inactive spectators of the victory freely offered to them. [...] They won a victory by faith and not by might.

The Alleluia victory was one of believers over unbelievers, composed of Picts and Saxons; while such a perspective would have been meaningless to Æthelfrith, it would certainly have been uppermost in the minds of the Bangor monks (we need only think of Gildas, at the time of the battle a fairly recent writer, seeing the persecution of the British by the English as punishment for their profligacy).

St Germanus arrayed his newly baptised troops—who are presented as being almost like monks, inexperienced, as if unarmed—in the area of a valley surrounded by hills, and awaited the pagan hordes coming from the direction of the sea and crossing a river. The topography matches that of Heronbridge, just to the south of Chester, where we now know the battle to have taken place after the excavation of the battle cemetery (most recently in 2002–5: see Mason 2007, ch. 3, and the previous chapter in this book), although the Heronbridge landscape is far less pronounced than that implied for the Alleluia encounter. Heronbridge itself is on the southern end of a plateau extending from just above the Dee at Chester, and it overlooks a wide hollow, with gentle slopes on three sides, and the River Dee to the east, just beyond which a quite noticeable ridge stands, setting the Dee in something of a valley; the river flowed into the sea just to the west of Chester, a couple of miles downstream. In the midst of the Heronbridge hollow is a substantial earthwork rampart dating from roughly the same time as the battle. Thus the pagan Æthelfrith's approach from near the sea at Chester and his crossing the Dee there before descending into the hollow of Heronbridge matches that of Germanus.

Germanus led his army himself, even though he was a churchman, just as Bede's account singles out the churchmen as playing a prominent role in the battle (and ignores the other troops). The high point of the encounter, which secured victory for the Christians, was the loud shouting of 'Alleluia'; there is a parallel here with the actions of the monks of Bangor: Æthelfrith is made to say 'si aduersum nos ad Deum suum *clamant* [...]', 'if they *shout out* to their God against us [...]', then they should be attacked first, which could almost be a riposte to the request of Germanus that his men should 'uno *clamore* respondeant', 'answer with one *shout*', at which the priests shouted out the Alleluia, 'alleluiam [...] sacerdotes *exclamabant*'. Here the two histories diverge: for Germanus, the Alleluia chorus resounded in the hills and terrified the pagans, securing a bloodless victory, whereas against Æthelfrith the tactic, far from working, is presented as enraging him, resulting in a very bloody massacre of the 'innocent' monks. The reason for featuring Brocmail so prominently could be to contrast him implicitly with someone who did just the opposite, leading churchmen to victory instead of defeat, namely the legendary St Germanus.

Although it did not work out for the monks of Bangor, St Germanus's victory may provide the template they hoped to follow in the battle, and the model followed in retrospect when the battle was interpreted and written up at the monastery. I suggest that what we find here is a multilayered typology underlying Bede's account. Joshua, in his storming of Jericho and leading of the Israelites into the Promised Land, acted as a type to the antitype of Christ, leading his Church into heaven. Germanus acts as a metatype to the Joshua–Christ type–antitype, storming the pagan/heretical land, defeating the foe by the power of faith-filled noise, just as Joshua destroyed Jericho with his trumpets (Joshua 6:1–27), and bringing salvation to his followers. St Germanus and his followers in turn then become a type to their metatype, the monks of Bangor, led by Brocmail (who proves a travesty-inversion metatype to Germanus).

If a connection is admitted between the Alleluia victory and the battle of Chester, it is unlikely to be the creation of Bede: the verbal parallels between the accounts are not great, focusing solely on the 'shouting' of prayers, and the circumstantial geographical and other features that link the accounts would have been unknown to Bede, but would have been obvious to a monk of Bangor involved in the battle or informed about it, who would also have realised that Æthelfrith, coming from the north, could look down on the British forces in the enclosure from the Heronbridge rise, and could even realistically be imagined to have been able to pick out the monks from the other contestants.

It suited Bede to have an account of a battle in which British churchmen were the object of aggression, but viewed objectively the account of the battle is very odd in its purely ecclesiastical focus. What, really, was a large group of monks doing participating in a battle—even if we allow that they may have come to bless the beginnings of a campaign and got caught up in an unexpected attack? Arguing that they were predominantly laybrethren sidesteps the issue (and is not directly supported by the text): the monks had a religious purpose in being there, and their numbers suggest this purpose was more than to act as chaplains to the troops; and victory could have been prayed for just as well from Bangor. The winning of a victory for Christ by St Germanus's band of inexperienced neophytes against the Saxons offers a model they may have hoped to follow.

Moreover, Plummer (1896, II, 34) notes that in local tradition St Germanus was held to have won his Alleluia victory near Mold, just ten miles from Chester, at Maes Garmon (the field of Germanus); while Constantius appears to have had no such place in mind (his mix of Saxon and Pictish pirates implies an east-coast setting), it is certainly the case that Germanus is widely commemorated in church foundations and place-names in Wales such as Maes Garmon, and traditions associating him with the area may well be ancient, and, whether historically accurate or not, could have inspired followers in such districts to follow his example. What we see through Æthelfrith's eyes in Bede's recasting of the story in fact represents a British perspective on the enmeshed involvement of religious in battle.

It is difficult to corroborate the suspicion that St Germanus was an important inspiration—in exegetical terms a type—to the actions of the monks of Bangor, but some further circumstantial evidence is worth presenting.

One of the earliest concrete pieces of evidence for the early realm of Powys is the Pillar of Eliseg in Valle Crucis, erected by Cyngen, king of Powys, who died in 854. Its purpose was to proclaim the might of Cyngen's ancestors, and it did this in part by bringing in a series of legendary figures, among them Britu (Brydw), son of Vortigern, a child blessed by Germanus (who is named in the inscription).[2] The legends accruing around St Germanus were therefore part of the legendary history of Powys by the mid-ninth century. In fact, the story of the child blessed by Germanus, along with a series of other legends about the saint, is given in a somewhat different form in the contemporary *Historia Brittonum*, and indeed are central to its narrative.[3] It is impossible to say how far back this adoption of the legends of St Germanus as political propaganda for the realm of Powys may go, but it is by no means impossible that it existed already at the time of the battle of Chester; indeed, the monastery of Bangor is likely to have been a place where such hagiographical legends were fostered. In terms of the pillar, Charles-Edwards notes (2013, 451) that the postulated book of St Germanus which the *Historia Brittonum* made use of was likely to have been composed for a church dedicated to St Germanus; Llanarmon-yn-Iâl was

---

[2] The precise purposes of the pillar, and the form of Powys history that it seeks to present, are difficult to ascertain in view of the damage already suffered to the inscription by the time of its first recording (it is now wholly illegible): see Charles-Edwards (2013, 447–52) for discussion.

[3] Charles-Edwards (2013, 447–51) offers an analysis of the differences, reflecting rival political interpretations of history, between the ninth-century genealogies of the ancestral (fifth-century) founders of Powys in the *Historia Brittonum*, a Gwynedd work, and the Pillar of Eliseg, a royal artefact of Powys; where the former talks of an illegitimate son of an incestuous Vortigern, Faustus, who later became a great Church leader (illegitimacy being of no consequence here), the Pillar mentions an equivalent son, Brydw, and seems to posit a descent of the royal house of Powys from Vortigern via a legitimate marriage to a daughter of the mighty Magnus Maximus, slayer of the king of the Romans.

quite close to the pillar. Moreover, Llanarmon-yn-Iâl is not much more distant from Bangor; and Llanarmon Dyffryn Ceiriog is also only slightly further, to the south-west from the monastery.

Selyf, who according to the *Annales Cambriae* fell in the battle of Chester, was a descendant of Cadell Ddyrnllug (the Catel dunlurc of Harleian Genealogy 22: Bartrum 1966, 12); his and his descendants' authority over Powys is given a founding legend in the *Historia Brittonum* (ch. 35), where he hosts St Germanus, who then blesses him for rule. In sending monks to support the British forces at Heronbridge, the monastery of Bangor was standing in the role of St Germanus, blessing the successor of Cadell for victory and rule. It is also notable—though perhaps too much should not be made of a saint exerting power through fasting—that in the *Historia Brittonum* (ch. 47) St Germanus along with his clergy fasted for three nights, after which the fortress of Vortigern along with all its denizens was suddenly destroyed by heavenly fire; the monks of Bangor were no doubt hoping for something similar after their three-day fast.

Towill (1979) discusses a further interesting legendary motif that highlights the possible importance of Germanus in early insular Christianity. In early legendary accounts of St Patrick (notes to *Fiacc's Hymn* in the Franciscan *Liber Hymnorum*, the *Lebar Brecc*, the *Tripartite Life*), the saint is said to visit an island inhabited by an eternally young couple, who wish to present him with a *baculus*, a staff of ordination, acting as a symbol of his adopting his mission, and one which opened the way to the Otherworld (he traces the entrance to St Patrick's Purgatory with it, where pilgrims received experiences of the Otherworld), but he refuses, and goes over to the mainland to get the staff directly from the Lord on Mount Arnon (or Harmon, Hermon). Traditionally, the site of this event was interpreted as being on the Continent; this seems to have derived from the association of St Patrick with St Germanus, but, as Towill (*ibid.*, 59) argues, Patrick need only have visited his homeland of Britannia to meet Germanus, given the latter's visit in 429. While the mountain's name has apparently been adapted to recall the biblical Mount Hermon (an impossible destination for Patrick), Towill suggests that it originated as a place commemorating St Germanus, of which several exist in Wales, as noted. Towill argues the tradition was already developing away from this notion towards a continental setting for Mount Arnon by the seventh century; this would be consistent with the strong Irish presence in north Wales, which appears to have been absorbed by around 600 (Charles-Edwards 2013, 178–9, 190).

The degree of historical truth in the legend is not so important in the present context: the point is that St Germanus was regarded, arguably, as sufficiently prestigious not only to give rise to a number of church dedications, but also, in legendary tradition preserved in Ireland, to act as guardian of a venue for the apostle of Ireland to receive his staff of missionary power from the Lord. Moreover, native traditions originally unconnected with Christianity, in the form of the island of youth (compare the Tír na n-Óg of Irish myth, as well as the fruitful isles discussed below), are woven into the legend. This independently parallels what I am suggesting in the case of Bangor and the battle of Chester: the Church authorities were manipulating the traditions of the victorious Germanus and probably weaving into them some native traditions to boot. This is, of course, conjectural—as it must be, given the sparseness of records from this time.

Thus the topography of the battle, and their own hagiographical warrior traditions, may have led the monks of Bangor to see the battle in terms of the Alleluia victory of St Germanus, which took place in a valley surrounded by hills, with which, on a moderate scale, the landscape of Heronbridge is comparable. Unfortunately, instead of being led to victory by their leader, as had happened with Germanus, they were betrayed by Brocmail, a sort of Judas-like antithesis of an antitype, and defeat followed; however, in hagiographical terms they had still won the victory of martyrdom.

The Welsh Annals

The *Annales Cambriae* (A text, MS Harley 3859, from *c.* 1100) record the battle of Chester *s.a.* 613 (which most probably stands for 615/616: Charles-Edwards 2006, 128; 2013, 352; Plummer 1896, II, 77):

Gueith cair legion . et ibi cecidit selim filíí cinan .

The battle of Chester. And Selim son of Cinan fell there.

As has been noted in the previous chapter, the *Annales* were composed in the late tenth century, and the association of Selim (Selyf) with the battle may merely reflect a desire to link recorded events with legendary heroes (Selyf, along with his father Cynan, being a major figure of saints' lives and poetry), although in essence the annal may be correct, in that it is likely that a leader from the Powys area fell in the battle at Heronbridge. Beyond this, the annal adds nothing to Bede's account.

Thus Selyf, or some other local leader, may well have been slain at the battle, but neither Bede nor any other source corroborates this. Annal entries tend to show an association of legendary figures who lived at approximately the right time with events derived from a 'good' historical source, in this case Bede. Implicit in this process is an understanding of history as a reification of the politicised world of legend, rather than a 'factual' account of what happened in the past.

Welsh poetry

The application of legend to history meant resorting to poetic tradition, and creating 'facts' from artefacts whose purpose from their inception was literary, not historical: the purpose of a poem was not to relate events, but, for example, to praise a ruler or to evoke the pathos of loss. Events are therefore incidental, and motives of the protagonists subject to the literary whims of the poet.

The battle of Chester in fact scarcely seems to feature in extant Welsh verse. This may be due to the vicissitudes of transmission, but the fact that the British were defeated would not have disposed poets to celebrate it. Yet we might imagine that Selyf's fall at the battle has made its way into the *Annales Cambriae* from a *marwnad* upon him. The only reference we appear to have to the battle is by Cynddelw, who in the later twelfth century speaks of the 'gweith y berllan', 'battle of the orchard' (see Bromwich 2014, 172). The identity of the 'orchard' is revealed after a somewhat tortuous visit to the *Trioedd Ynys Prydain*, to the interpretation of which the above general remarks about poetry are relevant: triads were summations of poetic tradition for the use of bards.

The Orchard of Bangor in Triad 60

Triad 60 of the *Trioedd Ynys Prydain* reads (Bromwich 2014, 171):

Tri Phortha6r G6eith Perllan Vangor:
  G6gon Gledyfrud,
  A Mada6c ap Run,
  A G6ia6n ap Kyndr6yn.
A thri ereill o bleit Loegyr:
  Ha6ystyl Draha6c,
  a G6aetcym Herwuden,
  a G6iner.

Three Gate-Keepers at the Contest of Bangor Orchard:
  Gwgon Red Sword,
  and Madawg son of Rhun,
  and Gwiawn son of Cyndrwyn.
And three others on the side of Lloegr:
  Hawystyl the Arrogant,
  and Gwaetcym Herwuden,
  and Gwiner.

The triad is discussed in depth by Bromwich (*ibid.*, 171–4). The fifteenth-century BL Cotton Cleopatra B.v version of the *Brut y Brenhinedd*, a Welsh rendering of Geoffrey of Monmouth's *Historia Regum Britanniae*, is the only authority for identifying the battle of Perllan Fangor with the battle of Chester, but Bromwich (*ibid.*, 172) regards this as representing a genuine tradition.[4] She argues that 'gweith Perllan Vangor', 'the battle of the Orchard of Bangor', could be the traditional Welsh designation of the battle of Chester. It would be difficult, indeed, to relate it to any other battle that is known of; the triad points to a connection with the Powys area, and Bangor-is-Coed is the only site with this name

---

[4] The situation is actually a little more complex. Geoffrey, and following him the *Brut*, has a contest at Bangor separate from and consequent upon the battle at Chester; the battle of the Orchard of Bangor could have been drawn in here just because of Geoffrey's battle at Bangor. Geoffrey's account is, in fact, garbled and of no historical value (as discussed in the previous chapter). We may be sure that just one battle took place, the site of which has been uncovered at Heronbridge, between Chester and Bangor (but much closer to Chester); cf. also Bartrum 1993, *s.v.* 'Caerlleon (Chester), Battles of'. Yet Bede's account associates the contest, specified as being near Chester, closely with the monks of Bangor, so the link between the Orchard of Bangor and the battle is reasonable, without bringing in Geoffrey's supposed testimony.

in the right area, and the only one with a battle independently associated with it (through the monks of Bangor present at the battle of Chester in Bede's account).

The information contained within the triad, it must be remembered, is found within a poetic tradition marked by strong symbolism and allusion. Thus Bromwich points out that *porthawr* could also be interpreted as 'supporter, assistant', and the choice of this ambivalent word was deliberate: the warriors were both gate-keepers of the orchard, and supporters in the *gweith*, the action (fighting).

Two of the three gate-keepers, Gwiawn and Madawg, are associated with minor dynasties of Powys, and were contemporaries of Selyf, who the *Annales Cambriae* say fell at the battle; they probably held authority under Selyf, and hence assisted at the battle (or were imagined to have done so in poetic tradition); from genealogies, it is clear that Selyf belonged to the Cadelling dynasty, but here the rival Cyndrwynyn, to which Cynddylan also belonged, are made his assistants through their representative Gwiawn (Rowland 1990, 126). Gwgon is a known character from a later time and different area; he may be one of a small set of such characters deliberately interposed among the heroes of yesteryear in the triads.[5]

Bromwich finds the coupling of three Welsh with three English gate-keepers historically rather unlikely, implying they shifted places during the action. Yet this could be a poetic way of saying the English took control of the orchard, which is to say the battle field. Alternatively, it could represent an alliance, the Englishmen here being Mercians working alongside the Welsh (though the triad seems to envisage two opposing sides, Welsh and English). The names of the English refer to their being hostages (*gwystyl*) and exiles (*herw*), designations which characterise them as being far from their own lands, which could apply particularly to Æthelfrith's Northumbrians around Chester at this date.

---

[5] The sixteenth-century antiquarian John Leland (1906–10, III, 68) records Porth Hwgan, the Gate of Gwgan, as one of the gateways of Bangor monastery, which may suggest Gwgan was an otherwise unknown contemporary of Selyf—yet this 'tradition' of the Bangor gate name could surely be derived from a version of the triad in question. (Porth Hwgan itself was real, however: it is listed among the houses of Bangor in a 1699 survey, just to the north-west of the village: see www.bangor-on-dee.co.uk.)

Bromwich does not suggest further ambivalences beyond the *porthawr*, but they are not far to seek if we accept that poets would have resorted to what may be surmised to have been traditional spiritual imagery, derived from both native worldviews and the exegetical approaches of the Church. The ultimate source of information about the battle is likely, after all, to have lain with the monks, who were the main focus of Bede's, and therefore the original British, account.

The triad seems to present the 'assistants at the battle of the orchard of Bangor' — a battle does not have 'gate-keepers'; yet this literal meaning turns the triad into a riddle, and calls for us to look at the rest of what it says.

Gweith is a regular word for a contest or battle in early sources, but it has a range of meanings, which could no doubt be played upon in a poetic context. Relevant are these entries from *Geiriadur Prifysgol Cymru, s.v.* 'gwaith[1]' masc.: 1a, labour, 1b, product of a mental or physical effort, 2, fortification, earthwork, fort; 'gwaith[2]' fem.: 2b, action, battle.

Labour, or the result of mental or physical effort, is an apt description of the struggle of monastic life, the result of spiritual labours being heavenly reward. In the anagogical terms espoused by the early Church the 'action' — whether a battle or labour — at the orchard has a significance as the monastic toil (of which the work in the orchard is a metonym) which results in heavenly reward, in this case in the form of martyrdom effected by the physical contest in the form of a battle.

Such an interpretation calls for further comment on the imagery of the orchard. The orchard could well have been a real orchard, owned by the monastery of Bangor; the metaphorical significances suggested here certainly work better if the orchard was more than a fiction, but it is possible that the 'orchard of Bangor' simply means the monastery of Bangor, metaphorised as an orchard. In terms of Christian exegesis, the most relevant orchard that came to take on a metaphorical sense is that of pomegranates in the Song of Solomon 4:13 ('perllan o Bomgranadau' in the Welsh Bible of 1588). The Song of Solomon was widely taken, from Origen onwards, as expounding a metaphor for the relationship between Christ and the Church. The patristic interpretation of 'thy plants are an orchard of pomegranates' is distinctly relevant (Littledale 1869, 184):

Thy plants. More exactly, *thy shoots,* and accordingly the Septuagint and Vulgate read *thy sendings-forth* (ἀποστολαί, *emissiones*). Further, the word translated *orchard* in the Authorised Version is *paradise* [...] The apostolates, then, or emissions of the Bride, are her augments of faith and spreading of preaching, that is her planting local Churches throughout the world, each of which is a *paradise*, resembling that first and central one which is their source and model. Or you may take them to be the Apostles themselves, ruddy, like the pomegranates, with the blood of martyrdom, and bringing forth many spiritual children to Christ by their toils and sufferings.

Pomegranates may not grow in Wales—an orchard here is more readily associable with apples—but this does not preclude some familiarity with this exegesis. An orchard is a paradise, and the way to paradise is through the cross, or martyrdom, as exemplified in Christ's declaration to his faithful companion as he was crucified (Luke 23:43); Bede, writing relatively close in time and place to the monastery of Bangor, in his commentary on the Song of Solomon stresses in particular how this verse points to the baptism in Christ's blood (Patrologia Latina 91, col. 1145). Yet the symbolism of the orchard also implies mission, according to the exegesis quoted. We might infer that the Orchard of Bangor was not the main monastery of Bangor, but a sort of daughter-house, an *emissio* from Bangor itself. This would be consistent with Bede's account, which makes it clear that monks came up from Bangor to a sort of compound, near which the actual battle took place; in fact, we now know the battle to have taken place some twelve miles north of Bangor, just to the north of the village of Eccleston at Heronbridge.

Yet the Christian symbolism of the orchard as a form of paradise, won by toil or martyrdom, is intertwined with more secular motifs of the Celtic Otherworld, which in fact reinforce the paradisal imagery. The most notable memorable example is the isle of Avalon of the Arthurian legends, to which the king retires after his struggles (implicitly to die) in Geoffrey of Monmouth's *Historia Regum Britanniae* (XI, ch. 2); this is the equivalent of his 'isle of apples which is called Fortunate' ('insula pomorum que Fortunata vocatur') in his *Vita Merlini*. The *Brut y Brenhinedd* has 'enys Auallach' ('the island of Afallach', *afal* being 'apple') for Geoffrey's 'insula Avallonis', referring to the abundant apples that mark out the Celtic Otherworld; Geoffrey's form is possibly influenced by the town of Avallon in Burgundy, whose name derives from the Gallic Aballone, 'place of apples' (Bromwich 2014, *s.v.* 'Auallach'). *Abhlach* occurs in Irish in reference to an Otherworld island, home to the god Manannán mac Lir; the Irish form was arguably borrowed into Welsh, though its occurrence is only late medieval, and hence the direction of any influence remains uncertain.

Glorious trees form a notable feature in the depictions of the Otherworld in medieval Irish literature (see Koch 2006, *s.v.* 'Otherworld'). In his comprehensive study of Avalon, Egeler (2015, 365) notes how early texts such as *Echtrae Chonnlai* and *Immram Brain*, from the eighth or possibly even seventh century, already have the idea of the Otherworld island, and combine the motifs of the island, the supernatural/otherworld woman, fruitfulness, particularly in the form of an apple branch, and the land of immortality. Egeler notes the use of a basically pre-Christian motif within a Christian monastic milieu; Christian and pre-Christian motifs are intertwined from the start (*ibid.*, 366): 'for Echtrae Chonnlai and Immram Brain, there is the possibility that the author's intention in designing the overall composition of these narratives might have been the construction of a Christian allegory based on monastic life'.[6] Between the fruitful cluster of grapes of the *Navigatio Sancti Brendani* to the apple branch of *Immram Máile Dúin* there is even a reversion to a more native image of the Otherworld isle of apples (*ibid.*, 368); the love of an island woman in the latter text, although rejected in favour of something morally more acceptable, harks back to the more primitive image of an island of pleasure. In Christian terms, the island virgin evokes the pure Church, or salvation; this accords with the identical patristic interpretation of the Bride of the Song of Solomon's orchard. The Irish voyage literature uses a traditional motif to present a monastic search for a paradisal place of withdrawal at the edge of the world; passage to it is through *peregrinatio*, a metaphor for the ascetical monastic endeavour.

---

[6] Original: 'für Echtrae Chonnlai und Immram Brain mit der Möglichkeit zu rechnen ist, dass die Intention des Autors bei der Gestaltung der Gesamtkomposition dieser Erzählungen in der Konstruktion einer christlichen, auf das monastische Leben bezogenen Allegorie bestanden haben könnte.'

Yet *peregrinatio* is a form of martyrdom: Johnston (2016, 39–40) points out how an early text from *c.* 700, the *Cambrai Homily*, equates renunciation of the world in favour of asceticism with martyrdom; in order to win this metaphorical martyrdom, the ascetic must separate from the familiar. It was a short step to see *peregrinatio* as a form of (ascetical) martyrdom (even though *peregrinatio* was not simply synonymous with making voyages to the ends of the earth). Johnston concludes that 'it does seem clear that in the course of the sixth and seventh centuries religious ideals, centred on exile and ascetic martyrdom, coalesced among Irish ecclesiastics' (cf. Stancliffe 1982; Malone 1951). In short, it may be said that the paradisal Otherworld is reached through an act of martyrdom, and martyrdom might be conceived in different ways, but its prototype was the red martyrdom of the early Christians.

The rich intertwined native and Christian Otherworld imagery of the Irish voyage literature cannot be paralleled in Welsh sources, but we do find supernatural apple trees, in particular in the *Afallenau* verses of the thirteenth-century Black Book of Carmarthen, associated with Myrddin, whose legend apparently derives ultimately from the sixth-century British realm of Strathclyde (see Jarman and Hughes 1992, 103–4; Clarkson 2016). The apple tree affords protection from his enemies in some supernatural fashion (perhaps through invisibility) to the wild Myrddin, who has entered a state of madness after a traumatic battle experience, but it also somehow represents a state of lost jubilance, when Myrddin sat at its foot with a fair maiden; its sweet fruit is unattainable by ordinary means, as it is protected by a current, and by its own strangeness. The otherworldly apple tree, on a sort of 'island' (protected by currents: the river is a commonplace separator of the Otherworld), all but unattainable, and associated with a fair maiden, clearly has a good deal in common with its Irish counterparts, and probably belongs to the same tradition.

There are differences, of course; yet some of them are circumstantial. The Irish monks were seeking out a form of lost Eden, retrieved through their ascetic efforts, and their *peregrinatio* was a metaphor for their inward journey; Myrddin's inner journey into the retreat within his madness is represented by his fleeing to his apple tree, the symbol of the paradisal state he enjoyed before his madness, and which survives as a fastness within his mind. The tree therefore emerges as a symbol of the bliss within Myrddin's deranged mind, made inaccessible to others by the defences of his madness. We may compare Myrddin with Sir Orfeo in the fourteenth-century English Breton lay, *Sir Orfeo*, who enters into a state of madness and, like Myrddin, withdraws to the woods as a wild man in order to enter the depths of Hades, whither his wife had been abducted as she sat beneath a special imp-tree (a grafted tree, which thus stood metaphorically between worlds as it stood between species), but which is inaccessible by ordinary means; it is, to some degree, clearly a mental state of withdrawal, but one where he glimpses fantastic beauty among the misery, much as Myrddin sees his sweet tree and, in particular, has visions of his maiden.

We may also suspect, in Myrddin's case, an implicit reference to Annwfyn, ambiguously a deep world (of the mind), or a non-world (Higley 1993, 212); it is from Annwfyn that *awen*, poetic or mantic inspiration, derives, but the *awenyddion*, those particularly inspired by *awen* to utter mantic answers to inquirers, are seen as deranged ('quasi mente ductos') in Giraldus Cambrensis's description of them (*Descriptio Kambriae* 1.16, pp. 194–5). Myrddin, of course, utters prophecies in his deranged state in the *Afallenau*. (I discuss *awen* and *awenyddion* further in Tolley, forthcoming.)

A further hint at the Otherworld connections of Bangor occurs in Triad 90 (Bromwich 2014, 232–3), the only other one the monastery is mentioned in; here, the topic is the three places (monasteries) where perpetual harmony is heard, these being the Island of Afallach, Caer Garadawg and Bangor. Caer Garadawg is uncertain, but the Island of Afallach is Glastonbury—but it is referred to under the term that links it with the traditions of Avalon and the isle of apples. The perpetual harmony, then, is one that characterises the monasteries as places of Otherworld peace, in the intertwined Christian and Celtic symbolism described above.

The 'orchard' could thus be a symbolic representation of the place where the monks of Bangor achieved their passage to the Otherworld through their glorious martyrdom, whether or not it was also a real orchard. We may note too that a sort of *peregrinatio* was involved (when looked at *post factum*) in the group of monks coming from the monastery to the site of the battle, identifiable from Triad 60 as the arguably symbolically paradisal orchard. The 'action' or 'labour' of the orchard is the attainment of the paradise it stands for.

Unlike a battle, an orchard, particularly one that was set aside as an ecclesiastical compound, might well have gate-keepers; but a gate-keeper or assistant of the action is one that helps the orchard-keepers on their way to paradise. It is difficult, too, not to recall the gate-keeper of heaven, St Peter, allowing in those who had won their due rewards. In the later verse of the *gogynfeirdd*, at least, St Peter as the *porthawr* of heaven is a common motif; he is treated as equivalent to the *porthawr* of a royal court, a designated official (McKenna 1991, 126–7). This further suggests, if a similar notion existed in earlier times (as seems likely), that the orchard guarded by the gate-keepers is a form of (heavenly) court.

A gate-keeper would certainly, in physical terms, most naturally be associated with something like a fort—and here we may turn to another meaning of *gweith*, 'fortification, earthwork, fort'. In its ambivalence the word is directly comparable with Old English *geweorc*, 'work, accomplishment', often used in poetry to describe things like monumental Roman remains (notably in *The Ruin*). What possible relevance does this have to the Orchard of Bangor as a name for the battle of Chester?

At the site of the battle at Heronbridge, the cemetery, which probably but not certainly belonged to the Northumbrians, appears to have been deliberately placed within a large rampart, which covers some six hectares, and which has been dated to the time of the battle. It is far from clear whether its construction precedes or follows the battle, but it is generally comparable with structures from this period found in British areas, some of which were ecclesiastical compounds, rather than anything produced by the English (examples such as the Northumbrian royal fort of Bamburgh were taken over from the British). My suggestion is that the battle consisted of the storming of this British stronghold to the south of Chester (see the more detailed discussion in the previous chapter).

Of interest too is the name of the nearby Eccleston. Research (particularly Hough 2009 and James 2009) into Eccles- place-names has shown that an *eglēs* was an ecclesiastical landholding, with its buildings and fields (not just a church building); the term was used as a pseudo-place-name, and then adopted as a place-name proper by English speakers in the seventh century (thus, shortly following the battle of Chester). Bede's account of the monks of Bangor at the battle, combined with the archaeological evidence that the battle took place close to Eccleston, suggests that the ecclesiastical estate or *eglēs* from which Eccleston took its name belonged to the monastery of Bangor. Triad 60's Orchard of Bangor may perhaps be identified with this *eglēs*; the actual orchard may thus have been the area demarcated by the large rampart at Heronbridge, at which the battle took place.

Just how much historical fact lies behind Triad 60 is difficult to say, but in principle we may have a reminiscence of a battle at an orchard of Bangor monastery — something which might well, in the vocabulary of the early seventh century, be called an *eglēs* — which was also characterised as an earthwork or fortification. It was guarded by gate-keepers, who were also supporters, we are to understand, of the king of Powys (Selyf); yet these gate-keepers were apparently ousted by English counterparts, characterised as exiles. The gate-keepers were also assistants in the labour of the orchard; they were understood in a metaphorical sense as helping the monks in the achievement of their work of martyrdom, by which they won through to the Otherworld symbolically represented by the orchard they toiled in.

Conclusion

It seems uncontroversial to suggest that texts emanating from a monastery should reflect the exegetical and hagiographical culture of the Church (the continued links with continental learning, both ecclesiastical and classical, are outlined by Davies 1995, ch. 1). It is more problematic to argue that such approaches could be maintained or picked up in bardic tradition, which is the likely source of the triad relating to the Orchard of Bangor.

Later tradition leaves us in little doubt that the period leading up to and around the battle of Chester was one of concerted Church effort, in fields of learning as well as spirituality, with figures such as the learned St Illtud looming large (Davies 1995, 9–11); we are less well informed, in truth, about the bardic tradition at this time, and, even allowing that some of the heroic poetry ascribed to Taliesin and Aneirin may go back in some form to the sixth or seventh centuries, we have scant record of the no doubt rich array of poetry in general that must have existed, so it is difficult to infer anything with certainty about its content or field of reference.

McKenna notes (1991, 17–19) that the existence of religious verse cannot be demonstrated before the earliest source containing such verse, the ninth-century Juvencus manuscript. Some twenty-four religious poems exist in the Black Book of Carmarthen and the Book of Taliesin, it is true, but their date is uncertain. McKenna even inclines (*ibid.*, 22) to the view that Gildas's diatribe against Maelgwn for listening to praises of himself while not hearing the divine message may imply the absence of religious verse in the sixth century. She concludes that 'Certainly it would have been difficult in the early period for laymen, which most of the bards were, to compose good religious poetry, simply because of their ignorance of theological or devotional matters'. Yet none of these inferences can be drawn with any certainty, or even likelihood. Gildas's statement is worthless: apart from the fact that it does not clearly refer to bards, it could just as well be interpreted as indicating that there was religious verse around, but Maelgwn chose not to listen to it. We know so little of early bards that we can make no assessment of their level of theological training.

There are two main reasons for regarding it as more likely that religious verse, or religious themes or motifs in verse, go back to the beginnings of verse composition in Welsh. One is what the neighbours were doing, and the other is what happens in Welsh verse later, with the *gogynfeirdd*. Irish verse incorporates religious themes from the beginning, the earliest extant poems (some examples are mentioned above) being probably from the eighth or even seventh century—though with the proviso that manuscripts are much later. The Anglo-Saxons managed, in the late seventh century, to gear their traditional heroic verse towards religious themes within fifty years of their conversion, in the form of the hymn produced by Cædmon (Bede, *Historia Ecclesiastica* iv.24, pp. 414–18), a poet, moreover, whose British name points in all likelihood to his having come from the recently overrun British areas of the Hen Gogledd. Cædmon is said by

Bede to have spent his life in a monastery, churning out religious verse once he had the knack of it; he forms an archetype of the sort of poet that is assumed to have been responsible for much of our Old English verse, most of which is either religious or infused with a familiarity with religious themes while focusing on ostensibly secular matters such as exile. Much of the verse is likely to have emanated from the many members of monastic communities who came from a cultural background inured to traditional heroic verse (as was the case with Cædmon). This contrasts with the stark division between secular bards and monks that McKenna seems to assume for the early period, but is there any well-founded reason to assume that the intertwining of the religious with the secular in poetic tradition was markedly different or absent in Wales at this period? The absence of religious themes in the few verses which come down to us, in some form, from the early period may simply reflect the vicissitudes of preservation. Sources such as the *Life of St Beuno*, set at just the time of the battle of Chester, indicate a tradition (for of course it is recorded long after the events described) of members of noble families, such as would have been familiar with heroic verse, being deeply involved in the monastic or eremitical life, much as was the case in England.

Bromwich (2014, lxvi) notes that the degree of interplay of bardic and ecclesiastical learning is uncertain even for the twelfth century, let alone the seventh, but she notes that twelfth-century poets were indeed influenced by the rhetorical teaching of the ecclesiastical schools. McKenna points, indeed, to several aspects of the verse of the *gogynfeirdd* and other poets from the twelfth century on that indicate an involvement with monastic life. Some of the poems of the Black Book of Carmarthen and the Book of Taliesin include themes such as the ten plagues of Egypt and the twelve tribes of Israel; one includes a pairing of the Latinate 'masculine and feminine' in a call for everything to praise God. Clerics were clearly acting as poets here (McKenna 1991, 74). The 'three hosts of tribulation' ('tri llu trallawd') at judgement day are derived from a learned source, a seventh- or eighth-century treatise, *De Numero*, knowledge of which must originally have seeped out of a monastery to become a commonplace convention of religious poetry (*ibid.*, 103–4). The poem *Canu Tyssilyaw* appears to have been composed as a thank-offering to the monastery of St Tisilio at Meifod after Cynddelw stayed there; it eulogises Tysilio and his noble lineage and aristocratic virtues, and notes the clerics are no weaklings as far as mead is concerned (they act like nobles, offering it to their guests and perhaps imbibing it themselves); here, perhaps, the poet 'fulfilled the double responsibility of the bard for sacred and secular poetry' that is noted in the laws of Hywel Dda, written down *c.* 1200 (*ibid.*, 7, 31). We cannot demonstrate this sort of involvement of bards with monastic life and themes at an earlier period, but it is surely difficult to believe the situation would have been drastically different in the sixth to seventh centuries, when Bangor, alongside other centres such as Llanilltud Fawr (Davies 1995, 11), must certainly have acted as a school of learning.

It is, in any case, not necessary to postulate a strictly religious poem as underlying Triad 60, merely imagery with an exegetical background. It might, however, be felt that the sort of complex imagery and word-play suggested as underlying the triad on the Orchard of Bangor would be more typical of the rhetorical devices that came to be developed in Ireland — the postulated complexity has something in common, for example, with that found in texts such as the eighth-century *Cauldron of Poesy*, where we encounter a complex set of metaphors employed to communicate a philosophical point about the gaining of wisdom (Breatnach 1981). The Irish voyage literature, moreover, illustrates the sort of interplay between traditional and Christian imagery that my interpretation of the Orchard of Bangor calls for.

An Irish connection is quite possible, in fact: north Wales was heavily settled by Irish in the post-Roman period, and the name Gwynedd indeed probably derives from the Irish Féni (Charles-Edwards 2013, 178–9, 190); the court of Gwynedd continued to be an important meeting place for Irish scholars on the way to the Continent, notably in the ninth century under Merfyn Frich and his son Rhodri Mawr (Davies 1995, 13); and the Juvencus poems were written out by an Irish scribe. The complexity of imagery that can arise in a Welsh poem under Irish influence is illustrated by *Preideu Annwfyn*, where a raid on the Otherworld, Annwfyn, otherwise referred to by the Irish term Caer Sidi, acts as a metaphor for the acquisition of poetic skill (the poem is most perceptively discussed by Higley 1996; see also the discussion in the edition of Haycock 2015); pertinent to the interpretation of the Orchard of Bangor is that the attainment of entry to the Otherworld (of which paradise is a variant) could readily be conceived as a *gweith*, a military action. Secular, bardic lore is also intertwined with, and in this case opposed to, the learned lore of the monks (Adderley 2009); such an awareness and interplay of different traditions could well have been found too in the tradition antecedent to *Preideu Annwfyn*, though in the absence of texts this is naturally impossible to prove.

There is no need to doubt the essential reliability of Bede's account of the battle of Chester, and the Welsh bardic tradition, surviving in this instance only in Triad 60, may well preserve a memory that the military action took place at the Orchard of Bangor monastery. The focus of interest in the present study, however, has been how this historical event was conceived by the monks who must have produced the first account of it, in terms of their typological and anagogical understanding of history as a process of salvation, and how some elements of this understanding may have been adopted and played upon poetically in the bardic tradition.

EADWINE

✣

KING EADWINE OF NORTHUMBRIA was baptised on Easter Day, 12 April 627, in York. His conversion was a drawn-out affair, but the decisive moment was a conference he held with his leading men in his hall. This is described by Bede in his *Historia Ecclesiastica* II.13, pp. 182–7 (Eadwine's baptism follows immediately, in ch. 14, pp. 186–7):

Quibus auditis, rex suscipere quidem se fidem, quam docebat, et uelle et debere respondebat; uerum adhuc cum amicis principibus et consiliariis suis sese de hoc conlaturum esse dicebat, ut, si et illi eadem cum eo sentire uellent, omnes pariter in fonte uitae Christo consecrarentur. Et adnuente Paulino fecit ut dixerat; habito enim cum sapientibus consilio, sciscitabatur singillatim ab omnibus, qualis sibi doctrina haec eatenus inaudita et nouus diuinitatis, qui praedicabatur, cultus uideretur.

Cui primus pontificum ipsius Coifi continuo respondit: 'Tu uide, rex, quale sit hoc, quod nobis modo praedicatur; ego autem tibi uerissime, quod certum didici, profiteor, quia nihil omnino uirtutis habet, nihil utilitatis religio illa, quam hucusque tenuimus. Nullus enim tuorum studiosius quam ego culturae deorum nostrorum se subdidit; et nihilominus multi sunt qui ampliora a te beneficia quam ego et maiores accipiunt dignitates, magisque prosperantur in omnibus, quae agenda uel adquirenda disponunt. Si autem dii aliquid ualerent, me potius iuuare uellent, qui illis inpensius seruire curaui. Vnde restat ut, si ea quae nunc nobis noua praedicantur, meliora esse et fortiora habita examinatione perspexeris, absque ullo cunctamine suscipere illa festinemus.'

Cuius suasioni uerbisque prudentibus alius optimatum regis tribuens assensum continuo subdidit, 'Talis' inquiens 'mihi uidetur, rex, uita hominum praesens in terris, ad conparationem eius quod nobis incertum est temporis, quale cum te residente ad caenam cum ducibus ac ministris tuis tempore brumali, accenso quidem foco in medio et calido effecto cenaculo, furentibus autem foris per omnia turbinibus hiemalium pluuiarum uel niuium, adueniens unus passerum domum citissime peruolauerit; qui cum per unum ostium ingrediens mox per aliud exierit, ipso quidem tempore quo intus est, hiemis tempestate non tangitur, sed tamen paruissimo spatio serenitatis ad momentum excurso, mox de hieme in hiemem regrediens tuis oculis elabitur. Ita haec uita hominum ad modicum apparet; quid autem sequatur, quidue praecesserit, prorsus ignoramus. Vnde, si haec noua doctrina certius aliquid attulit, merito esse sequenda uidetur.' His similia et ceteri maiores natu ac regis consiliarii diuinitus admoniti prosequebantur.

Adiecit autem Coifi, quia uellet ipsum Paulinum diligentius audire de Deo quem praedicabat uerbum facientem. Quod cum iubente rege faceret, exclamauit auditis eius sermonibus dicens: 'Iam olim intellexeram nihil esse, quod colebamus, quia uidelicet quanto studiosius in eo cultu ueritatem quaerebam, tanto minus inueniebam. Nunc autem aperte profiteor, quia in hac praedicatione ueritas claret illa, quae nobis uitae salutis et beatitudinis aeternae dona ualet tribuere. Vnde suggero, rex, ut templa et altaria, quae sine fructu utilitatis sacrauimus, ocius anathemati et igni contradamus.' Quid plura? Praebuit palam adsensum euangelizanti beato Paulino rex, et abrenuntiata idolatria fidem se Christi suscipere confessus est. Cumque a praefato pontifice sacrorum suorum quaereret, quis aras et fana idolorum cum septis quibus erant circumdata primus profanare deberet, ille respondit: 'Ego: quis enim ea, quae per stultitiam colui, nunc ad exemplum omnium aptius quam ipse per sapientiam mihi a Deo uero donatam destruam?' Statimque, abiecta superstitione uanitatis, rogauit sibi regem arma dare et equum emissarium, quem ascendens ad idola destruenda ueniret. Non enim licuerat pontificem sacrorum uel arma ferre uel praeter in equa equitare. Accinctus ergo gladio accepit lanceam in manu, et ascendens emissarium regis pergebat ad idola. Quod aspiciens uulgus aestimabat eum insanire. Nec distulit ille, mox ut adpropiabat ad fanum, profanare illud, iniecta in eo lancea quam tenebat, multumque gauisus de agnitione ueri Dei cultus, iussit sociis destruere ac succendere fanum cum omnibus septis suis. Ostenditur autem locus ille quondam idolorum non longe ab Eburaco ad orientem ultra amnem Deruuentionem, et uocatur hodie Godmunddingaham, ubi pontifex ipse inspirante Deo uero polluit ac destruxit eas, quas ipse sacrauerat aras.

When the king had heard these words, he answered that he was both willing and bound to accept the faith which Paulinus taught. He said, however, that he would confer about this with his loyal chief men and his counsellors so that, if they agreed with him, they might all be consecrated together in the waters of life. Paulinus agreed and the king did as he had said. A meeting of his council was held and each one was asked in turn what he thought of this doctrine hitherto unknown to them and this new worship of God which was being proclaimed.

Coifi, the chief of the priests, answered at once, 'Notice carefully, King, this doctrine which is now being expounded to us. I frankly admit that, for my part, I have found that the religion which we have hitherto held has no virtue nor profit in it. None of your followers has devoted himself more earnestly than I have to the worship of our gods, but nevertheless there are many who receive greater benefits and greater honour from you than I do and are more successful in all their undertakings. If the gods had any power they would have helped me more readily, seeing that I have always served them with greater zeal. So it follows that if, on examination, these new doctrines which have now been explained to us are found to be better and more effectual, let us accept them at once without any delay.'

Another of the king's chief men agreed with this advice and with these wise words and then added, 'This is how the present life of man on earth, King, appears to me in comparison with that time which is unknown to us. You are sitting feasting with your ealdormen and thegns in winter time; the fire is burning on the hearth in the middle of the hall and all inside is warm, while outside the wintry storms of rain and snow are raging; and a sparrow flies swiftly through the hall. It enters in at one door and quickly flies out through the other. For the few moments it is inside, the storm and wintry tempest cannot touch it, but after the briefest moment of calm, it flits from your sight, out of the wintry storm and into it again. So this life of man appears but for a moment; what follows or indeed what went before, we know not at all. If this new doctrine brings us more certain information, it seems right that we should accept it.' Other elders and counsellors of the king continued in the same manner, being divinely prompted to do so.

Coifi added that he would like to listen still more carefully to what Paulinus himself had to say about God. The king ordered Paulinus to speak, and when he had said his say, Coifi exclaimed, 'For a long time now I have realized that our religion is worthless; for the more diligently I sought the truth in our cult, the less I found it. Now I confess openly that the truth shines out clearly in this teaching which can bestow on us the gift of life, salvation, and eternal happiness. Therefore I advise your Majesty that we should promptly abandon and commit to the flames the temples and the altars which we have held sacred without reaping any benefit.' Why need I say more? The king publicly accepted the gospel which Paulinus preached, renounced idolatry, and confessed his faith in Christ. When he asked the high priest of their religion which of them should be the first to profane the altars and the shrines of the idols, together with their precincts, Coifi answered, 'I will; for through the wisdom the true God has given me no one can more suitably destroy those things which I once foolishly worshipped, and so set an example to all.' And at once, casting aside his vain superstitions, he asked the king to provide him with arms and a stallion; and mounting it he set out to destroy the idols. Now a high priest of their religion was not allowed to carry arms or to ride except on a mare. So, girded with a sword, he took a spear in his hand and mounting the king's stallion he set off to where the idols were. The common people who saw him thought he was mad. But as soon as he approached the shrine, without any hesitation he profaned it by casting the spear which he held into it; and greatly rejoicing in the knowledge of the worship of the true God, he ordered his companions to destroy and set fire to the shrine and all the enclosures. The place where the idols once stood is still shown, not far from York, to the east, over the river Derwent. Today it is called Goodmanham, the place where the high priest, through the inspiration of the true God, profaned and destroyed the altars which he himself had consecrated.

The Politics of
Coifi's Desecration of the Temple

THE ACT OF DESECRATION PERPETRATED BY COIFI, the priest of the pagan temple at Goodmanham,[1] in casting a spear at the sacred enclosure and rejecting all it stood for is interpreted by Bede as a rejection of paganism in favour of the enlightenment of Christianity. Yet it is much more than this (if indeed it was ever this at all). A substantial part of Bede's account is clearly his own invention: no pagan priest would have been able to envisage or use the highly Christianised concepts that Bede ascribes to him (indeed, much of this would have been beyond the capabilities of the English language to express at all at this stage), and even notions of a pagan 'priesthood', as a sort of counterpart to the Christian clergy, are open to question. Yet if we may assume there is some truth to the story, then it is possible to see behind Bede's spiritual interpretation one in which both political and spiritual concerns are enmeshed in equal measure.

---

[1] Despite acceptance by Plummer and the English Place-Name Society (and most historians) that Goodmanham is Bede's *Godmunddingaham*, Wallace-Hadrill (1988, 73) asserts that the place has not been identified. Apart from the plausibility of Goodmanham deriving from Bede's form of the name, the situation of Goodmanham so close to the primary early Anglian cemetery at Sancton argues in favour of this as the site of an early religious focal point for the first Anglian settlers of the area. Wallace-Hadrill is also entirely dismissive of Turville-Petre's suggestion (1953–7, 283) that *Godmunddingaham* could conceal a reference to a group of priestly acolytes here (such a group is, of course, implied in Coifi's appeal to his companions to help in the desecration); while Godmund may be a perfectly good Anglo-Saxon name, after whose family the village would be named, *godmundingas* could also mean 'the people of the divine favour', and to dismiss the possibility merely reflects Wallace-Hadrill's own interpretative predilections.

Fig. 5. The church at Goodmanham, which is likely to be
on the site of the pagan sanctuary desecrated by Coifi.

The key to such an interpretation lies not so much in the act
of desecration itself, as where this, and Eadwine's subsequent
baptism, take place: Goodmanham and York. The sanctuary
at Goodmanham—assuming it was situated where the church
now stands (Fig. 5)—was on a small and distinct plateau; the
churchyard would appear to offer a peculiarly apt site for a
sanctuary, a small discrete area at the end of a spur of the Wolds.
Standing here (and imagining away the modern houses), one
looks down over the low lands towards the Derwent and the
Vale of York (Fig. 6). Behind stands the past; in front, one looks
out on a vista of the future—if we put ourselves in the position
of someone at the point where Eadwine is about to convert. To
explain this, let us look briefly at the history that led up to the
event Bede describes as taking place here.

What happened during the transition from Roman Britannia
to Anglo-Saxon England is a contentious issue in every respect,
and every piece of evidence is interpreted in a multitude of
ways—it is truly a case of *quot homines, tot sententiae*. Given their
complexity, it is impossible here even to review these arguments
or most of the evidence on which they are based.[2] It seems clear

---

[2] For a measured outline account, relating to Northumbria, see Higham
(1993*b*, ch. 2–3). The most detailed archaeological report for Deira

Fig. 6. Looking out over the Derwent valley towards the Vale of York from Nunburnholme, just to the north-west of Goodmanham.

that at least some migrants moved from northern Germany and surrounding regions from the early fifth century on, and at least some groups were deliberately invited as mercenaries.[3] It is also clear that the local British population was acculturated to the new Anglo-Saxon culture, to a greater or lesser degree according to local circumstances, and the original proportions of migrants to locals almost certainly varied considerably from

remains that of Eagles (1979), but a major project is currently under way, which may well alter our whole perception of the rise of Deira: https:// www.leverhulme.ac.uk/awards-made/awards-focus/people-and-place -making-kingdom-northumbria-300%E2%80%93800-ce.

[3] Archaeological evidence rarely, if ever, indicates that a burial is that of a mercenary—but conversely, it can scarcely rule the possibility out. The interpretation of early settlers as mercenaries is chiefly derived from two factors: the literary evidence that this took place (Gildas, ch. 23, indicates the 'superbus tyrannus' (Vortigern) invited Saxons in as mercenaries), and the likelihood that British municipal authorities, faced with attacks from marauders (Saxons, Picts) yet lacking any army themselves after the withdrawal of Roman forces, would seek to employ foreign fighters rather than try to raise their own native armies (though the latter option was always there, particularly in less urbanised areas in the west of Britannia). In the 1970s, archaeologists were often inclined to interpret early Anglian presence as that of mercenaries, but seem less keen to do so nowadays. It is difficult to detect any substantial change in the data that form the basis of such arguments, but the interpretation of these very sparse data has certainly changed in line with academic trends.

one locality to another. However, the precise origin of any group that at a given point regarded itself as English (or whatever other term they used to emphasise their Germanic heritage) is not important for the present argument, which focuses on cultural identity and the implications this has for political action that are the focus of attention: what people *believed* about their history as a motivating factor for their actions.

To simplify things hugely, then, the germ—or at least one of the germs—of the kingdom of Deira surely lay at Sancton, within a couple of miles of Goodmanham. A huge Anglian cemetery (Sancton I, on top of the wold, largely cremation) has been excavated here, its origin dating from at least the mid-fifth century;[4] there appears to have been settlement extending for some miles along the edge of the Wolds from south of Sancton up towards Malton,[5] as well as further into the Wolds at Driffield (Eagles 1979, 228), which is likely to have been a royal centre in the pagan period and after (King Aldfrith died there in 705, according to the *Anglo-Saxon Chronicle, s.a.*, suggesting a long-standing royal connection). Apart from a small cemetery near York, Sancton represents the only cemetery in the East Riding definitely dating from as early as the fifth century (Eagles 1979, 243).

Why is the settlement here? The interpretation of Myres (1986, 188), although now somewhat dated, has much to commend it: it is the result of the deliberate posting of mercenaries here by the British authorities.[6] Sancton is in the perfect situation to serve such a mercenary guardian role: it overlooks the Roman road

---

[4] Faull (1976) sees Sancton I as serving a wider area than the Sancton II cemetery in the village itself; this is mixed cremation and inhumation, and dates from the sixth century. More generally on the Sancton cemeteries, see Myres and Southern (1973) and Timby (1993). The findings are now housed predominantly in Hull Museum and the Ashmolean Museum in Oxford.

[5] There are other early Anglian cemeteries further into the Wolds, and along the east coast, as well as a scattering around York and Catterick, and some on the Moors, but the western edge of the Wolds forms a particular concentration (Higham 1993*b*, 66–70; Eagles 1979, 206).

[6] This is also the conclusion of Eagles (1979, 240). Rather surprisingly, given his usual emphasis on continuity between post-Roman and Anglo-Saxon England, Higham (1993*b*, 67) rejects this idea, on the grounds that no-one would make the mistake of copying Vortigern's folly in inviting mercenaries in—as if politicians ever learn from history; he sees the settlement as the result of an intrusion by a Germanic warlord taking control of the Derwent valley—even though there is no evidence of settlement in the flood-prone lower Derwent.

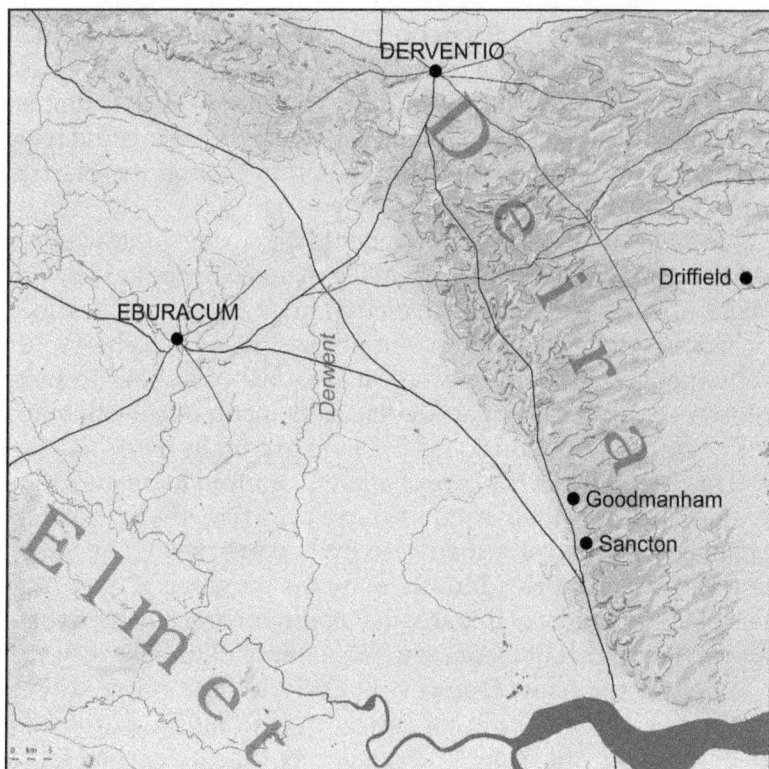

Fig. 7. The Vale of York, the Derwent valley and the edge of the Wolds, showing the heart of the realm of Deira and the eastern edge of the British kingdom of Elmet, with Roman roads highlighted.

from the south as it proceeds from nearby Brough-on-Humber, and lies close to its division, the one route going on to York and further north, the other to Malton, and thus it keeps watch over passage between the sea and the cities inland; it is close enough to the Humber to guard against maritime incursions and intercept any passage up the Derwent towards York; it is at the foot of the Wolds, and thus guards any passage between the hill district and the lowlands of the Derwent.[7] The earliest Anglian settlement of the western Wolds, then, was surely the

[7] If York was guarded to the south in this way, a counterpart defence to the north might also be expected; it may not be connected, but early Anglian presence (fifth to sixth century) is also clear at Catterick, at the northern end of the Vale of York (O'Brien 1999, 76).

result of deliberate decisions on the part of the early post-Roman authorities: the seat of authority was probably York,[8] the base for the *dux Britanniarum*, the military commander in late Roman Britain (Eagles 1979, 190), or Malton, or the decision could have been made by a wider regional collaborative authority. (See Fig. 7 for a map of the areas discussed.)

However, it makes little difference to the current topic whether the Anglian settlement was originally planned by the local British authorities or the result of an incursion by a Germanic warlord or lesser settlers. Whatever the origins, it is from the Wolds settlements that Deira may most reasonably be said to have grown, with other, smaller Anglian settlements outside this area (at York, Catterick and so forth) being gradually absorbed into it. This, I suggest, is the core of what Deirans in Eadwine's time would have held their origins to have been (whether or not they believed their ancestors had been invited in or settled by force), and this was confirmed for them by the presence of the pagan temple in the midst of this area at Goodmanham. (On the debate about the origins of Deira, see for example Dumville 1989.)

What of the name Deira? It is likely to be connected with the native British name for the Derwent (Fig. 8), but if it is, then it can only have been adopted once the English had taken the Derwent, or something named after the river, under their own control, but early enough for them to adopt an originally British regional name (suggestive of an existing British political structure).[9] I would suggest that taking the lower Derwent lands—where indeed there is no sign of early Anglian settlement—would not initially have been enticing: they are prone to flooding, and require heavy farming methods—they would have suited pasture, but scarcely agriculture to any degree. The

[8] Brough-on-Humber had apparently been more or less abandoned in the fourth century owing to silting and flooding (Eagles 1979, 188–9; Myres 1986, 187; Timby 1993, 247). However, York itself must have been much weakened by floods, which before the end of the Roman period had destroyed its bridge and harbour (Eagles 1979, 192).

[9] Reconstructing history on the basis of the name 'Deira' is, admittedly, problematic, given the uncertainty of the word's derivation. The term is also recorded in 'Derawudu' ('wood of the Deirans') around Beverley (Bede, *Historia Ecclesiastica* v.2, pp. 456–7), though of course this name may have been formed after the kingdom, rather than before it.

Fig. 8. The River Derwent
crossed by a medieval bridge at Sutton-on-Derwent.

upper Derwent presents a different picture; the difficulties it shares with the lower course of the river are less severe, and it is much closer to the Wolds, where the Anglians were settled.

However, I suggest that it is not so much the river name that has given rise to 'Deira' as the important Roman town of Malton, which was called *Derventio*. The reason for the asterisk is that, as Rivet and Smith note (1979, *s.v.* 'Derventio[1]'), the name always occurs in documents in the locative ablative (or, exceptionally, other inclined cases), *Derventione*, the meaning of which is probably 'at the [river] Derwent'. Hence the Deirans were 'the people of Derventio', where it was impossible to differentiate between the river and the town named after it.

Bede mentions the Derwent twice, and his usage arouses interest. The first time (*Historia Ecclesiastica* II.9, pp. 164–5) is the account of an assassination attempt on King Eadwine in his hall, which Bede says was 'next to the Derwent'. To give a location merely in terms of a nearby river is patently imprecise; moreover, the exact form of expression here is suspicious, 'Peruenit autem ad regem primo die paschae iuxta amnem Deruuentionem, ubi tunc erat uilla regalis' ('He approached the king on the first day of Easter beside the River Derwent, where at that time there was a royal hall'). This would read far more naturally if 'beside the Derwent' is interpreted as a place name: and this recalls the normal form of the Latin name for Malton, 'at the Derwent' (to which might be added that a number of other names occur in the locative in Bede, such as 'ad Gefrin' for Yeavering, *Historia Ecclesiastica* II.14, pp. 188–9). Hence, the meaning would be 'he approached the king . . . at Malton'. In this connection, it may be mentioned that the name 'Malton' probably means 'place of the assembly' (Smith 1928, *s.v.* 'Malton', p. 43), hence a centre of local government such as suits the site of a royal hall. If Eadwine's hall was at or near Malton, then it would symbolise a connection with the place whose take-over marked the founding of Deira as an independent kingdom several generations earlier.[10]

A likely scenario, then, is that the descendants of English settlers dwelling mainly on the edge of the Wolds embarked on a policy of expansion, the first stage of which included taking control of the area of the town of Derventio (along with some of the river valley). This must have taken place at some point in the later fifth century. Such an expansion, it may be surmised, coincided (and perhaps depended on) a growing sense of self-identification as a people; the assumption of authority over an existing administrative area (Deira) was marked by the adoption of the name of this area and its erstwhile chief town. I would regard it as implicit in this account that any such folk memory of history was a simplification and interpretation of 'reality' in terms of who the populace felt themselves to be at any point.[11] The English occupation of Deira was in any case

[10] Occupation of Derventio appears to have continued into the fifth century, and Anglian finds from the sixth century have been made there (Eagles 1979, 200–2; Eagles also suggests Eadwine's hall may have been at Malton). A few miles to the east of Malton, the settlement of West Heslerton was occupied, though not necessarily continuously, from the late fourth to early ninth century, covering the change-over from British to Anglian culture, with the densest occupation occurring in the late sixth century (Powlesland 1997, 111).

[11] Although it is questionable what, if any, historical basis there is to traditions recorded in the *Historia Brittonum*, it is interest that this work (ch. 61) relates that Soemil, great-great-grandfather of Ælle (the ruler of Deira in the late sixth century), divided Deira from Bernicia, which might be taken as meaning he established Deira as an Anglian realm distinct from the British kingdom of the region (given that the Anglian kingdom of Bernicia did not yet exist).

early enough to preclude the survival of any memory of the British kingdom or administration which existed here earlier—which probably dates it before the mid-sixth century (kingdoms surviving into the later sixth century such as Elmet tend to leave a slightly more substantial record in written sources). By Eadwine's time, and probably a generation or more earlier (the time of his father Ælle), the expansion had encompassed York and Catterick (taking in areas with an existing Anglian presence)—in other words, the whole Vale of York.

Where, then, was the royal hall where the religious conference took place? Bede does not specify it as the one on the Derwent, and his failure to mention any geographical location in the story apart from Goodmanham implies the hall was close by—yet far enough for Coifi to call for a horse to ride there. Higham (1993b, 81) argues the hall was most probably at Sancton.[12] There must surely have been a hall of the earliest period close to Sancton, the main Anglian cemetery, and by inference settlement, in this region of the Wolds. At a distance of a few miles from Goodmanham, this would suit the story as presented by Bede well.

The hall debate is presented by Bede as the culmination of a series of events which gradually persuaded Eadwine to adopt Christianity. More widely, the stage was set when Æthelberht of Kent took a Christian wife, Berhta, from Frankland—or, more accurately, it was set when he made a decision to form an alliance with a Christian realm through this marriage. The result was the conversion of Æthelberht and his kingdom by Augustine in 597. An alliance with a powerful continental kingdom clearly advantaged Kent politically and in terms of the greater trade possibilities it opened; the price was to yield spiritual control—and potentially a certain degree of concomitant political direction—to the Roman Church rather than controlling it internally. The same choice weighed upon each successive conversion of the English kingdoms, and has dogged English politics in some form or other to this day.

Æthelberht acted as an overlord to a number of lesser English rulers. One of these was Rædwald, king of East Anglia (in reality, a much wider realm than the modern East Anglia). Rædwald

---

[12] Higham unnecessarily and carelessly identifies the hall he argues existed at Sancton with the hall on the Derwent: Sancton is nowhere near the river.

appears to have tolerated Christianity to a degree, probably to avoid problems with Æthelberht, but remained a pagan—his ambiguous attitude towards Christianity is indicated by his worshipping both Christian and pagan gods (*Historia Ecclesiastica* ii.15, pp. 190–1).

Eadwine was of the royal house of Deira, but his realm was conquered by Æthelfrith of Bernicia around 604, and Eadwine was forced into exile. Bede indicates he spent time in many realms, but mentions specifically only Mercia (where he married his first wife, the daughter of King Cearl) and then East Anglia, where he was protected, falteringly, by Rædwald. Æthelberht died in 616, and Rædwald was freed to pursue his own foreign policy without Kentish interference. At first he seems to have been inclined to yield up Eadwine to Æthelfrith, but changed his mind, and instead marched against Æthelfrith with Eadwine and defeated him, putting Eadwine onto the throne of Northumbria.

As a protégé of the pagan Rædwald, Eadwine may well not have felt inclined to adopt Christianity, despite, according to Bede, receiving mysterious promptings to do so even while in exile. Rædwald died around 625, and Eadwine was then free from the constraints of East Anglian control, both political and religious (Mayr-Harting 1991, 66–7; Higham 1995, 79–81). He appears to have launched a campaign of conquest, but he also adopted Christianity in 627. This coincided with his marrying Æthelburh, the daughter of Æthelberht of Kent. This must have been a calculation to increase his political power: after an attempt on his life by Cwichelm, the king of Wessex, Eadwine effectively destroyed the power of Wessex (it was at this time a relatively insignificant kingdom), and East Anglia was less powerful after Rædwald's demise. An alliance with Kent would serve to bolster Eadwine's position, in particular against the other main power, Mercia, which was expanding northwards from its historic base around the middle Trent and was hostile towards Northumbria. The Kentish connection also offered the opportunities of links with continental powers, as has been noted.

Eadwine's dithering over the adoption of Christianity may, to a degree, be a reflection of Bede's attempts to reconcile differing accounts of how it took place (as Colgrave and Mynors, p. 182 n. in Bede's *Historia Ecclesiastica*, suggest). It may indicate a guardedness in balancing the relations with both Kent (Christian) and

East Anglia (pagan). It also implies deliberation over whether the yielding of a certain degree of independence in the choice of cultural affiliation and alliances for the sake of the greater security and trade arising from belonging to the wider Christian world was worth while or not. The materials Bede had to work with may not have been wholly conducive to his desire to show Eadwine as a great Christian king, unwavering in his loyalty to the faith, but he nonetheless manifests God's purpose in Eadwine's story, and showing how the king's ultimate success derived from a divine recognition of his Christian virtue, the spread of Christian virtue among his people being a reflection of his divinely determined power. The conversion of Coifi forms part of this developing narrative, and contributes to its aims.

The king's choice of York for his baptism, and the subsequent establishment of the city as the main centre of royal power in the region, seems only natural from the perspective of later centuries, during which York became a mighty city and the second archbishopric of the realm of England. Yet York was a quite different place in the early seventh century, and Eadwine's choice is a very definite statement. York had probably only been in Deiran hands for a few decades; the *Annales Cambriae* mention a battle in 580 in which a prince with the surname 'York' (Evrauc) was killed, and this could possibly be some memory of its fall. York was probably of only minor significance by this stage (and must have been in a somewhat ruinous state), and the English were certainly not accustomed to inhabit old Roman cities: yet it retained sufficient prestige for Eadwine to use it as a focus of his move to Christianity. It is difficult to imagine it as having been abandoned for more than about fifty years for this to be feasible, so a date of around 580 for its take-over by Deira seems credible, particularly when it is remembered that the British kingdom of Elmet, the eastern boundary of which appears to have been the River Wharfe, a fairly short distance from York, remained independent into Eadwine's reign. Whilst Deira may have controlled York and regions beyond for some decades by the time of Eadwine's baptism, these lands would appear to have been peripheral to Deira (as indicated by the royal halls on or to the east of the Derwent in which Eadwine held court) until Eadwine chose to shift the focus of his kingdom from the Derwent lands to this once important city.

Adopting Christianity had wider implications: it was an alignment of the realm with the concerns of Europe, as had been the case for Æthelberht. Eadwine was surely aware that the great emperor Constantine, who converted the Roman empire to Christianity, was proclaimed emperor in York. His linking of his baptism to this historically focal site was a declaration of his adoption not merely of Roman Christianity, but of Roman *imperium*, albeit expressed within just one province of the former empire; it is this *imperium* that forms a pointed part of Bede's introduction to Eadwine (*Historia Ecclesiastica* ii.9, pp. 162–3): 'ita ut quod nemo Anglorum ante eum, omnes Brittaniae fines, qua uel ipsorum uel Brettonum prouinciae habitabant, sub dicione acciperet' ('so, like no other English king before him, he held under his sway the whole realm of Britain, not only English kingdoms but those ruled over by the Britons as well').

The balance of probability is that Coifi did indeed desecrate the pagan shrine, or at least that he existed as a *persona* of traditional narrative who embodied the process of conversion in a way that made sense within the symbolism of the belief system people were familiar with: Bede chose to preserve this, as a clear rejection of paganism, but, as ever, eschewed revealing any explicit connection with the pagan beliefs that underlay it.

When Coifi turned back from the royal court to the sanctuary at the heart of the ancestral homelands, and cast the spear into its midst, he was not just murdering paganism: he was rejecting the confinement of the past, and was looking to the future, to new horizons—geographical, spiritual and imperial. Deira may have begun as a small settlement of mercenaries or adventurers on the edge of the Wolds, but it expanded westwards and northwards to include Malton and the Derwent valley, and thereafter York, whence royal authority was to extend across the land: under Eadwine's Christian leadership, Deira, releasing itself from the limits of being merely the pagan 'Derwent land', was now to be graced with an imperial city, and imperial religion, at its new heart, from which Eadwine would rule not just Deira but much of Britannia, the future England, a development that was cut short only by his untimely death. Whatever the historical reality, such, I suggest, was the historical narrative that Eadwine and his successors promulgated.

✝ B ✝

King Eadwine's Conversion:
A Typological Analysis

THE DECISIVE DEBATE, described by Bede in his *Historia Ecclesiastica* II.13, pp. 182–7, which took place in King Eadwine's hall in Northumbria in 627, and led to the king's conversion and baptism, was part of Bede's wider presentation of the life of Northumbria's first Christian monarch.

In the previous chapter, I have suggested the following points that bear on the present consideration. Eadwine's realm of Deira was named after *Derventio*, the Latinised name of both the River Derwent and the settlement of Malton on the river. One of Eadwine's halls was 'on the Derwent', which may mean specifically Malton; the hall in which the debate about adopting Christianity took place, however, was probably closer to the site of the pagan temple whose destruction is recounted. This pagan temple (whatever precisely that meant) was situated at Goodmanham, at the edge of the Wolds, close to Market Weighton; this site was a couple of miles from the very early, and large, Anglo-Saxon cemetery at Sancton. Goodmanham was therefore the spiritual heart of the most ancient core of Deira. In contrast, the later centre of Deira, York, and its surrounding area were probably not taken by the Deirans until a generation or so before Eadwine's time.

Bede presents the wider history of Eadwine in his *Historia Ecclesiastica* II.9–20, pp. 162–207; in the order in which he presents them, the main points are:

> Eadwine accepts the faith through the preaching of Paulinus, who has been sent from the mission in Kent: 'the king's earthly power had increased as an augury that he was to become a believer and have a share in the heavenly kingdom' ('cui uidelicet regi, in auspicium suscipiendae fidei et regni caelestis, potestas

etiam terreni creuerat imperii'); Eadwine rules all of Britain
except Kent (with which he was in alliance through marriage),
including even Anglesey and the Isle of Man.

The occasion of his conversion is marriage to Æthelburh,
daughter of Æthelberht, king of Kent: to bring this about, Eadwine promises to allow freedom of worship to his wife, with the
hint that he may adopt Christianity himself if his counsellors
regard it as a better religion. Paulinus, consecrated bishop in
July 625, comes with Æthelburh to Northumbria.

Paulinus is to yield up a Christian virgin to a heathen king;
but his real purpose is to bring the kingdom of Northumbria
as a virgin bride to her husband, Christ. In this endeavour he
at first has no success.

In 626 an assassin sent by Cwichelm, king of Wessex, makes
an attempt on Eadwine's life on Easter day in his hall on the
Derwent. The same night, a daughter, Eanflæd, is born to the
king, and he thanks his gods for this; Paulinus, however, tells
the king that the successful birth is due to his prayers to Christ.
Eadwine replies that if God grants him victory over Cwichelm,
he will become Christian, and he gives Eanflæd to Paulinus to
baptise as a pledge. Eadwine sets off and defeats those who had
plotted to kill him, but still does not become Christian, though
he gave up worshipping idols. Instead, he asks Paulinus to
instruct him in Christianity, and he consults his wise men over
it, whilst pondering which faith it will be best to follow.

Two letters are reproduced from Pope Boniface to Eadwine
and his wife, exhorting him to turn his back on idol-worship
and follow the Christian faith, and her to encourage him (these
must have been written somewhat earlier, as Boniface's papacy
ended in October 625).[1]

Bede returns to Eadwine. Paulinus sees how difficult it is
for the king's proud mind ('sublimitatem animi') to accept the
precepts of salvation, but he urges him to fulfil the promise he
made when he received the 'heavenly vision' while in exile with
Rædwald, king of East Anglia. Rædwald had been pleased to
receive the exiled Eadwine (who had been forced to leave Deira
when it was conquered by Æthelfrith of Bernicia), but Eadwine's
enemy Æthelfrith approached and threatened Rædwald, urging

---

[1] These are in such complex language, and imbued with such involved
theology, as to defy interpretation into the English that Eadwine would
have spoken; yet he would have grasped that his kingship depended on the
favour of the Christian God, and on rejecting his native religion: the gift of
a gold-embroidered robe and garment from Ancyra no doubt hinted at the
desirability of being on good terms with the pope and the lands he held
spiritual sway over. For Bede, however, the point was to stress the care of the
Roman see for the king's salvation, and with it that of his people.

him to put Eadwine to death; the threats were made on several occasions. Rædwald eventually promised to do as Æthelfrith requested. Eadwine was warned of Rædwald's plans, but refused to flee, as so far the king had done nothing to offend him, and, he noted, where could he now flee after spending so long avoiding the snares of his enemies?[2] Eadwine was 'consumed with inner fire', as he was approached by a strangely clad individual. He asked the prince what he would give if someone could persuade Rædwald to change his mind and support him, and moreover assure him that his enemies would be overthrown, making him a king unsurpassed in power. Eadwine promised him whatever he could give. The man then also assured the king of salvation, if Eadwine were willing to pay for this by obeying him. Eadwine immediately promised he would follow the teaching of one who would save him from so many troubles and raise him to the throne. The spiritual being laid his hand on Eadwine's head as a sign, and told him to fulfil his promise when he encountered the same sign again. Thereupon, the spirit immediately disappeared. Eadwine soon after received the news that Rædwald, at the urging of his queen, had changed his mind, and together they marched against Æthelfrith, defeating him and putting Eadwine on the throne. In due course, Paulinus makes the sign on Eadwine's head, and reminds him of his oath, promising that as God had rescued him and rewarded him with an earthly kingdom, so too by fulfilling his vow he will now be assured a place in the heavenly kingdom.

The next chapter relates the meeting in the hall, where the wise men discuss the option of adopting Christianity; this has been given above.

Eadwine, along with his nobles and vast numbers of common folk, receives baptism in 627 at York on Easter day in the church of St Peter, which had been hastily raised in timber. He makes Paulinus bishop, and sets about building a more splendid church in stone (completed by his successor, Oswald). Among those baptised are Osfrith and Eadfrith, sons of Eadwine by Cwœnburh, the daughter of Cearl, king of Mercia, whom he married in exile. Paulinus proceeds to baptise many near Yeavering, the royal hall of Bernicia, as well as in the Swale near Catterick in Deira.

Eadwine persuades Eorpwald, king of East Anglia, to become Christian. Bede mentions that Eorpwald's father, Rædwald,

---

[2] Here, Bede surely intends a reference to Psalm 38:12, 'They also that seek after my life lay snares for me: and they that seek my hurt speak mischievous things, and imagine deceits all the day long', along with Psalm 91:3, 'Surely he shall deliver thee from the snare of the fowler, and from the noisome pestilence' — something which the personage of the vision delivers.

had become Christian in Kent, but proved a recidivist, keeping an altar to Christ and another to the pagan gods within one temple. After a three-year interlude, Sigeberht succeeds to the throne, and continues the evangelisation of East Anglia under Bishop Felix.

Paulinus engages in missionary work in the kingdom of Lindsey. Also mentioned is the great peace under Eadwine, such that no-one dared lay hands on the drinking cups he set up for people's convenience throughout his realm, other than to use them for their intended purpose. Eadwine is said to have traversed his realm in due pomp, a standard borne before him in the way of Roman rulers.

A letter from Pope Honorius is reproduced, encouraging Eadwine to persist in the faith. The letter again emphasises that Eadwine's kingship is dependent on his faith in the King of Heaven, and urges him to read the works of Gregory. The pope sends a pallium each to his bishops, in a move designed to affirm the position of the Church in Britain. A further letter from Pope Honorius is quoted, granting the archbishop of either York or Canterbury the right to consecrate a successor, to avoid the need to go to Rome. The next chapter deals with papal letters to the Irish, urging them to correct their way of calculating Easter, and reject the heresy of Pelagianism.

After ruling for seventeen years, Eadwine is slain by Cædwalla (Cadwallon), king of the Britons, supported by Penda, pagan king of the Mercians, in a battle at Hatfield Chase, resulting in the destruction of the Church in Northumbria. Bede attacks Penda for his heathenism, but reserves his greatest ire for the cruel Cadwallon, who was supposedly a Christian, but worse than a heathen. Paulinus flees with Queen Æthelburh back to Kent. The Church in Northumbria is to a degree preserved by James, a deacon, whom Paulinus leaves behind; he helps restore the Church when peace returns (in other words, under the Christian King Oswald), and instructs many in church singing in the Roman way. It is implied that James acted as an informant to Bede on Eadwine's reign, possibly indirectly.

Bede's account reads as a mainly chronological description of Eadwine's reign and the Church events that took place then—a commonplace medieval presentation of history as *res gestae*, tempered by the concern to present a specifically ecclesiastical history of the nation, so that Bede for example appears always to give *in extenso* any papal letters he has copies of. Yet this narrative framework masks, I would argue, a series of underlying typological and symbolic readings of history; this is particularly evident in the details of the process of conversion.

Bede begins with Eadwine's conversion, then gives us a glimpse of his life in exile before this; he passes on to the king's baptism and his mission to his own people and those around (East Anglia, Lindsey); he concludes with his premature death in battle against a pagan (Penda) and apostate (Cadwallon), marking him out as almost a martyr (see Introduction), and his Christian followers are scattered. His life broadly mirrors Christ's, but within this general framework the typological connection is not strongly drawn (yet we may ponder if Penda and Cadwallon are to a degree to be read as metatypes of Pilate and Caiaphas).

The debate in the hall is the decisive turning point in Eadwine's adoption of Christianity, but Bede builds up to this with a three-crested crescendo: Eadwine promises not to stand in the way of Æthelburh's Christianity, and hints he may think about adopting the faith himself; he promises to adopt Christianity after being delivered from an assassination attempt, and has his daughter baptised as a pledge of this; he is persuaded to adopt the faith in earnest, subject to the approval of his wise men, by Paulinus, who reminds him of his earlier vision. The vision is surely meant to recall the emperor Constantine, and his vision that 'in this sign you shall be victorious', the sign being the cross; the sign of blessing that the spirit makes on Eadwine is not spelled out, but can surely only be the cross, delivered by a priest or the High Priest himself. Eadwine's acceptance of the blessing leads to his victory and the establishment of his Christian empire. Given the Constantinian imagery, it may be that the hesitation Eadwine shows hitherto is meant to reflect that of Constantine himself, who famously did not accept baptism until his death-bed — though this is scarcely hinted at. The spirit makes a three-fold promise to Eadwine:

- to deliver him from the threat posed by Rædwald;
- to grant him great power as a king;
- to effect the salvation of his soul.

We are surely meant to recall the temptations of Christ in the wilderness (Eadwine, of course, is at this stage in the wilderness of exile): according to his tempter, he can make bread from stones to save his body, he can have all the kingdoms of the world, and he can save himself from falling from a high place. Eadwine's spirit is, however, the inverse of Christ's tempter, and represents Christ himself, so Eadwine is rewarded for his true worship (thus: Christ, the perfect man, is tempted into sin by an evil spirit; Eadwine, a fallen pagan, is drawn into salvation by a good spirit).

The description of Eadwine as 'consumed with inner fire' just as the good spirit approaches him is a short quotation from Vergil's *Aeneid*, book ɪᴠ, line 2. Here, the subject is Dido of Carthage, on fire with love for the new arrival, Aeneas, whom she believes to be of divine descent—yet book ɪᴠ above all highlights how Aeneas, in comfortable exile at Dido's court, is stunned by a messenger from the gods, urging him on to fulfil his destiny and found a realm in Italy, just as Eadwine must forego the dubious (and potentially treacherous) comforts of Rædwald's court and claim his true homeland—conceived materially as Deira, but spiritually as the kingdom of heaven realised in the Church— urged on by the messenger, strangely attired and clearly divine, who comes up to him at this point. Hence Bede's allusion is, I think, more than a casual demonstration of familiarity with the classics; as noted in the Introduction, the story of Aeneas acted as a type for the metatype of the establishment of a Christian realm in England, and the allusion here particularises this notion to Eadwine, who thus stands as a sort of metonym for the whole migration from the pagan realms to the promised land that was to be a beacon of the true faith.

Such a symbolic presentation of Eadwine would, of course, work better if he had been the first Christian English king. Bede could scarcely ignore the fact that Æthelberht of Kent had anticipated him; yet even in this story Bede manages to intertwine a sort of Deiran supremacy through what he relates of the preamble to Augustine's mission. The conversion of England began not so much with Æthelberht himself, as with Pope Gregory the Great (before he became pope): Bede recounts, in his *Historia Ecclesiastica* ɪɪ.1, pp. 132–5, how Gregory is supposed to have been walking in the market, where he encountered some slaves for sale, and asked who they were (my translation).

> Dicunt quia die quadam, cum aduenientibus nuper mercatoribus multa uenalia in forum fuissent conlata, multi ad emendum confluxissent, et ipsum Gregorium inter alios aduenisse, ac uidisse inter alia pueros uenales positos candidi corporis ac uenusti uultus, capillorum quoque forma egregia. Quos cum aspiceret,

interrogauit, ut aiunt, de qua regione uel terra essent adlati; dictumque est quia de Brittania insula, cuius incolae talis essent aspectus. Rursus interrogauit utrum idem insulani Christiani, an paganis adhuc erroribus essent inplicati. Dictum est quod essent pagani. At ille, intimo ex corde longa trahens suspiria, 'Heu, pro dolor!' inquit 'quod tam lucidi uultus homines tenebrarum auctor possidet, tantaque gratia frontispicii mentem ab interna gratia uacuam gestat!' Rursus ergo interrogauit, quod esset uocabulum gentis illius. Responsum est quod Angli uocarentur. At ille: 'Bene' inquit; 'nam et angelicam habent faciem, et tales Angelorum in caelis decet esse coheredes. Quod habet nomen ipsa prouincia, de qua isti sunt adlati?' Responsum est quia Deiri uocarentur idem prouinciales. At ille 'Bene' inquit 'Deiri, de ira eruti et ad misericordiam Christi uocati. Rex prouinciae illius quomodo appellatur?' Responsum est quod Aelle diceretur. At ille adludens ad nomen ait: 'Alleluia, laudem Dei Creatoris illis in partibus oportet cantari.'

They say that one day, when merchants had just arrived and brought many goods for sale to the market, people thronged there to shop, and Gregory himself came along with the others, and among other things saw some boys put up for sale, with white bodies and handsome in appearance, and with outstandingly beautiful hair. When he saw them, he asked, so they say, what region or land they had been brought from; it was said that they came from the island of Britain, whose inhabitants looked like that. Again, he asked whether these island people were Christians, or were still embroiled in the errors of paganism. It was related that they were pagans. He drew a long breath from the depths of his heart and said, 'Alas, that people of such bright appearance should be in the possession of the author of shadows, and that such grace of face should mask a mind devoid of inner grace.' Again, he asked what the name of their race was. The answer was that they were called Angles. He said 'Fine, since they have an angelic appearance, and such people should be co-heirs with the angels in heaven. What name does the country have that they have been brought from?' The answer was that the men of their country were called Deirans. He said 'Fine. Deirans, wrested from wrath (*de ira*) and called to the mercy of Christ. And the king of that country, what is he called?' The answer was that he was called Ælle. Alluding to this name, he said 'Alleluia, the praise of God the Creator should be sung in those parts'.

The angelic appearance of the youths, which inspires Gregory to fill their countrymen with inner grace, acts as a precursor to the spiritual beauty of Deira which is achieved by Ælle's son, Eadwine.

The debate in the king's hall, which follows upon the recollection of Eadwine's vision at Rædwald's court, is the centrepiece of Bede's conversion narrative, and has proved the most memorable part of his account of Eadwine, most notably for the striking metaphor of the sparrow's brief flight through the warm winter hall, standing for a human life, and for the vivid reaction of Coifi to the coming of the new faith. However, the hall scene also has an important structural and symbolic role within Bede's overall narrative. The scene forms a sort of *recapitulatio* of the Christian message, representing three stages of conversion, a ladder of spiritual ascent passing from the material benefits afforded by true faith to salvation of the soul. In summary, the points made are:

- Coifi: Christianity may make us (especially me) richer;
- Nameless counsellor: Christianity may tell us what happens before and after life on earth;
- Coifi: Christianity offers the gift of life, salvation, eternal happiness; paganism is worthless.

The three points correspond to those portrayed by the good spirit that visited Eadwine: physical or material benefit; a secure position in the world based on knowledge of the truth; salvation. To an extent, therefore, the good spirit's lure is an adumbration (or type) of what is on offer at the debate, and as Eadwine was bound to accept the first, so he must surely accept the second. The three stages of the benefits of Christianity are reflected also in Eadwine's *curriculum vitae*: material welfare is seen in his gaining his kingdom after committing to convert; his position in the world is thereby assured, after years of exile outside the 'hall' of his kingdom; his true faith is clearly read as a promise of his salvation, following upon his quasi-martyr's death (and in terms of the pattern of Christ's temptations, it is the gaining of the kingdom of heaven that is the inverse of the kingdoms of this world that the devil offers Christ).

There is also some hint of the debate in the hall acting as a collocation of the Old Testament types of the anointed one. Three Old Testament offices were characterised by anointing: prophets (I Kings 19:16), priests (Exodus 28:41) and kings (I Samuel 10:1). These combined into the antitype of Christ, 'the anointed' (cf. Daniel 9:25, 26) prophet (Acts 3:22), priest (Hebrews 3:1) and king (Revelation 17:14). The hall scene has three actors: the king, Paulinus (the priest) and the counsellors, epitomised by Coifi (who is also, of course, the antithesis of a Christian priest), who act as a collective prophet, 'speaking forth' the truth and declaring for the new faith; the king and priest are in the background in this specific scene, but it is part of a wider tableau whose two main actors are very much Eadwine and Paulinus. The three offices do not coalesce in the converted Eadwine in the way they do in Christ, yet, just as Christ is revealed as the threefold anointed in the city of Jerusalem, so too Eadwine moves to York to establish it as the centre of his earthly and spiritual realm, ruling from there, giving Paulinus a bishopric there, and going forth to preach to other kingdoms from there (either himself or with Paulinus acting as the means of bringing Christianity to East Anglia and Lindsey).

The equation of York with Jerusalem calls for a closer look at the symbolism of place as the arena of spirituality in Bede's account (Fig. 9). This is manifested in a variety of ways.

The hall/temple presents various patterns. Eadwine's conversion takes place mainly in three royal halls:

- Rædwald's hall, where Eadwine is in exile;
- Eadwine's hall 'on the Derwent' (*Historia Ecclesiastica* ii.9, pp. 164–5), where an assassination attempt is made on him by Cwichelm, king of Wessex; as noted in the previous chapter, Bede may have meant specifically Malton as the site of this hall;
- Eadwine's hall where the debate about adopting Christianity takes place. This was presumably close to Goodmanham (though it could have been the same hall as that 'on the Derwent', but Bede does not make this identification), but far enough away to justify using a horse to get there; somewhere near the settlement associated with the Sancton cemetery is likely.

A progression may be discerned here: the first presents Eadwine as a landless exile, the second as a king with secular power, the third as a king with spiritual power, which passes from being pagan to Christian. We observe a geographical approach towards Goodmanham, the centre of paganism, going hand in hand with the spiritual march towards Christianity, and the progression results in the overthrow of that spiritual centre and its replacement with a Christian spiritual focus. The overthrow

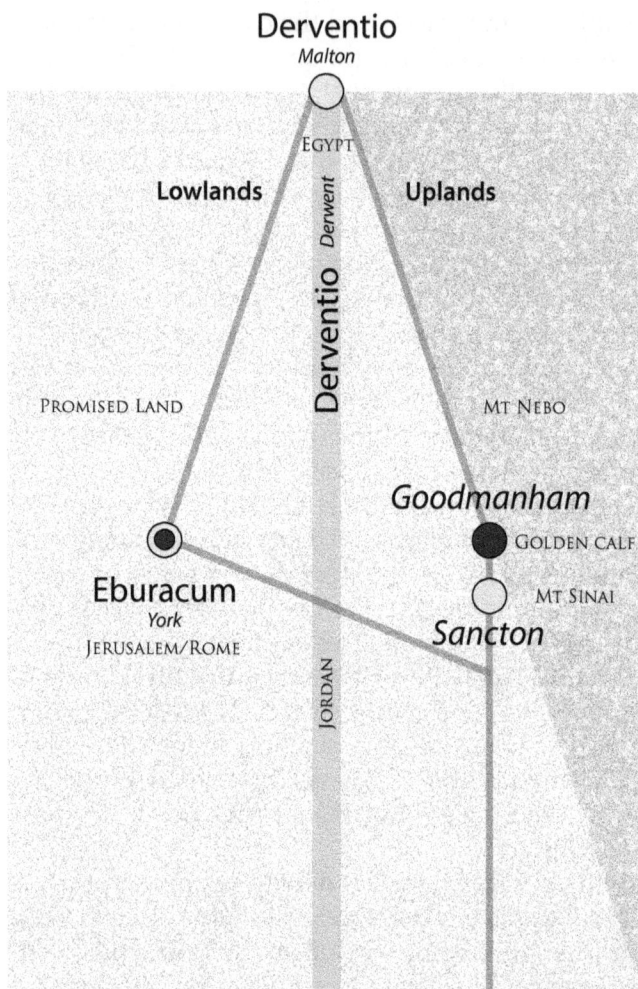

Fig. 9. A schematic representation of the realm of Deira, with sacred sites represented with light circles, and secular halls with dark; Roman roads are also indicated. Suggested typological interpretations are included.

of the idols of Goodmanham may be intended to recall the destruction of the golden calf that the Israelites worshipped on their path to the Promised Land (Exodus 32): only when this idolatry was rejected was it possible to pass (eventually) over the Jordan and establish a true centre of worship there.

An interesting narrative balance arises between the two incidents within Deira which spurred Eadwine on to convert. The first was a political affair: an attempt on Eadwine's life by the king of Wessex. This took place in the hall which, as suggested above, had symbolic and political significance as marking the foundation of Deira as a kingdom. The conference near Goodmanham, by contrast, takes place in a venue which marks the *spiritual* foundation of Deira, near the heart of the ancient settlement marked by an ancestral shrine. Whilst Eadwine was already inclined to accept Christianity as a result of political connivings against him, it is here, close to Goodmanham (certainly in narrative terms, and probably in historical geographical terms), that the spiritual conversion truly takes place, and is marked by the overturning of the pagan shrine. The spiritual conversion is, nonetheless, given a symbolic political twist, in that the conference to discuss it was instigated by the king upon his recalling an earlier vision when in exile at Rædwald's court which saved his life and led on to his defeating his enemy, Æthelfrith, and taking on the kingship of Northumbria: hence the twin threads of political and religious motivation are here intertwined, and the achievement of spiritual conversion reflects the political success with which Bede hails Eadwine at the beginning of his description of his reign (*Historia Ecclesiastica* ii.9, pp. 162–3).

Several further dualities may also be observed in the figure of the hall/temple. The pagan halls taken together are contrasted with Eadwine's Christian hall in York, situated presumably in the still-standing *principia* building of the Roman fortress, the remains of which are visible beneath York Minster.[3] In particular, the pagan temple of Goodmanham is contrasted with the Christian church in York. It is interesting that a further contrast appears to be implicit between wood and stone; all the pagan halls would have been of wood (and this would hardly have needed stating), whereas by settling in York, Eadwine was presumably adopting Roman customs of living in a stone palace. Eadwine's church was at first of wood, but then he begins a stone edifice, left unfinished at his death, just as the establishment of the Church in his realm is similarly left unfinished, both the church and the Church being completed in York and Northumbria by his successor, Oswald. The temple

---

[3] Eagles (1979, 192) notes that the *principia* building was standing at least into the ninth century.

at Goodmanham and the presumably nearby royal hall of the debate are both in a sense 'Christianised', the hall through the decision taken in it to adopt Christianity, and the temple through its destruction (and replacement with a small church, though this is not stated by Bede); the disparate hall and temple are brought into one complex in York, the new church being right beside Eadwine's headquarters. The implicit abandonment of the old hall is contrasted with the restoration of an old Roman 'hall', and the destruction of the pagan temple is matched by the construction of a new church.

Both of Eadwine's pagan-period halls are defined in relation to the River Derwent; the one where the assassination attempt took place is said to be on the river, and the pagan temple, fairly near which the debate hall must have stood, is described as beyond the Derwent. The association with the Derwent implicitly contrasts them with York, nowhere near the river, but the river appears to have a deeper symbolism. The two mentions of the river imply a symbolic link with Deira itself, the kingdom named after it:

* The assassination-attempt marks this hall out as a symbolic political site; the hall acts as a microcosm of the realm of Deira as a political entity;
* The spiritual debate marks the hall in question as a microcosm of Deira as a 'spiritual' entity.

Bede's account relates the destruction of the shrine which must have defined the heart of Deira at (and indeed before) its inception, the site of the sanctuary reflecting the very oldest traditions of attachment to the land that the Anglian settlers could muster, and we may well infer that in Eadwine's time, perhaps some seven or so generations after the first Anglian settlers, this area was still regarded as their heartland. The mention of the river whose name gave rise to that of the kingdom is, I suggest, intended to evoke this ancient tradition—but in a particular way, which is marked by the observation that Goodmanham is *beyond* the Derwent. This is only true if one travels thither from York, which is also mentioned in the account. In Bede's time, York was the metropolis of Deira, but it was Eadwine that made it so: to go to Goodmanham from York is to retrace the steps by which Deira emerged from the dark limitations, geographical as well as spiritual, of paganism on the path to the *imperium*, based in

York, that came with the adoption of Christianity.

The river thus becomes a spiritual boundary between the pagan past and the Christian present, something that may possibly be further rooted in history, as the Derwent may at an early stage of Deira's development have acted as a political boundary (as suggested by Eagles 1979, 203, who notes greater signs of continuity, and an absence of Anglian settlement in the fifth century west and north of the river around Malton). Hence the Derwent acts as a metatype of the Jordan, a river which the exiled Israelites crossed in order to take possession of the Promised Land. The crossing of the Jordan is, of course, a type to the baptism of Christ in that same river and his possession of the promised land of the heavenly kingdom. By moving over the Derwent to York upon his decision to accept the new faith, Eadwine acts as a metatype, leading his people into the promised land of Christianity. Allusion is also surely made to the other biblical type of baptism: the exiled Moses leading the Israelites across the Red Sea, leaving Pharaoh's forces (the deceits of the pagan world) destroyed. As noted (see Introduction), this could act also as a type for the English passage over the sea to the 'promised land' that is their due upon accepting baptism into the true faith. Hence Eadwine, in 'crossing' the Derwent, is seen as a metonym of the whole English crossing-over into the 'promised land' of England.

Baptism is linked specifically with the Derwent in the events described as taking place at the hall on the river: Eadwine's daughter Eanflæd was born on the day of an attempted assassination, and Eadwine offers her up to be baptised as an act of thanksgiving for his delivery. He also set off to wreak retribution on his enemy, the king of Wessex. Bede emphasises that the events took place at Easter—which directly links it with Eadwine's own baptism later, also at Easter. But the collocation of Easter with baptism emphasises the meaning of baptism itself as a participation in Christ's death (and resurrection): 'Know ye not, that so many of us as were baptized into Jesus Christ were baptized into his death?' (Romans 6:3). Like Christ, and symbolically like the baptismal neophyte, Eadwine 'dies' in the hall; he then spends some time in the pagan darkness outside his realm, as it were 'harrowing' Wessex, and is 'reborn' with the course of events that lead up to his actual baptism, but also in his daughter, who is not only physically born at this time, but is born into new life through baptism. The cluster of events acts as a symbolic dry run for the baptism of Eadwine himself, and the Easter setting hints at how Eadwine's baptism, as a metatype of Christ's death and resurrection, is a metonym for his whole martyric reign. Eanflæd was, moreover, not merely the first fruits of the conversion of Northumbria, but an important agent in the rebirth of Christianity after Eadwine's fall, since she married Oswald's brother King Oswiu, and later became abbess of the important monastery of Whitby.

There are further indications that Eadwine is a metatype of Moses. Æthelfrith attempts to take Eadwine's life, and forces him into exile; Pharaoh attempts to murder Moses (Exodus 2:15), who is eventually forced into exile. Eadwine avenges the attempt on his life by a powerful king (Cwichelm), and Moses slays the overbearing Egyptian overseer (Exodus 2:11–12). The hall 'on the Derwent' in this respect thus signifies Egypt, a land of spiritual exile for the Israelites where they had exercised authority, but where worldly powers could now betray them: a land that must be abandoned to find the true spiritual home in the Promised Land. Moses in exile marries Zipporah and has a son by her (Exodus 2:21), and has a vision of God, who tells him to go back and lead his people to their Promised Land (Exodus 3). Eadwine is forced into exile, where (in Mercia) he marries his first wife and has children by her (and the mention of this marriage, the sole thing we learn of his exile in Mercia, may have been deliberately intended to draw the parallel with Moses' marriage), then later (in East Anglia) has a vision of a man, implicitly Christ or a representative of Christ, who assures him of victory and his kingdom. Egypt, the land of exile, represents a state of bondage such as holds the sinner prior to his conversion (Galatians 4:1–7; Romans 6:17; I Corinthians 10:1–4, which identifies the crossing of the Red Sea as a type for baptism), which fits Eadwine's state at this stage. The ultimate goal of the Israelites is Jerusalem (or Zion), a metonym for the promised land in general; the city typifies the Church and finally heaven (cf. Galatians 4:25–6; Hebrews 12:22; Revelation 21:2).[4]

---

[4] Moses, of course, did not attain his goal, but is said to have gazed out over the Promised Land from Mount Nebo (Deuteronomy 34:1–4). From the

This leads on to a consideration of the symbolism of York. The York area had been in Deiran hands for a generation or so, but was peripheral to the English realm; the English were not city-dwellers and had little use for Roman cities. Yet Eadwine made a deliberate choice to move his centre of power here. In view of the symbolism of the river, York, to the west of the Derwent as Jerusalem was to the west of the Jordan, combined secular and spiritual power as a new centre in the 'promised land', bringing together and cleansing all the former secular and religious centres of Deira, in the form of the two halls and the Goodmanham sanctuary.[5] The symbolism of 'Jerusalem', however, is affirmed as specifically Christian; hence York symbolises the 'new Jerusalem' of Rome, the centre of the Catholic Church.

The symbolism of Rome is complex—just a few points can be made here. The paradox of this city, the worldly *caput mundi*, being the pagan centre of persecution of the faithful, and yet the seat of the first among patriarchs of the Church, was apparent from an early date, and forms the basis of the central imagery of St Augustine's *City of God*, where the worldly city, founded on the fratricide of Remus by Romulus (to Augustine, a typological analogue of Abel and Cain), is the antithesis of the spiritual City of God, which gathers all the faithful into it over the ages. Rome, viewed as a spiritual city, thus forms a type to the antitype (or anatype) of the new Jerusalem of the fulfilled kingdom of heaven: the perspective is anagogical, looking forward to this fulfilment at the eschaton.

The symbolism of Rome was affirmed liturgically and ritually (as discussed by Ó Carragáin 1994, 9–12). By the seventh century, a system had developed whereby the pope would undertake a circuit of the various basilicas of Rome in a particular order, the stational procession. A stational list of the sites was known

---

Goodmanham sanctuary it would have been possible (it is not today, but see Fig. 6, taken from nearby) to glimpse the 'promised land' of the lowlands of the Derwent valley towards York. The symbolism of this view is not explicit in Bede, but could have been apparent to Deirans with local knowledge (which Bede may well not have had, unless he visited Goodmanham during his visit to York).

[5] In reality, of course, there is no reason to think the earlier halls were abandoned; the 'abandonment' is symbolic, within the terms of the spiritual reading of Bede's text.

in Northumbria, and probably specifically in Bede's monastery. It is likely (but unproven) that some form of imitation of the Roman procession was effected between or within churches and monasteries in Northumbria: this emphasised the unity of the Church as a whole. Some parts of the stational procession emphasised the links with Jerusalem: in particular, a procession from the Lateran to the church of the Holy Cross of Jerusalem, which housed a relic of the cross brought back from Jerusalem by Constantine's mother Helena, took place on the fourth Sunday of Lent, which was particularly laden with ceremonies focused on the catechumenate. The introit begins 'Laetare Ierusalem' ('Rejoice, Jerusalem'), and the faithful are expected as it were to focus on 'going up to Jerusalem' (Luke 9:51) for Passiontide; the procession was symbolically equivalent to the passage from the Temple to Golgotha, and the Good Friday liturgy for the hour of Christ's death involved Christ's followers coming together at the church of the Holy Cross in Rome to worship before the cross, as was noted in the Northumbrian stational list. The implications of Ó Carragáin's discussion are that Rome was identified with Jerusalem figurally, and also that the procession was one from this earthly life to the life of the new Jerusalem (symbolised in the cross, but also in the focus on the catechumenate, which passes through the death of baptism at Easter). In Augustinian terms, it might be said that Rome is becoming the City of God, the new Jerusalem, and Rome acts as a metonym for the whole Church through local participation in its liturgy, and the Roman catechumenate similarly acts as a metonym for converts in all the nations.

Eadwine, then, is baptised in York and in doing so adopts a web of spiritual connotations: Christ acceded to the Promised Land of the new covenant through baptism in the Jordan, marking passage into this promised land. Moreover, Constantine, who converted the Roman empire to Christianity, was proclaimed emperor in York.[6] Hence Eadwine through his baptism and

---

[6] The symbolism of Rome as the 'new Jerusalem' is slightly complicated in a Constantinean context. Constantine moved his capital to Constantinople, 'Nova Roma', in 330; the reasons may have been practical, but in terms of Church spirituality this might be seen as a rejection of the pagan associations of the old city in favour of a new Rome, untainted by any heathen past. The establishment of York might, in such terms, be viewed as the foundation of

establishment of power in York proclaims that he is adopting Roman Christianity, and along with it Roman *imperium*: he aspires to be an English Constantine, albeit on a smaller scale. Eadwine's dedication of his new church to St Peter is a declaration that York is a metonym for Rome as the foundation stone of Christianity, at least in this land. Bede sums up Eadwine's achievements: 'so, like no other English king before him, he held under his sway the whole realm of Britain, not only English kingdoms but those ruled over by the Britons as well' (*Historia Ecclesiastica* II.9, pp. 162–3).

For Bede, the various stages of Eadwine's conversion are carefully manipulated into leading towards a culminating victorious interweaving of *Christianitas* and *imperium*. He acts as a metatype of Moses and Joshua, leading the Israelites from exile over the Red Sea and the Jordan into the promised land, which for the English is secured through baptism into the kingdom of heaven; he may, perhaps, also have acted as a metonym for the passage of the English in general from paganism to Christianity. His Christian capital of York is a metatype of Jerusalem, and a metonym for Rome, the centre of the Catholic Church. Eadwine is also a metatype of Constantine, the first Christian emperor, who, relying on the sign of the cross, established his capital (whether we view it as Rome or Constantinople) as the 'new Jerusalem', the centre of the Christian world, which itself anagogically stands for the new Jerusalem of Revelation, the kingdom of heaven. Ultimately, Eadwine may be seen as a metatype of Christ himself, one who is baptised, preaches to his people for whom he secures the kingdom of heaven, and is slain before his time by the godless, his message apparently overthrown along with his life, yet who in defeat achieves an ultimate spiritual victory for his kingdom.

a new spiritual capital, untainted by the heathenism of Goodmanham (and its associated hall).

Eadwine's deeds (metatypes)	Antitype	Type
Exiled by enemy king	Christ in wilderness	Moses in wilderness
Attempted assassination by enemy king	Herod kills the innocents, attempting to destroy Christ	Pharaoh attempts to kill Moses
Takes vengeance on assassins		Moses kills Egyptian overseer, and eventually Pharaoh perishes in pursuit of Israelites
Marries daughter of King Cearl while in exile		Moses marries Zipporah, daughter of chieftain while in exile
Divine vision at Rædwald's court		God appears in the Burning Bush to Moses
Promises of the spirit at Rædwald's court (inverse metatype) / Debate in the hall	Temptations of Christ in the wilderness	
Debate in the hall (Paulinus/ Coifi, counsellors, king)	Christ	Anointed ones: priest, prophet, king
Destroys the people's idols		Moses destroys the golden calf
Brings centre of power over the Derwent and is baptised	Baptism in the Jordan	Crossing the Red Sea / Crossing the Jordan
Converts or preaches to his people and surrounding nations	Christ's ministry	The prophets
Slain by pagan (Penda) and apostate (Cadwallon)	Destroyed by Pilate and Caiaphas	

Places

York (St Peter's)	Rome (St Peter's)	Jerusalem (Temple)
Goodmanham temple	Temple as den of money-changers	Golden calf
Sancton (?) hall of debate	Sermon on Mount	Mt Sinai
Wolds near Goodmanham	Christ sees kingdoms of world / (Calvary)	Mt Nebo
Malton (?) hall of assassination		Egypt, land of power but spiritual exile
Derwent		Jordan (Red Sea)

Some suggested typological interpretations
of the events of Eadwine's reign

Coifi's desecration as an act of pagan spirituality at the transition to Christianity

How did the tale of Coifi's act of desecration arise? It must remain a possibility that the conversion to Christianity was not marked by any dramatic temple destruction such as Bede depicts, but that the holy places were simply abandoned or turned into churches, and that tales such as that of Coifi are later inventions serving Christian propaganda purposes.[7] Even if the tale of Coifi is a *post factum* creation, however, it may still be read as part of the tradition of the conversion and as reflecting concerns wider than just Bede's. Thus Barrow (2011) follows a Christian interpretation, arguing that the casting of the spear into the sanctuary is an inversion of the piercing of Christ by the lance in John 19:34: as the waters of salvation flowed from Christ, so the waters of baptism cleansed Northumbria of pagan belief. If Bede's account reflects any historical reality, then naturally no such symbolism could have been apparent to the protagonists of the story, unless we assume they were already well versed in the Gospel (which is scarcely a convincing proposition); if, on the other hand, we take this as Bede's intended slant on the story, we are confronted by the difficulty that he makes nothing of it — and as it relies on an inversion (the desecration of something to be rejected, wicked paganism, rather than of the Saviour as in the Gospel), it is not a symbolism that would have been obvious without some hint that this is what was intended. If such an interpretation had existed in tradition, it is difficult to see why Bede should not have exploited it.

A more fruitful approach may be to interpret the action in terms of Germanic pagan belief, the details of which Bede would be keen to suppress, but which would have been of pressing concern to the actual participants in the process of conversion.[8]

---

[7] Thus Wallace-Hadrill (1988, 72) compares Sulpicius Severus, *Vita Martini* (ch. 15), where the preaching of the saint persuades the people to destroy their own temples.

[8] Wallace-Hadrill (1988, 72) notes that Mayr-Harting interpreted the Coifi story as showing clear signs of the existence of a cult of Woden, yet, in typical fashion, dismisses this on the basis that Bede would have known nothing of such a cult — which is to argue on the basis of absence of evidence. The question of Anglo-Saxon paganism is dealt with far more provocatively and

This implies a traditional understanding of what was thought to have happened, current among people who continued to maintain some sort of pagan mind-set well after the conversion: the account would have taken shape among people who sought to understand how their traditional belief as it were self-destructed, by being overturned from within—which is a different matter from Bede's more straightforward concern, namely to present Christianity as patently superior to paganism.

Riding a stallion and casting a spear at an enemy to ensure its complete and unfailing destruction is the characteristic of the god Óðinn in Norse myth, as in the poem *Vǫluspá*; Óðinn's name is cognate with the Old English Woden, who must have shared at least basic characteristics with his Norse counterpart, such as being a warrior god. Coifi, however, had been accustomed to ride a mare, *equa*. Clunies Ross (2014, 66) has pointed out that this feminises him, and by taking up arms and riding the king's stallion, he stands *in loco regis*, taking on masculine royal authority in destroying the pagan cult. We might add that the priest's effeminacy further links him with Óðinn in his pursuit of effeminate practices such as that of magic (*seiðr*: see Tolley 2009, I, 155–64), and it both ridicules the straits of the paganism he is forced to follow, and, in his mounting a stallion, shows Christianity to be the antithesis of its emasculating limitations; now, a bold *Christianitas* will allow the establishment of a virile *imperium*, a motif that would be welcomed in what was still essentially a warrior society. One further detail is also interesting: Coifi is said to *insanire* ('act madly') in the eyes of onlookers as he rides to desecrate the sanctuary: the meaning of Woden/Óðinn is the 'raging one', and *wood* continued into Middle English in the sense of '(raging) mad'. Coifi may therefore be understood, within the terms of his own belief system (as we may surmise it to have been), to be turning his own god against himself, finishing paganism in the most certain manner available to him.[9]

thoroughly, if perhaps too imaginatively, by North, who deals with the Coifi story in some detail (1997, 332–8).

[9] Matters should not be overmilked, however; attempts at seeing further Óðinnic features in my opinion run onto the sands; it is possible, but unprovable, that further Óðinnic features may have existed in the traditional account Bede used, but he would have eschewed giving them too much heed. North (*ibid.*, 333–4) would see in the name *Coifi* a derivative of Latin *cofium*, a hood

The pagan understanding may have run deeper than this, however. In Norse myth, as recounted in the poem *Hávamál*, st. 138, the supreme god Óðinn hanged himself, offering himself as a victim to himself, which enabled him to gain power over runes (which may be seen as a symbol for supernatural power and knowledge). The sacrificer is thus identified with the victim: Coifi may thus be seen as embodying his god, who sacrifices himself in a final act of self-destruction for the gaining of the greater knowledge and power afforded by Christianity. This notion would readily have been accommodated within the growing cult of Christianity, where of course God, in the form of Christ, similarly sacrifices himself for the gaining of the ultimate power of life and salvation for his followers.

(a characteristic feature of Óðinn), but it is difficult to explain how a pagan priest at this stage could have a name derived from Latin, or why he should do so (or, if we take it to be a later invention, why Bede should thus include a reference, albeit obscure, to pagan belief)—although North constructs a complex, and highly speculative, picture to explain this, in which Coifi is actually the Christian missionary Paulinus in a hood, understood by the pagan populace as identifying him as Woden. Among other things, this interpretation faces the difficulty that at the conference Coifi is presented in Bede's account as listening to, and responding to, Paulinus. North is correct to point out that the image of a pagan priest, as an antithesis of a Christian priest or like something derived from classical sources, is not borne out by evidence from Norse sources, where the role of priest coincides with that of chieftain (*goði*), but in fact the Norse sources are, apart from a few runic inscriptions which mention *goðar*, all well post-conversion, and it is difficult to determine anything reliable from them about priestly roles in pagan times in Scandinavia, let alone in England. Even if we assume that priesthood and chieftaincy coincided across the pagan Germanic world, there is no reason to assume that Coifi could not also have been one of Eadwine's chieftains—and his petulant complaint that his honouring of the gods had not brought him as much worldly renown as others in the king's service could be interpreted as a reflection of this dual role, if we feel inclined to lend the details of this speech any credence as at all historically reliable. Bede's characterisation of Coifi as 'chief priest' need not imply a hierarchy within pagan priesthood (though Bede could have wished to imply this: Coifi is on a footing with Paulinus): Coifi is the most significant priest merely in that it is he that oversees the ancestral temple of the Deirans. Of course, even if Coifi was a historical priest, Bede is likely to have had only a fuzzy idea of the ritual requirements of priesthood: the stipulation that a priest could not bear arms, for example, is scarcely credible in such an age, and is more likely to relate to traditions such as the inviolability of the assembly place or sanctuary, such as is found in Norse sources: hence, that he could not bear arms when carrying out his sacral duties is a more likely historical reading of what lies behind Bede's statement.

In pagan understanding, it was the king or chieftain himself (as preserved in the Norse term *goði*, which indicates both 'priest' and 'chieftain') who, almost certainly, was the ultimate sacrificer. Coifi, while standing as an embodiment of the god, represents the king: hence it would be implicit to the still-pagan community that the king himself was perpetrating an act of self-destruction through the agency of his priest, but one which resulted in a 'resurrection' to a new man, a member of Christ's flock. Again, with the growing understanding of Christianity, a ready epistemological transition could be made, and the king's followers could understand what was happening in terms both of their former systems of beliefs, and of the new faith. Eadwine may be seen as a Christ figure: from a pagan perspective as an embodiment of a new god, and from a perhaps more refined Christian understanding as being in a typological relationship with the new god, a metatype.

The notion of resurrection, or recreation, may have been apparent in another symbolism that may have been evident within a pagan understanding. In Norse myth, in an image that is likely to go back to the most ancient layers of religious understanding, the world was made through an initial act of 'sacrifice', when the giant Ymir was slain, and his body used to make the various parts of the cosmos (*Grímnismál*, st. 40): the notion is of one order being violently overthrown in order to create a new one, overseen by those responsible for the sacrifice; hence Coifi's act of desecration could also be seen as a re-enactment of the slaying of Ymir by Óðinn (and his brothers), to make way for the new world of Christianity (Ymir's place being taken by Óðinn himself, in an act of self-sacrifice).

The notion of paganism ritually destroying itself is difficult to exemplify, in so far as records invariably come from a time after a new religion has displaced the old. I suggest, however, that something similar may have been understood to have happened just a few centuries after Coifi, when Prince Vladimir adopted Christianity in Russia (traditionally dated to 988). The monastic *Primary Chronicle*, recording the details a couple of centuries later, gives us a few glimpses into an earlier worldview that was then displaced by Orthodox Christianity. It is clear that there were growing numbers of Christians within or close to Vladimir's realm, and the main trading partner he had to deal with, the Byzantine Empire, was Christian; his grandmother, Ol'ga, had also been Christian. He was therefore faced with a similar situation to that of Eadwine. His initial response appears to have been to codify his native religion: he set up a sanctuary dedicated to a group of Slavic gods in Kiev, with Perun, the god of thunder and ruler of heaven, at their head. Clearly, matters did not work out, and Vladimir desecrated his sanctuary a few years later when he adopted Christianity. It is said that he cast the image of Perun down from its high place and had it dragged, tied to a horse's tail, into the river (*Primary Chronicle*, *s.a.* 988, p. 116).

Given the paucity of information on pagan Slavic religion, any interpretation is bound to be speculative. Yet it is probable that Vladimir, as king, embodied the god he worshipped, and acted as chief sacrificer: hence his destruction of Perun was an act of self-sacrifice to make way for a new order. Being cast into the river almost certainly also involved a more complex symbolism than mere degradation (which is all the *Primary Chronicle* suggests, the idols being whipped to this purpose): in other Indo-European mythologies, the god of thunder (Þórr in Norse, Indra in Indian) contended against, and mastered, disordered powers of water (Tolley 2009, I, 285–8). Hence, Perun was being cast down into the power of the enemy forces that he had hitherto always mastered, and hence the pagan hierarchy came to be overturned from within.[10]

One matter in the account of Coifi that has caused some questioning is whether it is feasible to think of a temple, or sanctuary,

---

[10] The Rus' appear to have had two chief gods: Perun and Volos (for example, Oleg's men swear by these gods, *Primary Chronicle, s.a.* 907, p. 65). Vladimir is not said to have set up an image of the god Volos on the hill-top with Perun and other gods (*Primary Chronicle, s.a.* 980, p. 93); Volos, as god of cattle, may have been associated with the market place, towards the river, and may also have been a representative of the watery powers that were in opposition to Perun. It is also likely that Volos was lord of the underworld (with which cattle, explicitly said to be in his care, are associated in various Indo-European traditions), and that the horse, like cattle, was his animal: hence Perun is dragged to the (watery) underworld by his enemy's beast. Little can be said with even a modicum of certainty, given that 'sources' for Volos consist very largely of much later folk tradition from various Slavic and Baltic lands, and comparative Indo-European mythology: see Ivanov and Toporov (1973) for a full philological discussion (but one that has not met with universal approval).

of pagan gods at all. It does not seem unreasonable to suppose that the Germanic peoples had sacred places with some form of sacred images (Old Norse *vé*, Old English *weoh*, related to *victima*, appear to relate to such things), but it is possible that the more organised sanctuary implied in Bede's description of Goodmanham may have been a counterpart to Vladimir's attempt to form a pagan sanctuary in Kiev (it is interesting that Bede declares Coifi destroyed the very idols he had himself consecrated, perhaps implying a recent act of sanctuary construction, or, more probably, upgrading). The implication would then be that, in its developed form, Goodmanham was a short-lived attempt to provide a counterweight to the Christian temples that were arising, under royal patronage, in Kent (and further afield on the Continent). Bede would never reveal any political toying with paganism on Eadwine's part if it did exist, and it is impossible to prove, but must, I think, remain a possibility: Eadwine may have had his own sanctuary of Goodmanham destroyed in just the way Vladimir was to do at Kiev.

Determining what happened in 627 is impossible: it may be that the pagan 'priests' (if they existed as a discrete category at all) simply decided to go along with the king's decision to adopt Christianity, seeing it as politically expedient. Ordinary people, who were compelled to adopt the new faith, may have felt a need to put their old beliefs and practices to rest in a seemly manner, and, if Coifi did not in reality exist as a graphic deconsecrator of the pagan temple, a need to create him soon came into being in the tales folk told of how their old ways disappeared. Bede seized upon these traditions and no doubt refined them to fit his well-crafted picture of the arrival of Christianity in Deira.

OSWALD

✠

Shortly after returning from exile among the Scots, Oswald, the son of Æthelfrith, marched against the Britons who had overrun Northumbria. His victory, in 634 or (more probably) 635, is described by Bede in his *Historia Ecclesiastica* iii.1, pp. 214–15 (my translation).

Quo post occisionem fratris Eanfridi superueniente cum paruo exercitu, sed fide Christi munito, infandus Brettonum dux cum immensis illis copiis, quibus nihil resistere posse iactabat, interemtus est in loco, qui lingua Anglorum Denisesburna, id est Riuus Denisi, uocatur.

The wicked leader of the Britons with his numberless forces, which he used to boast nothing could resist, was done away with in a place called in English Denisesburna, which is to say the stream of Denis, by him [Oswald] sweeping down on him with a small army, but protected by his faith in Christ, after the murder of his brother Eanfrith.

Bede is more interested in what happened just before the battle, which he describes in the next chapter (ch. 2, pp. 214–17):

Ostenditur autem usque hodie et in magna ueneratione habetur locus ille, ubi uenturus ad hanc pugnam Osuald signum sanctae crucis erexit, ac flexis genibus Deum deprecatus est, ut in tanta rerum necessitate suis cultoribus caelesti succurreret auxilio. Denique fertur quia facta citato opere cruce, ac fouea praeparata in qua statui deberet, ipse fide feruens hanc arripuerit ac foueae imposuerit atque utraque manu erectam tenuerit, donec adgesto a militibus puluere terrae figeretur; et hoc facto, elata in altum uoce cuncto exercitui proclamauerit: 'Flectemus omnes genua, et Deum omnipotentem uiuum ac uerum in commune deprecemur, ut nos ab hoste superbo ac feroce sua miseratione defendat; scit enim ipse quia iusta pro salute gentis nostrae bella suscepimus.' Fecerunt omnes ut iusserat, et sic incipiente diluculo in hostem progressi, iuxta meritum suae fidei uictoria potiti sunt. In cuius loco orationis innumerae uirtutes sanitatum noscuntur esse patratae, ad indicium uidelicet ac memoriam fidei regis. Nam et usque hodie multi de ipso ligno sacrosanctae crucis astulas excidere solent, quas cum in aquas miserint, eique languentes homines aut pecudes potauerint siue asperserint, mox sanitati restituuntur.

Vocatur locus ille lingua Anglorum Hefenfeld, quod dici potest latine Caelestis Campus, quod certo utique praesagio futurorum antiquitus nomen accepit; significans nimirum quod ibidem caeleste erigendum tropeum, caelestis inchoanda uictoria, caelestia usque hodie forent miracula celebranda. Est autem locus iuxta murum illum ad aquilonem, quo Romani quondam ob arcendos barbarorum impetus totam a mari ad mare praecinxere Brittaniam, ut supra docuimus. In quo uidelicet loco consuetudinem multo iam tempore fecerant fratres Hagustaldensis ecclesiae, quae non longe abest, aduenientes omni anno pridie quam postea idem rex Osuald occisus est, uigilias pro salute animae eius facere, plurimaque psalmorum laude celebrata, uictimam pro eo mane sacrae oblationis offerre. Qui etiam crescente bona consuetudine, nuper ibidem ecclesia constructa, sacratiorem et cunctis honorabiliorem omnibus locum fecere. Nec inmerito, quia nullum, ut conperimus, fidei Christianae signum, nulla ecclesia, nullum altare in tota Berniciorum gente erectum est, priusquam hoc sacrae crucis uexillum nouus militiae ductor, dictante fidei deuotione, contra hostem inmanissimum pugnaturus statueret.

That place is shown even today and is held in great reverence where, when about to enter this battle, Oswald erected the sign of the holy cross, and on bended knees besought God to succour his worshippers with heavenly aid in such a strait. Then, it is said, once the cross was made by hurried labour, and a hole made ready to stand it in, Oswald with eager faith grasped it to himself and placed it in the hole, and with both hands held it erect until it was secured with the dust of the earth piled up by the soldiers. Once this was done, he lifted his voice up and shouted out to the whole army: 'Let us all bend our knees, and beseech the living and true and all-powerful God together to defend us from our proud and savage enemy through his mercy: for he himself knows that we are taking up a just war for the salvation of our people.' They all did as he had ordered, and as day broke they set out against the enemy, and won the victory that their faith had made them worthy of.

At the place of his speech, numberless powerful examples of healing have been revealed, a token and reminder of the king's faith. Even to this day many people scrape off shavings of the very wood of that sanctified cross, which they put in water and give to sick people or animals to drink, or sprinkle them with it, and they are soon restored to health.

That place is called in English Hefenfeld, which could be expressed in Latin as Caelestis Campus (heavenly field), a name it received in ancient times as a sure presaging of future events, signifying that in that same place a heavenly memorial would be raised, a heavenly victory would begin, and heavenly miracles would be celebrated to this day. The place is beside that wall, to its north [or, 'beside that wall in the north'],[1] where once the Romans sealed off the whole of Britain from sea to sea against the attacks of the barbarians, as we indicated above.

In this place, for a long time now the brothers of the church of Hexham, which is not far away, have maintained the tradition of coming every year on the eve of the day on which that same king, Oswald, was killed, in order to hold vigil for the salvation of his soul, celebrating his praise with the singing of many psalms, and making the offering of the holy sacrifice [the Mass] in the morning. This good custom is growing, indeed, and now a church has recently been built there, to make the place more sacred and honourable for everyone. And not without good cause, since, as we have learnt, no sign of the Christian faith, no church, no altar had been raised in the whole of Bernicia before the new leader of the army, egged on by devotion to his faith, set up this standard of the holy cross when about to do battle against his monstrous enemy.

---

[1] Colgrave and Mynors appear, in their translation, to have misinterpreted the Latin here: Bede is almost certainly indicating that Heavenfield lay to the north of the wall, where the chapel of St Oswald now lies, although the wall in fact passes through the midst of the 'field' (open ground) in question.

Bede is not the only early witness to Oswald's victory. Adomnán, the abbot of Iona (d. 704), tells the following tale about the battle in his *Life of Columba* (pp. 198–202):

Hujus talis honorificantiae viro honorabili ab omnipotente caelitus conlatae etiam unum proferemus exemplum, quod Ossualdo regnatori saxonico pridie quam contra Catlonem Britonum regem fortissimum proeliaretur ostensum erat. Nam cum idem Ossualdus rex esset in procinctu belli castrametatus quadam die in sua papillione supra pulvillum dormiens sanctum Columbam in visu videt forma coruscantem angelica cujus alta proceritas vertice nubes tangere videbatur. Qui scilicet vir beatus suum regi proprium revelans nomen in medio castrorum stans eadem castra, excepta quadam parva extremitate, sui protegebat fulgida veste. Et haec confirmatoria contulit verba, eadem scilicet quae dominus ad Jesue bén Nun ante transitum Jordanis mortuo Moyse proloqutus est, dicens: 'Confortare et age viriliter. Ecco ero tecum', et cetera. Sanctus itaque Columba haec ad regem in visu loquens addit: 'Hac sequenti nocte de castrís ad bellum procede. Hac enim vice mihi dominus donavit ut hostes in fugam vertantur tui, et tuus Catlon inimicus in manus tradatur tuas, et post bellum victor revertaris et feliciter regnes.'

Post haec verba expergitus rex senatui congregato hanc enarrat visionem; qua confortati omnes totus populus promittit sé post reversionem de bello crediturum et babtismum suscepturum. Nam usque in id temporis tota illa Saxonia gentilitatis et ignorantiae tenebrís obscurata erat, excepto ipso rege Ossualdo cum xii. virís qui cum eo Scotos inter exsolante babtizati sunt. Quid plura? Eadem subsequta nocte Ossualdus rex sicuti in visu edoctus fuerat ad bellum cum admodum pauciore exercitu contra milia numerosa progreditur. Cui a domino sicut ei promisum est felix et facilis est concessa victoria, et rege trucidato Catlone victor post bellum reversus postea totius Brittanniae imperator a deo ordinatus est.

Hanc mihi Adomnano narrationem meus decessor noster abbas Failbeus indubitanter enarravit. Qui sé ab ore ipsius Ossualdi regis Segineo abbati eandem enuntiantis visionem audisse protestatus est.

We shall offer one example of this sort of bestowal of honour on the honourable man, sent down from heaven by the Almighty. This was shown on the day before he was due to battle against Cadwallon, the mighty king of the Britons, to Oswald, the Saxon ruler. When this same king, Oswald, was preparing for war one day in his tent, sleeping on the ground, he saw Saint Columba in a vision, shining with an angelic form, whose highest tip seemed to touch the clouds. The blessed man revealed his own name to the king, standing in the midst of the camp and protecting this camp, other than some small corners, with his resplendent garment. In confirmation he came out with some words, the same, indeed, which the Lord spoke to Joshua son of Nun before the crossing of the Jordan when Moses had died: 'Be strong and act bravely. Behold, I will be with you', and so forth [Joshua 1:9]. And so Saint Columba added this to what he said to the king in the vision: 'The following night, proceed down from the camp into battle. On this occasion the Lord has granted me that your enemy will flee, and your foe Cadwallon will be given into your hands, and after the battle you will return as victor and rule happily.'

After these words the king woke up and told his vision to the elders gathered there. Strengthened by this, everyone—the whole people—promised that after returning from war they would believe and be baptised: for up to that time the whole of the land of the Saxons was overshadowed by the gloom of paganism and ignorance, except King Oswald himself with his twelve men, who had been baptised with him while in exile among the Scots. What more to add? The following night King Oswald, as instructed in the vision, set off for battle with a much smaller force against thousands. Just as the Lord had promised him, he was granted a happy and easy victory, and with King Cadwallon killed, he returned the victor after the battle and thereafter was ordained by God to be the emperor of all Britannia.

My predecessor, our abbot Failbe, told this story to me, Adomnán, without expressing any doubt. He asserted that he had heard it from the mouth of King Oswald himself as he related this same vision to Abbot Segineus.

→ A ←

Oswald's Victory at Denisesburna

A CLIMAX IN THE TURBULENT EARLY HISTORY of the northern English kingdom of Northumbria and its adoption of Christianity was reached when King Oswald, after camping at Heavenfield on Hadrian's Wall and receiving a divine vision, defeated the Welsh king, Cadwallon, at Denisesburna, some miles to the south. The battle has been analysed at some length by Tom Corfe (1997); whilst I cover much of the same ground, I refrain from dealing with all of the points which he raises and covers, instead offering a rather briefer and somewhat different analysis.

The early Anglo-Saxon kingdom of Northumbria was a fusion of two realms, Deira (roughly present-day Yorkshire) and Bernicia (roughly from the Tees to the Firth of Forth). Æthelfrith of Bernicia took over Deira around 604, and exiled the males of its royal line; one of these, Eadwine, with the assistance of Rædwald of East Anglia, attacked and defeated Æthelfrith in 616 and became king of Northumbria. He converted, and introduced Christianity. In 633 or 634,[1] however, King Penda of Mercia joined with King Cadwallon of the northern Welsh kingdom of Gwynedd, and defeated Eadwine at the battle of Hatfield Chase, near Doncaster. The kingdom split, Deira going to a cousin of Eadwine's, Osric, and Bernicia to a son of Æthelfrith, Eanfrith, who returned from exile among the Scots. However, Cadwallon managed to kill both of them, and there followed a year of savage looting of Northumbria by the Welsh king. (Bede, *Historia Ecclesiastica* II.12, pp. 180–1; III.1, pp. 212–15.)

[1] While the date is usually given as 633, Kirby (2000, 56) argues, on the basis of the date of papal letters, that Eadwine is likely to have been overthrown in the autumn of 634 rather than 633, and hence Oswald's victory must have taken place in 635.

The reasons for Cadwallon's treatment of Northumbria are not entirely clear. It is possible that he may have assisted Eadwine in his exile, only to find Eadwine then turning against him by occupying Anglesey and Man, both Welsh realms at this time (Bede, *Historia Ecclesiastica* ii.5, pp. 148–9); or it could have been a reaction against the growing encroachment of Northumbria on the British kingdoms of the north, which seems to have begun in earnest a few decades earlier, under Æthelfrith (Bede, *Historia Ecclesiastica* i.34, pp. 116–17). Whatever his motivations, Cadwallon's supremacy was not to last: another of Æthelfrith's sons, Oswald, attacked. The victory, in 634 or 635, secured his accession to the kingship of Northumbria and dashed any final chance of the British regaining control of northern Britain. Several points emerge from Bede's account, which need to be stressed, as many misconceptions about the battle have circulated which have no basis in anything Bede wrote:

+ The site of the battle was Denisesburna, not Heavenfield (commonplace references to the 'battle of Heavenfield' are misleading):[2] Bede gives no indication of fighting taking place there, merely that the troops set out at dawn from there to engage in battle. The identity of Denisesburna is established by recourse to an early-thirteenth-century charter that establishes that the stream in question is that now named Rowley Burn; how far up the burn the battle actually took place cannot, of course, be determined.[3]

---

[2] The history of the misidentification of the battle site as being at or near Heavenfield is dealt with in detail by Corfe (1997, 65–71); the misperception arose in large part through the disappearance of the name Denisesburna at some point in the medieval period.

[3] The relevance of the charter is noted by Plummer (1896, II, 123). The text is given in Raine (1864–5, Appendix, p. iv): 'Omnibus. Thomas de Whitinton, salutem. Noveritis me concessisse — Waltero, Ebor. archiepiscopo, tertiam partem de Hoggesty, quam tenui de dono Ranulphi de Porchet, de qua cartham suam habui. Pro hac concessione dedit mihi dictus archiepiscopus, in escambium, xx acras terrae de vasto suo in Ruleystal, inter istas divisas, videlicet, inter Deniseburn, et Divelis, incipiendo ex parte orientali super Divelis, et ascendendo ad magnam viam quae ducit usque ad forestam de Lilleswude.' ('To everyone. Thomas de Whittington, greetings. Know that I have granted to Walter, archbishop of York, a third part of 'Hogsty', which I held by gift of Ranulph de Porchet, on which I had his charter. For this concession the said archbishop gave me as pasture land twenty acres of his waste land in Rowley

- Bede does not indicate that fighting took place anywhere other than at Denisesburna. One proposal to explain the battle, which has been mooted a number of times (recently, for example, by Adams 2013, 156–9), is that the 'real' battle took place somewhere else, such as the crossing of the Tyne at Corbridge, and that the event at Denisesburna was merely the conclusion to this. In this case, Bede would surely have mentioned the Roman town, rather than a tiny stream, as the primary site of battle.
- The length of the sojourn at Heavenfield is not indicated, but at least one night's stay is implied by both Bede's and Adomnán's accounts.
- Almost certainly Bede had two sources of information, one concerning historical events, outlined in his first chapter of book III, the other relating to the cult of Oswald, which must be derived from the monks of Hexham, who were guardians of this cult: the focus on Heavenfield is entirely related to cult, not to battle. It was a matter of little interest to the monks where the fighting itself took place: what was important was where tradition related that Oswald set up the sign of the cross before the battle.
- The only other source on a par for reliability with Bede, namely the *Life of Columba* (pp. 198–202) by Abbot Adomnán of Iona (d. 704),[4] says nothing about raising a cross, but relates that Oswald, resting in his tent before the battle, had a vision of St Columba (the founder of Iona), who promised him victory, but there is no indication of the site of battle. The celebration of the raising of the cross was part of the Hexham cult of Oswald; Hexham was not founded until 674, several decades after Oswald's death, and the possibility must be entertained that the legend of Oswald's cross is a fabrication aimed at linking Oswald with Constantine's vision of the cross before the battle of the Milvian Bridge, which

---

Steel divided off between 'Deniseburn' (Rowley Water) and Devil's Water, beginning on the eastern side above Devil's Water and rising up to the main road which leads as far as the forest of Lilswood Moor.')

[4] Adomnán's source was his predecessor Failbe, who heard it from Oswald himself; Oswald, in exile among the Scots, and thereafter reliant on the community for his missionary efforts in Northumbria, would have had close contact with Iona. Adomnán at one point visited Bede's monastery.

led to Christianity becoming the established religion of the Roman Empire. Adomnán's account confirms, nonetheless, that something Oswald regarded as an exceptional religious experience that led on to his victory did indeed occur. This has little bearing on the tactics or course of battle, however, other than to suggest that Oswald would have been more inclined to take risks in the hope of victory; the renewed vigour, ascribed to spiritual causes, may also reflect Oswald's having ascertained Cadwallon's precise movements, thus enabling him to plan his battle manoeuvres.[5]

Understanding the battle calls for a consideration of the places mentioned, Heavenfield and Denisesburna, in both a wider geographical sense (see Fig. 10), and a more specific topographical one (see Fig. 11). Oswald was leading a small force including Scotsmen, and he had returned from exile in Scotland. However, his brother Eanfrith had been ruling Bernicia (not Deira) before him, so he had almost certainly returned from Scotland some months before (the reign of Eanfrith was under a year long)—indeed, Bede makes it clear that the sons of Æthelfrith (Eanfrith and Oswald) were able to return upon the death of Eadwine. Hence we may reasonably surmise that he had set out from the Bernician centre of power, most probably, to be more precise, the defended stronghold of Bamburgh. His destination was wherever Cadwallon was: if we draw a line from Bamburgh to Heavenfield, sticking as far as possible to Roman military roads (which soldiers would certainly have preferred marching on, even well after the Roman period), it continues over the Pennines towards the area of Penrith (which includes the Roman camp of Brocavum (Brougham) nearby) and Appleby. I will consider the implications of this in a moment. The Devil's Causeway, the Roman road from Berwick and the vicinity of Bamburgh, meets Dere Street a little to the north of Hadrian's Wall, and Dere Street then proceeds south through Coria (the

---

[5] The battle is also mentioned in the *Historia Brittonum* (ch. 64) and *Annales Cambriae* (*s.a.* 631) as taking place at Cantscaul; this is merely a translation of 'Hexham' (Corfe 1997, 77, with references). The name is interesting as showing that Welsh tradition, at least as recorded here, associated the battle neither with Heavenfield nor with Denisesburna specifically; but the name can hardly go back to the battle itself, as Hexham is unlikely to have existed at this time.

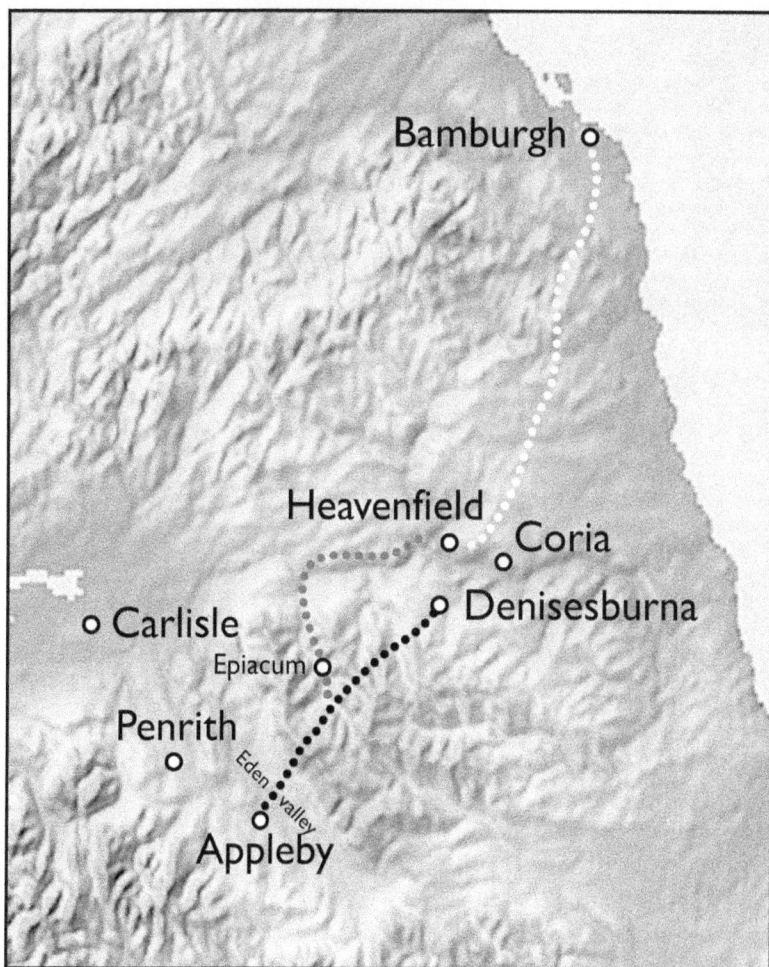

Fig. 10. The routes of Oswald (white) and Cadwallon (black), as argued in the article. The grey dots mark the easier route Oswald may have supposed Cadwallon would be taking.

Roman town to the west of Corbridge), and ultimately on to York much further south. Heavenfield lies directly in line with the last part of the Devil's Causeway, but Oswald would have had to cross country for a few miles to reach it, leaving the Roman roads behind (unless he went right up to the wall and followed that westwards). It therefore looks like a very deliberate act of maintaining a direct route to the south-west, rather than following the road to the south. The implication is that he knew

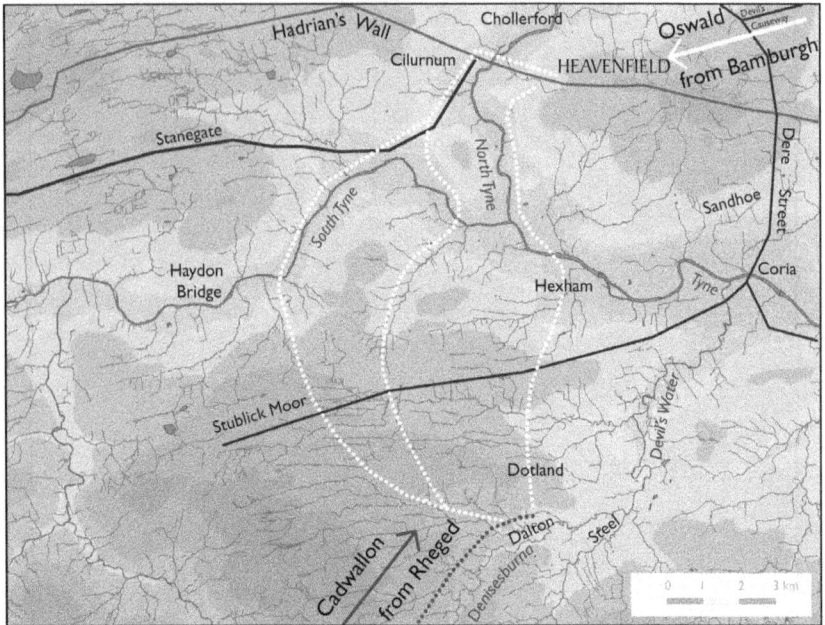

Fig. 11. The area of the battle, showing possible routes Oswald may have taken from Heavenfield to Denisesburna. Hadrian's Wall and Roman roads are marked (the precise course of the Roman road to the south of Hexham is conjectural for much of its route, and its existence west of Stublick unproved).

Cadwallon was advancing on him from the south-west, and Oswald was proceeding in a more or less straight line to meet him. He may have supposed that Cadwallon would be following the Roman road along the South Tyne, then eastwards along Stanegate: hence Oswald moved roughly along the Roman roads and wall in the direction of the route along which he surmised Cadwallon to be advancing.

The choice of Heavenfield was also defensive—all the more important, given Oswald's clear inferiority in forces: it is a raised plateau, with the Roman wall crossing it, and therefore offers an excellent strategic advantage to the defenders should an attack be launched here (see Figs. 12–13); it is comparable to the site chosen by Harold at Battle at the battle of Hastings, a high ridge that would look down on any enemy, which would be forced to attack upwards from lower ground. Had Oswald wished to find a similar defensive site, while remaining close to the main road south to Coria, it would not have been particularly difficult, for

Fig. 12. A view of the Heavenfield plateau
from the south-west (near to Wall).

Fig. 13. A view of the Heavenfield plateau from the south,
looking over Hexham in the middle distance.

example on the rise above Sandhoe (though that does not have
the direct protection of the Roman wall); this again suggests he
was deliberately maintaining a course south-westwards, rather
than southwards, as there would be no need to go out of his way
to find a defensible site. Had Cadwallon already been encamped
at Coria—which is likely to have been what he planned had he
got there in time—Oswald would surely have had little choice
but to attack him there; his camping at Heavenfield would then
only be reasonable if he were proceeding not from the north-
east (Bamburgh), but from the north-west, across unfavourable
terrain without Roman roads, on his way to the encounter. This
seems unlikely.

It may perhaps have been Oswald's intention to await Cadwallon at Heavenfield: but, if this was ever the plan (rather than the site being merely a stopping-place on a rapid trek towards Cadwallon), it appears to have altered after the vision or supernatural experience that Oswald had, which seems to have spurred him on to take the offensive, so that he left to seek out Cadwallon ('he came upon him'), convinced of the victory to come. Of course, it is possible that Cadwallon deliberately avoided confronting Oswald where he was at a topographical disadvantage, but the site of the final confrontation, at Denisesburna, a considerable distance from Heavenfield, suggests that Cadwallon had not advanced quite as far as Oswald may have thought when he camped at Heavenfield, and moreover had not followed the easier but rather longer route along the South Tyne, but had crossed the Pennine moors. It is surely likely that the mundane aspect of Oswald's realisation as he camped at Heavenfield was the more precise news of Cadwallon's route, which prompted Oswald to change course southwards and cross the Tyne to meet him.

Denisesburna may seem a strange place for a battle, especially to anyone that has visited the site (Figs. 14, 15). The area is full of small streams, many in quite deep gullies, and the moorland is not easy to move across, at least for troops engaged in battle. As noted above, the initial thought might be that the main battle took place elsewhere, such as near Coria and the crossing of the Tyne, and that Cadwallon was pursued up into the highlands here and slain (this is the line followed by Adams 2013, 159). Yet various factors militate against this idea. It is scarcely feasible to imagine a pursuit of what had clearly begun as a superior force over rough ground to Denisesburna, a considerable distance from the crossing—too far to be viable as a site of thwarted flight. There is also no explanation of why Oswald should have been at Heavenfield, to the west of Coria and off the Roman roads that led to the crossing there; the scenario would involve Oswald turning back from Heavenfield (but why then had he proceeded thither anyway?) and marching down Dere Street after all; he could, it might be supposed, have swept down on Cadwallon from the ridge above Coria and forced him back. Adams (2013, 159n.) is also rightly troubled by why Cadwallon, if he had been camped at Corbridge,

Fig. 14. The Rowley Burn (Denisesburna).

Fig. 15. The Devil's Water, near the confluence of the Rowley Burn.

should have diverted westwards when pursued, rather than sticking to the main roads southwards, which would have afforded a swifter flight. Bede gives no hint of any fighting at Coria, and the whole course of events is better explained without recourse to something for which there is no evidence, and which calls for special pleading on several counts.

The actual site of the battle on the Denisesburna makes more sense when we remember the small size of forces at this stage: an army consisted primarily of the personal retinue of a war leader—this is before the days of the more organised *fyrd* of later Anglo-Saxon times. Hence, at most a few hundred soldiers would be fighting on either side, and Bede stresses that Oswald's force was far less powerful than Cadwallon's; he was leading something that we might think of more as a unit of guerilla fighters than an army, and hence the site, which lends itself well to ambush, makes more sense.[6] As Oswald 'came upon' Cadwallon, it is more likely that the British king was still on the march to do battle with Oswald when he was surprised; Cadwallon's intent would appear to have been to move as rapidly as possible to secure the crossing of the Tyne at Coria, and the confluence of Roman military roads there, against Oswald's advance from the north.

We do not know where Cadwallon was when Oswald set out from the north. Oswald's route implies, however, that Cadwallon was coming from the south-west. I have suggested the Penrith/Appleby area: this is at a lesser distance from Heavenfield than Bamburgh is, but this supposition allows for the considerably more difficult terrain, and Cadwallon's much larger force. Bede presents a picture of Cadwallon ravaging widely across Northumbria in the year he occupied the country, but this should not be taken to imply that Cadwallon spent all this year in the firmly English areas of Deira or Bernicia close to the east coast. His aim was clearly to wrest control of the area from the English—it was, after all, less than twenty years since Æthelfrith first crossed the Pennines and defeated the British at Chester, *c.* 615, and the English hold on much of the land of the north that they had so recently acquired can hardly have been strong. Most of the areas to the west of the Pennines were probably still under British rule, and even Elmet, to the east of the Pennines, had only fallen a few years before to Eadwine. It is surely likely that Cadwallon,

---

[6] The size of forces at this stage of history is considered by Davies (2010, 153, with further references given) in his analysis of the battle of Chester, led by Oswald's father Æthelfrith, *c.* 615; Davies emphasises that a kingdom could be taken with fewer than a hundred men, and forces reaching into the hundreds were considered large.

rather than operating directly from his distant homeland of Gwynedd in what is now north Wales, would have fallen back on the British-ruled areas west of the Pennines to launch most of his Northumbrian campaigns from—particularly after his almost disastrous entrapment by the Deiran king, Osric, in a fortified city, perhaps York, from which Cadwallon managed to break free and defeat the English king.

Apart from being intent on seizing the kingship, Oswald was also, and perhaps primarily, on a campaign of vengeance for the treacherous murder of his brother Eanfrith, which can only have taken place shortly before. Bede relates that Eanfrith, with just twelve companions, went to visit Cadwallon to sue for peace, but was slaughtered. The tale may be read most convincingly as implying the Welsh king was on his own territory at this point, in an area where Eanfrith could not call upon his forces and was hence exposed to precisely the sort of treachery that was meted out to him. A likely scenario, therefore, is that this took place in a predominantly British area. Although we cannot trace the old British kingdoms of the north with any precision, it is probable that the Penrith area either formed part of, or was subject to, the realm of Rheged. Welsh poetry from this time may have undergone considerable development, or corruption, before it was written down many centuries later, but it is possible that the place-name Llwyfenydd, associated with the sixth-century lords of Rheged in this traditional verse (ascribed to the court poet Taliesin), is preserved in that of the River Lyvennet, south of Penrith and close to Appleby (Williams 1968, xliv–xlv; cf. Charles-Edwards 2013, 11).[7] It would therefore be from a secure

---

[7] Williams is tentative about the identification, and calls for more research on it; regrettably, this more detailed investigation has still, it seems, not been carried out. Clarkson (2010, 73–4) rightly views the identification of Llwyfenydd with scepticism, noting that it could have applied to any number of rivers, most of which would have lost their Welsh names once the areas in question became English, and in any case it occurs in a poetic, rather than historical, source (and one written down long after the events described). Clarkson demonstrates, in the chapter which mentions Llwyfenydd, that it is impossible to determine anything but the vaguest setting for Rheged, somewhere in northern England or southern Scotland. Yet for the present purposes, this is largely irrelevant; the Eden valley may have been part of some other, unnamed, realm rather than Rheged, but that the area must have been some sort of centre of power is determined by the geography, as it forms an extensive area of rich farmland

British base in Rheged (or whatever name the realm of the Eden valley went by) that Cadwallon set out towards the English upstart advancing on him from the north.

The position of Denisesburna suggests Cadwallon did not proceed along the South Tyne valley road, but took a more direct route over the moors towards the crossing of the Tyne at Coria. There is one uncertainty which affects matters somewhat at this point. It is possible that apart from the road along the South Tyne, a Roman road existed from Epiacum (Whitley Castle) that skirted Hexham to the south and proceeded to Coria. If Oswald established that Cadwallon was not following the road along the South Tyne, he might have anticipated that Cadwallon would be using this second route, and, if he knew in time, Oswald would surely have crossed the Tyne at Coria and proceeded along this route to meet him. Yet there is no indication that this route came into play at all. The reason for this may be that it did not in fact exist, or if it had once existed, it had fallen into such desuetude as not to be worth considering.[8] Even assuming it existed, its postulated course is, in any case, several miles to the north of Denisesburna, which makes it somewhat unlikely that

surrounded by inhospitable moorlands to east and west; that it was a British area at the time of Cadwallon's sojourn in Northumbria is beyond question. The balance of probability still seems to me, however, that the Eden valley would have been within the ambit of Rheged: this was the only British kingdom in the region whose name survived in poetic heroic tradition, along with the fame of its rulers, which implies a centre of power that must have exerted itself over a considerable area. As mentioned below, Oswald wished to secure an alliance with Rheged, by marrying his brother to its princess, which again implies an important political power base, although, admittedly, this tells us nothing about its geographical position beyond its proximity to Northumbria.

[8] The course of this postulated road, from Coria to Epiacum, is marked on the map in Fig. 11. I thank Michael Haken of the Roman Roads Research Association for working through the research of the late Hugh Toller and other information, based on lidar images, aerial photography and some fieldwork, and providing me with a map of the course of this road on which mine is based. While Haken is convinced of its existence, trial excavations have so far failed to uncover convincing evidence of its existence west of Stublick (in the direction of Epiacum): see the report, 'Lost Roads on Hexham Fell' (Altogether Archaeology, 2016), at https://www.altogetherarchaeology.org/reports.php. The report speculates that the road may not have been a route to Epiacum at all, but may have served local purposes such as transport from mines; it is also possible that it was an abortive attempt at a route to Epiacum, abandoned before completion.

Cadwallon was following it. The valley of the Denisesburna, however, along with the higher ground flanking it, itself forms a sort of pass across the moors, in a direct line from the south-west, and represents the last part of the shortest route from the Appleby area to Coria; moreover, the 'main road' ('magnam viam') mentioned in the charter that identifies Denisesburna proceeded parallel to the stream and may well have existed centuries earlier. Cadwallon was the king of a mountainous area of northern Wales, and would be accustomed to precisely the hilly moorland landscape found in the northern stretches of the Pennines. Whatever the precise details, by some means Oswald managed to use the topography to his advantage, as he would potentially have done with his choice of Heavenfield had the battle taken place there. The situation at Denisesburna is different, but, as noted, still favours a smaller force: Cadwallon was forced into the gully of a stream, where it was difficult for a large force to exploit its superiority in numbers (the terrain is not as extreme as at the ancient Greek encounter with the Persians at Thermopylae, but Oswald's tactics belong to the same school of thinking: to attempt to confine a larger enemy in a bottleneck).

Given that much of the land over the moors is high, one difficulty here is to explain how Oswald 'came down on Cadwallon' ('superueniente', which suggests both coming down from a higher position, and chancing upon him). There are, in general terms, three ways Oswald could have got from Heavenfield to Denisesburna. The most obvious is that he turned back, proceeded down to Coria, crossed the river, and marched up onto the high ground, confronting Cadwallon head on, and fighting him uphill. Such a course of action would expose him to danger at all stages. The second possibility is that Oswald continued over the North Tyne, using the Roman bridge at Cilurnum (Chesters) or the ford at Chollerford, and then proceeded to somewhere near Haydon Bridge, crossing the South Tyne there and proceeding south-eastwards once he had established where Cadwallon's army had got to; this route has the advantage of crossing two smaller rivers rather than the substantial united Tyne. Oswald could, on this route, perhaps have swept down on Cadwallon's army, surprising it from the rear, from Stublick Moor, forcing it down into the river valley near Dalton. Yet moving this far west might result in Cadwallon having advanced too far, eluding his enemy by the time Oswald came upon him; it would not appear the best course to follow, therefore. Alternatively, and perhaps most probably, Oswald may have moved south from Heavenfield, crossing the Tyne roughly at Hexham, where, as Corfe (1997, 77–9) notes, a ford existed, then proceeded southwards, sweeping down on Cadwallon from around Dotland and forcing him into the valley of the Denisesburna.[9] The description of the battle is not precise enough for us to be completely sure that Oswald attacked from higher ground, or that he struck from the rear, but, with a smaller force, these tactics would have made best sense, and are most consistent with what Bede says. My conclusions on this matter are thus in accord with those propounded by Corfe (1997), but it seems advisable to allow for the route actually followed by Oswald having been the result of his finding out just where Cadwallon was only late on in the campaign.

Cadwallon emerges from the events as an arrogant ruler — as Bede notes, he boasted of how his forces were unbeatable: he would have been keen to strike at Oswald with force, but without too much thought, perhaps — and hence would have been willing to march all the way to Bamburgh, if need be, in line with the widespread ravaging of Northumbria he had been committing over the last year. In his haste he decided, perhaps to Oswald's surprise, to march an army over moorland rather than following the slightly longer, but safer, road along the South Tyne. He appears to have expected his enemy still to be proceeding towards him along the Devil's Causeway, and so sped towards the crossing of the Tyne at Coria to reach him further north, or at least to intercept him at the crossing. Oswald, on the other hand, showed greater acumen. With his small force he had moved more quickly than Cadwallon anticipated, and proceeded westwards, in the direction from which he expected Cadwallon to come. Realising he was close, he encamped on a plateau, Heavenfield, that offered the best topographical advantage to him. His intention may have been to continue further

---

[9] I am placing the site of the battle close to Dalton, near the confluence of the Denisesburna with the Devil's Water. Had it taken place further upstream, Oswald would have had further to travel, making for less of a surprise attack, as well as having to cross a great many more small streams. Topographically, Dalton makes the best sense for the site.

west and then south if need be, but one factor, not immediately obvious today, may have made him reluctant to go too far: at this stage of history, the Pennines must have acted as a *de facto* border between English Northumbria (though, in truth, many of its inhabitants must still have been of British descent) and British kingdoms to the west; hence the Hexham area, on the eastern edge of the Pennine moors, was border country, and the battle took place at the intersection of English and British spheres of influence at this time.[10] Oswald may have been unwilling to proceed too deep into British territory and run the risk of being overwhelmed in a foreign country, as his brother may recently have been. Possibly he was intending to await Cadwallon at Heavenfield, when a vision or moving religious experience convinced him to take the offensive. Realising that Cadwallon was in fact crossing the moors, he set out to confront him, crossing the Tyne and coming down upon him from behind, again turning the topography to his advantage in a surprise attack. Such a reading, it need hardly be said, relies on a series of suppositions for which evidence is scarce. However, it does take account of the details of Bede's account, without adding imaginary events such as battles in multiple places, and it fits what can be determined about the historical context of the battle.

The result of the battle was to establish Northumbria as henceforth permanently both Christian and English, through the reigns of both Oswald and his long-reigning brother Oswiu. However, this future would not necessarily have been clear to Oswald on the day of his victory. Cadwallon had been defeated, but it may not at first have been obvious that the British were a spent force. Hence we find the ninth-century Welsh composition

---

[10]   I think it wiser to leave the description of the border region in these fairly vague terms, rather than enter into speculation of the sort entertained by Corfe (1997, 79–83). It may be tempting, for example, to see the young warrior commemorated in Hexham's name as Oswald, but there is no reason to do so. Hexhamshire as an administrative unit is likely to go back in some form to the grant whereby the ecclesiastical centre of Hexham was established some four decades after the battle, but it is pushing the 'evidence' too far to suppose that the Devil's Water was necessarily the eastern boundary of an earlier Rheged. Denisesburna almost certainly has a Celtic base to its first element, indicating a British cultural continuance in the area long enough for the name to be carried on into English; for grammatical reasons it cannot, as Corfe suggests (*ibid.*, 73), relate to a supposed English people, the *Denise.

ascribed to Nennius, the *Historia Brittonum* (ch. 57), recording
that Oswald's brother Oswiu married Riemmelth, a princess
of Rheged, we may assume soon after the battle.[11] This was
presumably an attempt to secure peace with a British neighbour
that had backed Cadwallon in his attempt to oust the English
from control of the North. Yet Riemmelth did not even warrant
a mention in English sources, and Oswiu went on to take an
English wife, Eanflæd, daughter of Eadwine and related to the
royal house of Kent, soon after his own accession in 642: the alliance between the two houses of Northumbria soon proved more
important than worrying about a dwindling British kingdom
in the Pennines. Cadwallon's foray into the English kingdoms
of the North had indeed marked the last, unsuccessful, bid to
maintain British sway in Britannia.

[11] I do not see any strong reason for supposing, as Corfe does (1997, 82–3),
that it took place while Oswald and his family were still in exile, though it is
possible. If it did take place at this earlier date, then complications of allegiance
arise: Rheged would then have been hoping to put someone on the throne of
Northumbria less aggressive towards it than (we are to suppose) Eadwine
may have been, yet an alliance with an unproved exile, who was nonetheless
the son of Æthelfrith, whom Bede records as being the greatest scourge of
the Britons, may not have seemed particularly appealing. Rheged's loyalty
would also have been divided once Cadwallon, a fellow Briton, opposed
himself to Oswald. Far more likely is an alliance formed after Oswald's victory,
through a marriage to the house which had supported Cadwallon (possibly
only luke-warmly), but with which it was important to settle peaceful terms
as Oswald established control of his kingdom.

✛ B ✛

Oswald's Tree

Cum ergo Deus omnipotens uos ad reverentissimum uirum fratrem nostrum Augustinum episcopum perduxerit, dicite ei quid diu mecum de causa Anglorum cogitans tractaui; uidelicet quia fana idolorum destrui in eadem gente minime debeant, sed ipsa quae in eis sunt idola destruantur, aqua benedicta fiat, in eisdem fanis aspergatur, altaria construantur, reliquiae ponantur. Quia si fana eadem bene constructa sunt, necesse est ut a cultu daemonum in obsequio ueri Dei debeant commutari, ut dum gens ipsa eadem fana sua non uidet destrui, de corde errorem deponat, et Deum uerum cognoscens ac adorans, ad loca quae consueuit familiarius concurrat.

When Almighty God has brought you to our most reverend brother Bishop Augustine, tell him what I have decided after long deliberation about the English people, namely that the idol temples of that race should by no means be destroyed, but only the idols in them. Take holy water and sprinkle it in these shrines, build altars and place relics in them. For if the shrines are well built, it is essential that they should be changed from the worship of devils to the service of the true God. When this people see that their shrines are not destroyed they will be able to banish error from their hearts and be more ready to come to the places they are familiar with, but now recognizing and worshipping the true God.

Pope Gregory to Abbot Mellitus
(Bede, *Historia Ecclesiastica* 1.30, pp. 106–7)

T‌HE SHORT REIGN (634/635–42) of St Oswald of Northumbria is both inaugurated and culminates with a concrete marker, a *trēow*, redolent of religious symbolism. A *trēow* is most obviously a Christian cross—but it is also a tree, something with roots reaching deep into pagan cult.[1] This ambiguity,

---

[1] A parallel example is the word *bēam*, which in modern English usually means a limb of a tree used for timber, but in earlier usage referred to the living tree as well, a meaning which survives in species names like *hornbeam*. *Trēow* as 'tree' is Bosworth and Toller (1898) sense I; as 'cross' several examples are

permeating both the beginning and the end of his reign, was arguably exploited along the lines suggested by Pope Gregory, starting already with Oswald, and expanding as the folk tradition developed. Yet if such was the reality of the case, we can glimpse it only darkly, through the glass of Bede's wholly Christian outlook: against Pope Gregory's words we may set those of the historian of England's conversion, Henry Mayr-Harting (1976, 1): 'In Bede we have the paradox of the greatest of all historians of a barbarian conversion who found this consideration to a quite exceptional degree unimportant'. It is to see a little behind Bede's indifference that I aspire in what follows.

Oswald's victory

Scarcely had Christianity arrived in Northumbria when King Eadwine was slain, the missionary Paulinus fled back to Kent, and the kingdom disintegrated into its two parts, Deira ruled by Osric, and Bernicia by Eanfrith, both of whom apostatised on taking their thrones. These rulers in their turn were destroyed by the British king, Cadwallon, who occupied Northumbria for a year, ruling it like a tyrant. At this point Eanfrith's brother Oswald led a small force against the Britons at Denisesburna, to the south of what was to become Hexham, in 634 or 635, and defeated them (Bede, *Historia Ecclesiastica* II.20, pp. 202–7; III.1, pp. 212–15).

Bede makes much of the apostasy of Osric and Eanfrith, and the just vengeance of Cadwallon upon them for it, contrasted with the faith of Oswald, victoriously overthrowing the foreign tyrant. This faith is illustrated graphically in what Oswald did before the battle, raising a cross which comes to act as a symbol of his imminent victory, which seems to be assured in Oswald's statement that God knew they were fighting a just war for the salvation of his people (Bede, *Historia Ecclesiastica* III.2, pp. 215–16). A good deal of Bede's account is devoted to the cult which had sprung up at the cross, which included people taking shavings of the cross and immersing them in water for healing purposes. It

given under IVa; and IV lists a usage where *of trēowe* glosses *de stipite*, the word used by Bede to describe the stakes on which Oswald's remains were fixed.

Fig. 16. The chapel at Heavenfield, marking the supposed spot
where Oswald raised the cross before setting off into battle.

is to be noted that the cult, sponsored by the brothers of Hexham
(and furthered by the recent establishment of a chapel on the site,
a successor to which is still to be found there: Fig. 16), focused
not on the date of the battle in which Oswald gained victory
after setting out from Heavenfield, but on the eve of the battle
in which he perished, in the far-off Welsh Marches.

Bede comments on the auspicious name of the place, Heavenfield, as being an omen of the heavenly victory that followed
Oswald's setting up of the heavenly sign of the cross there. He
therefore regarded the name as antedating Oswald's arrival,
which means it would have originated in pagan times, without
reference to Christian concepts; Bede eschews any speculation
on this background.

Adomnán, writing a few decades earlier than Bede, and with
a good pedigree for his information, gives a different account
of Oswald's experience on the eve of battle, one which involved
the patron of Adomnán's monastery of Iona, St Columba. It is
impossible to reconcile the accounts, but the common factor is
that some moving experience or vision, regarded as signalling
divine intervention, impressed itself upon Oswald.

The sixteenth-century antiquarian John Leland (1906–10, V,
61) also has something to say about Oswald's victory:

> There is a fame that Oswald wan the batelle at Halydene a 2.
> myles est from S. Oswaldes Asche. And that Haliden is it that
> Bede caullith Hevenfeld. And men there aboute yet finde smaule
> wod crossis in the grounde.

The meaning of Halydene is 'holy vale', perpetuating the
sacred associations. Toulmin-Smith, the editor of Leland's text,
identifies Halydene as Hazel Dean, just under two miles east
of the chapel of Oswald, and on the eastern end of the Heavenfield plateau. Leland's account over all seems garbled. Bede
says nothing about the battle taking place at Heavenfield;
rather, he makes it clear that it took place at Denisesburna,
some miles distant from Heavenfield to its south. Leland was
not the first to read into Bede what he wanted to see there—
the identification of Heavenfield as the battle site continues
to be made, including by scholars who should know better.
It is possible, however, that Leland was recording a local
folk tradition; it is easily forgotten that folk tradition is often
informed by learned tradition, and a misreading of Bede
could easily have entered local tradition at some point, especially if it helped the local pilgrimage trinket trade, which we
may suspect lies behind the finding of many wooden crosses
here. Yet there also seems to be a link between what Leland
records and the veneration at St Oswald's Ash noted by Reginald of Durham, but as taking place at Oswestry, the place
of Oswald's demise; I consider Reginald below. Leland may
have confused the sites of veneration of the saint, but it is also
possible that a connection more deeply rooted in tradition
existed, by which an ash 'tree'—encompassing both senses
of the word—was associated with Oswald both at his victory
and at his martyrdom.

Oswald's defeat

Just a few years after his victory at Denisesburna, Oswald was
defeated and killed in battle by Penda of Mercia in the Welsh
Marches, near Oswestry (at a site named Maserfelth by Bede), on
5 August 642, aged 38 (Bede, *Historia Ecclesiastica* III.9, pp. 240–3).[2]

---

[2] That Maserfelth was indeed Oswestry is argued strongly by Stancliffe
(1995*b*). Whether the conflict involved the Iron Age fort of Old Oswestry (Fig.

Fig. 17. Old Oswestry Iron Age hillfort.

Bede is more interested in the miracles associated with the site of Oswald's death than the politics of the events, but it is probable that Oswald was attempting to split Mercia from its Welsh allies (it was an alliance of Penda and Cadwallon that had overthrown Eadwine in 633/634); such an alliance posed a continuing threat to Northumbria. Bede recounts what happened after the battle (*Historia Ecclesiastica* iii.12, pp. 250–3, my translation):

> Porro caput et manus cum brachiis a corpore praecissas iussit rex, qui occiderat, in stipitibus suspendi. Quo post annum deueniens cum exercitu successor regni eius Osuiu abstulit ea, et caput quidem in cymiterio Lindisfarnensis ecclesiae, in regia uero ciuitate manus cum brachiis condidit.

> The king who slew him ordered his head and his hands along with the arms to be cut from his body and hung on stakes. A year afterwards, his successor Oswiu came down with an army and took them away. He interred the head in a burial place of the church of Lindisfarne, but the hands and arms he buried in the royal city [of Bamburgh].

Bede is brief, but Reginald of Durham, writing in the twelfth century, gives a full account in his *Vita Sancti Oswaldi* of the site of Maserfelth and the events that followed Oswald's death there. Although he is of little value as a critical historian—most

17), paralleling in some way what I have suggested as having occurred with Oswald's father Æthelfrith at Heronbridge, cannot be determined.

of his account is clearly lifted from Bede, and embellished with a tediously strained prolixity through his own imagination—he nonetheless appears to have had access to local traditions, which he duly recorded (Tudor 1995, 191). He gives a fairly precise location for Maserfelth, near Oswestry (ch. 14), and notes (ch. 12) that:

> In loco non longe ab ipso fons perennis exoritur, qui sancti Oswaldi fons ab incolis illius gentis nominatur. Et in ripa fonticuli arbor pergrandis radicari cernitur; sub umbra cujus culminis paene tota fontis amoenitas contegi videtur. Nam non longe inde, ubi nunc arbor nascitur, caput sancti Oswaldi cum manibus per annum integrum stipitibus [...] infixa fuerunt.

> In a place not far from it [the site of Oswald's death] a perpetual spring rises up, called St Oswald's Well by the inhabitants of the area. And on the banks of the spring a mighty tree can be seen to have taken root; almost the whole pleasantness of the spring seems to be concealed beneath the shadow of its crown. Not far from where the tree now grows the head of St Oswald along with his hands [...] remained whole, fixed to stakes for a year.

The sacred relics were retrieved, as Bede had recounted, and above the sepulchre where Oswald's head came to be kept in Lindisfarne shone a light (ch. 13). In ch. 17, Oswiu is said to have come to search for Oswald's arms and head but could not find one arm:

> Mira tamen Dei dispositione [...] ante regis Oswin [*recte* Oswiu] adventum, ales permaxima, olim in partibus illis tantae quantitatis invisa, comparuit, quae et manum dexteram de stipite cum brachio sustulit, et cum tanti pretii praeda ad vicini loci arborem cum reverentia convolavit. Eratque ales ipsa, ut putabatur, corvini generis; sed pro grandibus rostro et unguibus aquilarum similitudini conformis fuisse videbatur [...] Arbor etiam ipsa fraxinus est, qui a loco illius martyrii fere dimidii stadii longitudinis abest. [...] At fraxinus tunc temporis veteranus extitit, et foliis decidentibus ramisque prae vetustate et senio marcescentibus squalidus et importunus videntibus cunctis apparuit. Nam neque pulchritudine vel gratia vel frondium jocunditate serena vel foliorum ubertate amoena praestitit, sed eatenus senio contabuerat et ab omni viroris paene virtute deciderat, et fronde, folio, et cortice emarcuerat.

Yet by the wondrous arrangement of God [. . .] before the arrival of King Oswiu there appeared an enormous bird, of a size hitherto never seen in those parts, and it took the right hand down from the stake along with the arm, and with this valuable booty reverently resorted in its flight to a tree in the neighbourhood. The winged creature was, it is thought, of the crow type; but seemed, by the grandeur of its beak and talons, to conform rather with the appearance of eagles [. . .] The tree itself was an ash, scarcely half a furlong from the place of martyrdom [. . .] But the ash at that time was ancient, its leaves falling and its branches withering with age and feebleness, and appeared wretched and ill-favoured to all onlookers. It looked pleasant neither for any beauty or grace or serene burgeoning of foliage or fecundity of leaves, but so far had been decaying with age, while any strength and vigour had all but departed from it, and it was withered in leaf, foliage and bark.

The bird landed on this ash tree, causing its stiff limbs to creak, and thereafter the tree was returned to vigour:

Eodem itaque tempore arbor ipsa coepit florere et frondescere, nec unquam postea a viroris sui et decoris amoenitate deficere. [. . .] Neque aliquis hactenus impune de frondibus illius at foliis divellere seu distrahere poterat, quin statim ultrice poena suae temeritatis merita non susceperat. [. . .] Arborque ipsa sancti Oswaldi fraxinus ab omni populo terrae nominatur [. . .] Multi tamen illo languentes confluunt, et vel umbra arboris, seu tactu aut gustu folii ejus vel frondis, sanitatis opem beati martyris meritis consequi consuescunt.

And so at the same time the tree began to flourish and bud, and never to be lacking thenceforth in the pleasantness of its vigour and beauty [. . .] Nor could anyone thereafter to this day divest it of its leaves or rip off its foliage without at once being subjected to well-deserved vengeful punishment for his audacity [. . .] The tree is called St Oswald's Ash by all the people of the area [. . .] Many weary people gather there, and often, through the merits of the blessed martyr, attain the riches of health from the shade of the tree or by touching or tasting its leaves or foliage.

Reginald then returns to the matter of the spring (Figs. 18, 19) that arose at the tree (ch. 18):

Igitur dum avis cum tanti rapina thesauri in quavis arboris regione subsisteret, Dei disponente contigit, ut molem illius gravaminis ales ulterius minime sustineret. Unde de ore illius praeda delapsa decidit, et sacrata dextera cum brachio super

Fig. 18. St Oswald's Well, Oswestry.

asperae silicis duritiem deorsum corruit. Miranda igitur Dei
virtute statim ad attactum sacri brachii decidentis de saxo
durissimo prorupuit fons limpidissimus et perennis. [. . .] Igitur
Oswin [*recte* Oswiu] rex, divina virtute commonitus oraculi,
ad hunc fontem processit, et sicut noctu didicit in visione, sic
postmodum expletum repperit Dei miranda dispositione. Unde
de aquis ipsis brachium cum manu sustulit, et sicut ei per visum
jussum fuerat caput sanctissimum cum brachiis et manibus
inde secum asportavit.

So, while the bird along with the mighty treasure it had seized
was settling in some part of the tree, by God's arrangement it
happened that the winged creature could scarcely hold on any
longer to a burden of such weight. Hence the booty slipped
and fell from its mouth, and the sacred right hand with the
arm clattered down over a hard surface of sharp flint. By God's
astonishing power, a most limpid and everlasting spring immediately burst forth from the very hard rock at the touch of the
holy limb falling upon it [. . .] Thus King Oswiu, advised by the
divine power of an oracle, went up to this spring and what had
been spoken in a vision in the night he thereafter found fulfilled

Fig. 19. A modern statue of the eagle seizing Oswald's arm,
set above St Oswald's Well, Oswestry.

by the wondrous arrangement of God: he lifted the arm with
the hand from the waters and as he had been commanded in
the vision he took away the most sacred head along with the
arms and hands from there.

Reginald notes that people still came and healing was still
granted by drinking from the holy spring.

It is clear that Reginald took the name Oswestry to mean
'Oswald's tree', yet the Welsh version of the name, Croes-
oswallt, must have originated at an earlier time, when *trēow*
was readily taken to mean 'cross' (Stancliffe 1995*b*, 89). Bede
apparently did not know the name *Oswaldestreow, but he
gives the tale of how the sanctity of the place of the king's
death was established (*Historia Ecclesiastica* iii.9, pp. 242–3):
a man with a sick horse happened upon the place, and the
horse was healed when it rolled on the spot. The man left
there a *signum*—a word Bede uses for the cross set up by
Oswald at Heavenfield—and then others visited the place

and were healed. It is probable that this temporary sign was replaced by a more substantial cross (see Stancliffe 1995b, 90–1; she notes the widespread occurrence of free-standing crosses to mark sacred sites); Reginald's story of the ash tree, by contrast, is folklore. As such, however, it illustrates the sort of belief that readily attached to figures such as Oswald: the cross-*trēow* has come to be envisaged as a living, burgeoning *trēow* in the form of an ash. The same process of re-imaging probably took place at Heavenfield, to judge from Leland's account of St Oswald's Ash, which must refer to the original Heavenfield cross envisioned as an ash tree, or at least an ash tree that continued the presence of the erstwhile cross; it is possible that this is the result of cult imagery being shared between Oswestry and Heavenfield.

The nature of the accounts

All the accounts of Oswald are hagiographical, but there are differing interests at work within this general description, and various layers of manipulation of the events are evident. It is difficult, indeed, to disentangle the different elements in the legend. Reginald's account illustrates that the cult had developed since the time of Bede, but Bede's own account is a century removed from the events described, and incorporates a good deal of developed tradition within it.

Adomnán's account has a better provenance than Bede's, with a direct personal line back to Oswald himself. Adomnán agrees with Bede in that something Oswald took as a sign from God occurred just before the battle and led him on to victory, but the nature of the divine intervention differs: Adomnán knows nothing of a cross, and does not mention Heavenfield. The image of Oswald as a Christ-figure with his twelve followers is made explicit; the same image is at least implicit in Bede, and may well go back to how Oswald saw himself. Stancliffe (1995a, 51) notes that the political purpose of mentioning the vision of Columba was probably to remind King Aldfrith of Northumbria (r. 685–705), who like Oswald had spent much time in exile among Irish, of the efficacy of Iona's saint; nonetheless, this does not mean Adomnán invented it.

Reginald had a hagiographical view of history that is little tainted by any Bedean desire to confine himself to the realistic; he was quite willing to use folk traditions, and he was clearly interested in recognising and perhaps in promoting local cult. He was geographically remote from the events described, and his chief use is as a witness to the developing hagiographical folklore around the saint.

Bede remains the fullest and most reliable early witness both to the historical details and the cult of Oswald. In his version of the legend, he is concerned to present the glorious development of Northumbrian Christianity under royal patronage. As Wallace-Hadrill (1988, 89; cf. Stancliffe 1995a, 50, 63) comments, Bede's account places Oswald's success in a historical tradition of royal victories beginning with Constantine and including Clovis. Bede may well have been inspired by the cross at his own church of Jarrow (and still to be seen there), inscribed with the words taken from Rufinus's version of Eusebius, commemorating Constantine's victory: 'in hoc singulari signo vita redditur mundo' ('in this unique sign life is returned to the world'). Oswald's victory represents for Bede a victory over resurgent paganism (and heresy, Cadwallon being a British Christian), and the associated disorder of society (marked for example in the disintegration of the kingdom). All the miracles associated with Oswald were, ultimately, confirmation that God was working through his chosen English subjects to establish an ecclesiastical *imperium Romanum* here. More specifically, Wallace-Hadrill (1971, 86–7) points out that 'the personal virtues that Bede emphasises are more technical than they look; they correspond to the requirements of the Church: protection, endowment, largesse, the prosecution of Christian warfare, and, above all, obedience to its teaching'.

Behind Bede's account lie the intentions of the Hexham monks, who were undoubtedly his main informants. In essence the aims of the Hexham community may have been similar to Bede's, if perhaps less lofty. The monks' cult, as reported by Bede, was markedly local and personal in character: they were not concerned with the history of the Church in Deira, for example, let alone further afield. For them, Oswald's victory (and his subsequent 'martyrdom' at Maserfelth) marks the beginning of Christianity in their land. The story of the cross being raised at

Heavenfield must derive from the monks of Hexham, the guardians of the sacred site, which they had no doubt looked after since the founding of the monastery in 674. Yet the foundation was forty years after the battle, allowing time for traditions to have been manipulated. The victorious carrying of the cross against the Welsh would fit with the ideology of Hexham's founder, Wilfrith, whose gloating sermon outlining how the English had taken over many Welsh areas in Northumbria by the sword is summarised in the *Vita Wilfridi* (ch. 17); thus Oswald's victory over Cadwallon would be remembered in ecclesiastical circles as part of the victory over the British form of Christianity that Wilfrith opposed so vehemently at the Council of Whitby in 664, even though Oswald himself adhered to a form of British Christianity (but Scottish, not Welsh).

There were, then, good reasons to emphasise the story of the cross within ecclesiastical tradition, but it seems unlikely to have been a total invention—that would be to suppose that the monks, knowing Oswald's victory to have taken place nearby (namely at Denisesburna, to the south of the monastery), and realising a piece of ground to the north of the Tyne was fortuitously named Heavenfield, decided to link the two and place the king at Heavenfield the night before the battle, with a cross thrown in to add piquancy to the story. Far more likely is that Oswald found himself at a place called Heavenfield; he may even have gone slightly out of his way to camp there, given the auspicious name. His Christian credentials are beyond doubt, and his personal motivations were most probably thoroughly Christian; he may even have seen himself as a new Constantine (rather than this being merely Bede's emphasis). What of his followers? Some of these would have come with him from Scotland, and thus have been Christian—though how deeply is open to question, in view of Oswald's brother Eanfrith's immediate apostasy on reaching his homeland: we are left with an impression of Christianity assumed at the Scottish court, at least by some, for expediency. Such of his army as came from Bernicia (presumably most of it) were even less likely to have had a firm commitment to the new faith. In setting up a cross and praying for victory in front of it before the battle, Oswald was performing an act of Christian propaganda with a great risk attached, in terms of its all-important reception by his followers. Is it not likely that

Oswald shared Pope Gregory's wisdom, and adapted a pagan rite to Christian use?[3] Was the troops' enthusiasm fired not so much by pure Christian devotion focused on the novelty of seeing a cross of victory raised before battle, as by beholding a familiar pagan rite imbued with new spiritual power through the ingenuity of their leader, the pagan cult *trēow* transformed into the *trēow* of the Crucifixion?

Any motivation in Oswald's actions that would link him with paganism is eschewed by Bede. As Wallace-Hadrill notes (1988, xx–xxi), Bede the ecclesiastical historian conceived of the content of paganism as lacking any seriousness: yet

> It is right that we should know at least that Germanic paganisms were warband-religions and kin-religions, whereas Christianity was neither; and moreover, that pagan cultus as practised by warriors shared ethical concepts with the warrior's fighting-creed, from which indeed the Church borrowed some meaning-laden words when it faced the task of expressing Christian doctrine in the vernacular. Coifi's naïve equation of pagan honour and success with Christian salvation was the reaction of a high priest whose congregation was a royal court of warriors.

This observation makes it all the more probable that Oswald would exploit any warrior-based cultus his followers are likely to have adhered to, no doubt diverting it into serving his Christian purpose.

In its more developed form, the legend of Oswald has his reign marked at beginning and end with crosses; the beginnings of this are implicit in Bede's account, with the stakes (also a form of *trēow*) on which his body was mounted a sort of grotesque parody of the cross he had raised in victory (on the prototype of which, of course, Christ's body had been hung). The cross that gave rise to the name Oswestry was referred to ambiguously as a *trēow*, 'cross, tree', and in due course this came to be seen as a sacred ash tree, recalling the cosmic ash tree of Norse myth (e.g. *Vǫluspá*, st. 19, 45, *Grímnismál*, st. 29–35, 44); and

---

[3] Stancliffe (1995a, 64) rather simplistically dismisses the idea that the events at Heavenfield could have had any pagan aspect to them, given that Oswald was so firmly Christian. I am suggesting the converse, that because he was so Christian, he would seek to bring into the fold not only his devout followers, but also those more aligned to pagan spirituality, by Christianising motifs that they would be familiar with.

the cross which he set up at Heavenfield perhaps has parallels with world trees found widely in folk traditions, as discussed below. The folk tradition which developed around Oswald had three bases: long-standing indigenous perspectives, Germanic paganism, and the increasing influence of the Northumbrian Church. The legend of Oswald developed as an intertwined interaction between these elements.

The elements of the legend

I have hinted that the legend of Oswald appears to have become more structured as it developed; it may therefore be instructive to take a broadly structuralist approach to the legend, as recorded in the sources discussed above. Several elements of Oswald's victory and his martyrdom may be distinguished; I make no assessment of their historicity—the intention is to discern the motifs in the story.

OSWALD'S VICTORY

a. Oswald raises a *trēow* before battle, which gives him confidence of victory; the *trēow* here is envisaged as a cross.

b. In later tradition an ash tree associated with Oswald was found on the site (following Leland).

c. The place of the *trēow* is Heavenfield, a raised area of open ground.

d. Oswald displays a very physical connection with the *trēow*; he uses his own hands to pile up earth around it.

e. There is no eagle as such, but in the case of Constantine, upon whom Oswald is modelled (possibly already by himself), the cross itself acted as the *aquila*, the eagle-standard of victory, which Roman armies would take into battle.[4]

---

[4] Bede spells out that Oswald's cross was a battle standard, but he terms it a *vexillum*, an ensign or banner. This is surely meant to recall the famous hymn of Venantius Fortunatus, first used in 569 at a procession of a part of the true cross of Christ, a gift of the emperor Justin II to St Radegunda, from Tours to Poitiers; the hymn was absorbed into the liturgy of Passiontide. Kayser (1881, 397–8) clarifies the meaning of *vexilla*: they were, strictly speaking, the pieces of cloth suspended from the aquila, the eagle which surmounted the battle standard; in Christian usage, following Constantine's victory, the eagle came to be replaced with the cross, so the *vexilla* were adornments to

f. There is no clear association between the *trēow* and any springs, but it is interesting that Bede should mention the site of Oswald's victory by name, at the small stream called Denisesburna; the Halydene, 'holy vale', of Leland also has a small stream coming from a nearby spring.

OSWALD'S MARTYRDOM

a. Oswald's remains are raised on stakes—a sort of antithesis of a victorious cross, but reminiscent of the cross of the Crucifixion—after his defeat. The site of his martyrdom was marked originally by a *signum*, probably a cross.

b. His remains also end up in an ash tree close to the site of martyrdom.

c. The place of the stakes and the cross, and the ash tree, is Oswestry, 'Oswald's *trēow*' (although it is not named as such by Bede).

d. The physical connection of Oswald's body—in the form particularly of his hands, as well as his head—to both the stakes and the ash tree is emphasised.

e. An eagle-like *corvinus* (probably a raven) plays a significant part in the legend of the aftermath of Oswald's martyrdom, and is closely associated with the ash tree.

f. A sacred spring emerges at the place his relics are dropped.

The correspondences between victory and martyrdom are not worked out comprehensively, but there appears to be a parallelism which strengthened as the tradition developed; this

the cross, symbolising its power of victory, and hence could act as a metonym of the cross itself. The hymn's opening stanza reads: 'Vexilla regis prodeunt, fulget crucis mysterium, quo carne carnis conditor suspensus est patibulo' ('The banners of the king go forth; the mystery of the cross shines out: on its cross-beam the creator of flesh was hung in the flesh'). The image is one of a Church procession pictured as a battle assault, the victory, of course, being in reality spiritual, but conversely, just as a procession could be seen metaphorically as a battle, so too a march into battle could be seen as a metaphorical Christian procession. The king here can, then, be taken as either an earthly king winning victory in Christ through his cross, or as Christ himself, whose banner of victory is the cross itself—a victory which is achieved only by his fleshly sacrifice: Oswald, the earthly king, wins victory through the banner of the cross, and through his crucifixion-like passion, his flesh hung on stakes, he achieves a heavenly victory of martyrdom, becoming a metatype of Christ himself. Hence the allusion to the *vexilla regis* hints at a deep perception of Oswald as the agent of salvation for his nation.

could be the result of a sharing of features of the cult of the saint between the sites.

The following mythemes may thus be isolated, each of them occurring or implicit at both Oswald's rise and his fall:

a. A sacred area is prominently designated, associated with the *trēow*, and realised as the 'heavenly field' or the place of 'Oswald's tree'.

b. The *trēow* is realised as a cross or an ash tree, and in an antithetical image as a stake; the *trēow* has power in itself and physical contact with it is emphasised. The cross brings victory, but the ash tree returns the power of the saint, bringing health to pilgrims, its sustaining power symbolised in its own burgeoning foliage. The image of the *trēow* may thus be divided into three motifs:

- The *trēow* of victory;
- The sustaining tree;
- The stake or post.

c. An eagle-like bird is associated with the *trēow* and acts as a form of mediator between the saint and the cross/tree, both of which are endowed with supernatural power.

d. A sacred spring is associated with the *trēow* and saint.

e. The divinely appointed king achieves his authority through the power of the *trēow*. Initially this authority is expressed as military victory, then is overturned—as it seems—through slaughter in battle, Oswald's parts being displayed on stakes: yet this overthrow thwarts the intended contumely, achieving spiritual power through the king's martyrdom (he is slain by an avowed pagan). There is a reciprocal balance: first the king is charged with power from the *trēow* and the 'heavenly field' it is set up on, then the *trēow* and its associated well and ground are charged with spiritual power through their association with the martyr.

f. The king's head and hands act as a metonym—as it were a distillation—of his continuing power.

I would like to consider each of these mythemes in terms of analogues to be found elsewhere. Our records of English pagan belief are minimal; it is more rewarding to look at Scandinavian parallels, as recorded in Old Norse mythology, along with widespread motifs such as the world tree, which are found across a broad area of northern Eurasia. I am not arguing that English traditions would have been identical with any of these analogues, but that English paganism would have shared some of the basic features of other Germanic and northern cultures; a comparison may be suggestive of areas of belief beyond the explicit, Christian message that Bede and his successors are keen to convey.

Heavenfield

It may or may not have been chance that Oswald found himself in a place named, uniquely, 'Heavenfield', but he certainly made use of the fact. It is possible that the name was invented *post factum*, and the tale of Oswald raising a cross in the auspiciously named location was a fabrication, but Bede reveals that the name was ancient. If he is right, from an English perspective it was therefore pagan, unconnected with the Christian heaven in its origins.

The name is likely to have been a calque translation of a local British name: a few miles to the west, for example, on a comparable open piece of country on Hadrian's Wall, lies Vindolanda, a name recorded in Roman times, which means 'Bright plain/moor' (Rivet and Smith 1979, *s.v.*); *vindo-* probably had divine connotations (compare, for example, the ancient name of the Boyne, *Buvinda*, the sacred 'white cow': see MacKillop 1998, *s.v.* 'Boyne River'), and *landa* (developing into Welsh *llan*, 'churchyard') corresponding exactly to *feld*. The first element, 'heaven', would be expected to be **Neμ-* (modern Welsh *nef*). Yet this element does not seem to have been productive in Celtic place-names. It is intriguing, however, that a number of place-names are recorded from Roman Britain, and a good many more from continental Celtic areas, with the element *Nemeto-*, 'sacred grove',[5] such as Aquae Arnemetiae (Buxton; see the discussion

---

[5] The precise sense of *nemeton* is not clear: it certainly designated a sacred area, but how far it was necessarily a grove, a discrete collection of trees, is uncertain (it might in principle also have included, for example, a discrete, cleared area within a forest, or a sacred hilltop). The cognate Latin *nemus* certainly implied a grove, however, and place-names such as Drunemeton, 'Oak *nemeton*', in Asia Minor, as well as the Old Irish *fidnemed*, 'wood *nemeton*', imply a close connection with groves in most cases. Place-names with *nemeton*

Fig. 20. The Heavenfield plateau seen from near Wall,
illustrating how it forms a 'heavenly field'.

in Rivet and Smith 1979, *s.v.*). The word survived in Irish, but not (as far as I can tell) into recorded Welsh. One possibility must surely be that a name in * *Neμed-* (from **Nemetolanda*) was interpreted as containing **Neμ-*, 'heaven', at a time when the sense of 'grove' was already obsolete, and was translated accordingly into English (which, onomastically speaking, could well have occurred after the battle, for example at the time of the establishment of Hexham, and hence substantial English settlement, some decades later). Moreover, according to Rivet and Smith (*ibid.*, *s.v.* 'Aquae Arnemetiae'), **nemet-*, 'grove', derives from **nem-os*, 'heaven', so the words were probably always perceived as being related. The raised nature of Heavenfield, particularly when seen from the west (Fig. 20), would probably easily have led to a reading of the *Neμ-* in the postulated place-name as meaning 'heaven'. One particularly interesting place-name, in view of Heavenfield being an open area atop a definite rise, is Nemetobala (probably Lydney), which Rivet and Smith (*ibid.*, *s.v.*) regard as likely to mean 'grove-hill' or 'hill-sanctuary'. Heavenfield could then, perhaps, have been regarded as a sacred site before the coming of the English.

It hardly needs stating that a 'sacred' site in antiquity was bound to be concerned also with what we would regard as more secular functions, and the *nemeton* is no exception. The oldest recorded *nemeton*, Drunemeton in Asia Minor, was the sacred site

are reviewed in some detail in Watson (2011, 244–50)—an old study (originally published 1926) which is rather lacking in references, but still useful.

of three Celtic tribes that settled there; Strabo, in his *Geography* xii.5.1, describes how it functioned as the joint tribal meeting place for the dispensing of judgements, and similar associations are found in later instances of *nemeta* (see Watson 2011, 244–5).

A 'sacred-grove plain' atop a hill, associated with a summer religious procession (as conducted by the monks of Hexham in commemoration of Oswald's death on 5 August), can hardly fail to recall the *troménie* (peregrinatory processional circumambulation) of Locronan ('the sacred area of St Ronan') in Brittany, held in the middle of July (which, allowing for the difference in latitude, corresponds well with the Heavenfield ritual some three weeks later). This is recorded from the later Middle Ages on, but, according to the researches of Donitien Laurent (1996), has strong indications of going back to a pre-Christian procession which commemorated the seasons of the Gallic year, and was linked with the fertility and success of the land. The procession passed by the forest of Névet—a name derived directly from *nemeton*—and ascended to the top of the Locronan hill, where the station (ceremonial stopping place) of St Ronan himself was to be found, and back down again. The information about the cult at Heavenfield is too meagre to allow for any clear development from a pre-Christian ritual, but the possibility cannot be excluded; it is slightly strange, for example, how the monks processed to Heavenfield not on the celebration of Oswald's victory, but of his death, which took place elsewhere, yet in high summer. It is conceivable that in the name Heavenfield, and the cult conducted there, is concealed a memory of a more ancient religious rite that Oswald himself may have appealed to, and which was adopted and adapted by the monks of Hexham.

Such a ritual might have marked the place out as sacred in local tradition, yet a 'sacred-grove plain' could have had additional symbolic significance to Oswald, in view of his Gaelic upbringing. *Nemeton* does not appear to have been a productive term in place-names in Gaelic areas (though it was in Pictish regions: see Goldberg 2012, 178–9), but as an ordinary noun the word survived: thus Lucas (1963, 27) notes how the *fidnemed*, 'wood sanctuary, grove', of Armagh was burnt down along with the ecclesiastical settlement and town in 995 (according to the *Annals of the Four Masters* and *Annals of Ulster*); Lucas argues this grove was part of what was originally a pagan site,

Christianised by St Patrick. In connection with Heavenfield, it is worth noting that the sacred centre of Armagh, where this grove must have been situated, is on a sort of miniature plain atop a definite rise. Lucas (*ibid.*, 27–33) traces a rich array of groves associated with ecclesiastical sites in Ireland; in many instances, the arboreal connection is realised in the form of a single tree, such as at Cill Dara (Kildare), 'Church of the Oak', founded by St Brigid in the sixth century. If the proposed derivation of Heavenfield from *Nemetolanda is correct, and Oswald understood it to refer to the sort of *nemed* that existed at St Patrick's shrine in Armagh, he could well have been prompted to set up his own *trēow* as a particularisation of the sacred *neµed the place commemorated, hallowing it as a Christian sanctuary by specifying the *trēow* as a cross.

The sacred tree of Irish tradition, the *bile*, according to one definition (*ibid.*, 23) was a large tree standing in a plain or open space—much like Oswald's *trēow*. The *bile* had further symbolic meanings. Lucas (*ibid.*, 20–2) shows how a *bile* was regarded as a proper adjunct of a noble dwelling, and cites a twelfth-century poem from the Metrical Dindshenchas which uses the *bile* as a symbol for the king himself, residing on a hill free of battle and distributing bounty—in other words, he has achieved a plentiful victory. This notion is epitomised in the tree as a site for the inauguration of a king's reign; Lucas (*ibid.*, 25) cites several instances from annals relating events in the tenth and eleventh centuries where enemies uproot a tribe's inauguration tree, clearly symbolising an uprooting of their rule, such as the Craobh Tulcha, 'Mound Tree', in Co. Antrim in 1099. The converse, the establishment of a tree, declares the reimposition of the rightful accession to power. In planting the cross at Heavenfield, therefore, Oswald, in terms of the Gaelic traditions he must have grown up with (assuming the traditions cited did indeed stretch back that far, as seems quite likely), could well have understood himself both to be asserting his Christianity, making truly sacred a place whose name already intimated its holiness, and proclaiming himself the rightful hereditary king of the land, the whole realm of Northumbria ravaged by Cadwallon, through the raising of a sacred *trēow*.[6]

---

[6] Bintley (2014) argues that the removal of Oswald's relics to the new minster

The name 'Heavenfield' would nonetheless also have had resonances for pagan Germanic peoples. The heavenly field is suggestive of several mythological plains, both in Old English and Old Norse; several words designating, broadly, 'plain' may be mentioned: in Old English there is *feld*, 'open country', and *wang*, 'meadowland, open field'; in Old Norse there is *vangr*, 'meadow, homefield' (= Old English *wang*), *vǫllr* (pl. *vellir*), 'meadow, paddock, plain', and *akr* (= Old English *æcer*), 'cultivated field'.[7]

Paradise was referred to by Ulfilas in Gothic as *waggs*, and by the Anglo-Saxons as *neorxnawang*, a word of obscure, but not ostensibly Christian, origin; in *Beowulf*, line 93, God created the world as a 'wlitebeorhtne wang' ('beautiful-bright meadow'). The *Phoenix* refers to the paradise in which the phoenix lived as a *wang*: the bird dwelt in a tree on this plain. The poem is based on a Latin work of Lactantius, *De Ave Phoenice*: the Latin mentions the plain only twice (as *planities*, then as *campi*), whereas the *wang* or *feld* is frequently brought to the reader's attention by the Old English poet, perhaps indicating a preoccupation with (originally pagan) connotations of the supernatural plain. Old Norse poetry mentions *Himinvangar*, 'Heaven meadows' (*Helgakviða Hundingsbana I*, st. 15), adding a piece of mythological scenery to a heroic poem; in *Lokasenna*, st. 51, Skaði mentions her *vé*, 'sanctuaries', and *vangar*, 'meadows', together in an alliterating phrase suggesting a traditional association between plains and the dwellings of the gods.

Glasisvellir (or *Glæsisvellir*) is the name of a paradise in Norse (see Tolkien 1960, 84–6, for a survey of sources; Saxo gives the most information); the name apparently means 'the plains of Glasir': the glowing buds (*glóbarr*) of Glasir, 'the Gleaming', are

at Gloucester around the end of the tenth century was an act intended to symbolise the uniting of Wessex and Mercia, on the basis that Oswald was seen as the sainted establisher of the united Christian realm of Northumbria. It seems plausible to me that rather than this being merely a later, albeit long-standing, perspective, it could have been an explicit intention of Oswald himself to present himself as establisher of a united Christian realm after the chaos of Cadwallon's time, although of course he could not know how much of a founder figure he would prove to be, given the vicissitudes in the establishment of Anglo-Saxon power and Christianity that had so far been experienced.

[7] See Smith (1970) for the meaning of the English terms as they occur in place names; and Straubergs (1957, esp. 71–2) on plains as part of the topography of the Otherworld.

mentioned in the (possibly) tenth-century *Bjarkamál* (*Skjalde-digtning* B1 170) as a kenning for 'gold', and Snorri says Glasir is a golden-leaved *lundr* (which could mean either grove or tree) growing before Valhǫll. Also, a *Glasislundr* is mentioned in *Helgakviða Hjǫrvarðssonar*, st. 1, and a *Brálundr*, 'Bright grove' (a designation suggesting a grove similar to Glasislundr) in *Helga-kviða Hundingsbana I*, st. 1. The concept of a *vǫllr* that renews itself may have been made specific in *Vǫluspá* in the form of *Iðavǫllr*, 'Plain of industry/perpetual return', where at the beginning of the world the gods meet and engage in forging wealth, and where at the start of the new world (at the end of the poem) the gods meet again to *dœma*, 'discuss, pass judgement', on the old world. The poet seems to have adapted a tradition of a divine plain to serve his literary purpose—a main theme of the poem is the end and renewal of the world. If *Iðavǫllr* is the poet's invention then this confirms the conventionality of the belief in the 'plain' for living beings.[8] Among men the *þing*, 'assembly', was conventionally held on a plain, commemorated in names such as Þingvellir (Iceland), Tynwald (Man) and Tingwall (Shetland). At least at Þingvellir, the *lǫgberg* (law-rock), from which the laws were proclaimed, acts as a variant of the judgement tree or post (notably the *stapol* of the Anglo-Saxon king's hall, discussed below). In *Grímnismál*, st. 30, the place where the gods *dœma* (meet for council)—most naturally conceived as taking place on a *vǫllr* like the *þing* among men—is said to be at the world-tree Yggdrasill; it appears that the world-tree, judgement and plain may well have formed a traditional association. The tree, growing beside a spring, may well be imagined to have grown in the midst of a *vǫllr* (though this is nowhere stated), like the tree in the midst of the *wang* in the Old English *Phoenix*. De Vries (1956–7, §265) mentions Anglo-Saxon laws against setting up a *friðgeard* around a stone, tree or spring; and the Norse *stafgarðr* was a sacred area surrounding a wooden post. These practices confirm the connection between the *þing* and the sacred tree, situated in a designated area of ground (*vǫllr* or *garðr*).

---

[8] The word involves a punning play upon *ið*, 'activity', *iða*, 'eddy' (derived from the same base meaning 'perpetual motion'), and *iður-*, 'again' (cf. Old English *ed-*); the name of the goddess responsible for the 'ellilyf ása' ('medicine of old age for the gods', *Haustlǫng*, st. 9: *Skjaldedigtning* B1 16), Iðunn, 'Renewer', is also likely to have influenced the formation of *Iðavǫllr*.

The concept of fertile renewal is expressed through the use of *akr*, 'corn-field', in mythological names. Thus, for Þjóðólfr of Hvinir, composing in the late ninth century, the home of the goddess Iðunn, who renews the gods' youth, is *Brunnakr*, 'spring/well corn-field', in *Haustlǫng*, st. 9 (*Skjaldedigtning* BI 16). *Óðáinsakr*, 'the corn-field of the undead', is found in two thirteenth-century Icelandic sagas as a name of a paradise (see Tolkien 1960, 84–6); it is also found in place names from the pagan period, though it is not possible to specify how it was conceived at that time (de Vries 1956–7, §519). In Saxo, the form of the name is *Undensakre*, 'Underworld field'; Much (1904, 70–1) compares this with the German folk tradition, traceable to the fourteenth century, of the *Untersberg*.

Evidence from non-Germanic sources is consistent with the (sometimes tenuous) indications that in Germanic paganism there was a concept of a heavenly plain, associated with one or more trees. Thus the world tree is often stated to grow in the midst of a great meadow; for example, a Mordvin poem (recorded in modern times), which may be taken as exemplifying a widespread concept found across northern Eurasia, begins 'A very great, a great meadow! In the meadow a great hillock, on the hillock an apple tree. Its roots fill the whole earth, its branches fill all heaven, it has covered the sun with its leaves' (Paasonen 1938, 31). Likewise the Yakut tree of life, which heals and rejuvenates man and beast, grows in a meadow beside the dwelling of the first man; the goddess of the tree reveals his fate to him, paralleling the Norse connection of the tree with judgement and fate (Böhtlingk 1851, 82).

In Norse, the name of the god Heimdallr apparently means 'world tree' (*heimr* can mean either 'home' or 'world') — Heimdallr shares characteristics of guardianship with the Scandinavian 'guardian tree' of the home, and is also the guardian of the realm of the gods (see Pipping 1925, 7–9, and Tolley 2009, I, 365–6, 375–6); he may indeed be identified *as* the world tree (in a personal form: see Pipping 1925, 7–49, and 1926, 24–64, 107–24, and Tolley 2009, I, 371–3), as his name seems to indicate. He lives at *Himinbjǫrg*, 'Heaven mountains' (*Grímnismál*, st. 13). The world mountain, which Himinbjǫrg perhaps represents (though the mytheme is not strongly developed in extant Norse sources), is a well-recognised feature of many mythologies (though the idea is not traceable in Old English), where it is often stated to be the place where the world tree grows; for example, the Abakan Tatars believed that a seven-branched birch (representing the shaman's tree of ascent through the worlds) stands on an iron mountain in the middle of the world (Harva 1922, 33). There is some indication of a similar concept in Germanic tradition: apart from Heimdallr's dwelling at Himinbjǫrg, the Saxon world pillar Irminsul (see below) was set up on a hill, Eresburg. The evergreen ash (cf. the world ash tree Yggdrasill) growing on a mountain reported by Strelow (see below) exemplifies a tradition, surviving into Christian times, of a great sacred tree on a mountain, suggesting an origin in a concept of the world tree (Yggdrasill or an equivalent) growing in a similar position. (On the world tree and the mountain, see Tolley 2009, I, 329–30.)

The varying sitings of the world tree, on mountains or in the midst of meadows or open country, demonstrate the adaptability of the mytheme to local environments. It is little wonder that Scandinavia—in particular Norway and Iceland, where our myths primarily originated and were recorded—should tend to place the tree on a mountain, whereas the rolling countryside in which they lived (in part at least) should have predisposed the Mordvins to place it in a great meadow. A *feld*, that is a stretch of open countryside, would appear a natural setting for much of northern England, should its inhabitants have wished to find a site for a world tree. The distinguishing feature which unites all the settings is that the tree is made to stand out—it is not in the middle of a forest, for example, or down in a valley. The rarity of 'heaven' in Germanic names may suggest a connection between Heavenfield and the 'Heaven mountains' of Norse myth, the heavenly aspect setting the site apart as special, with the particularisation, as mountain or field, being dependent on local circumstances.

The *trēow* of victory

The physical emphasis is noticeable in Oswald's deed of raising the cross: he does not—at least in Bede's account—act on a vision, like Constantine, but sets up a tangible cross, made of wood, for all to see and touch. Oswald appears to be appealing to a pagan understanding of things as having power in themselves (as opposed to the official Christian view, that all power resides with God alone).[9] Chaney (1970, 117) argues that the raising of the Heavenfield cross was done 'perhaps in Christian *imitatio* of the cult-pillars, judgement pillars, and tree-cult of Germanic heathenism'. The clearest instance of the cult pillar is found among the continental Saxons. In 772, Charlemagne undertook a campaign in Germany and razed a Saxon sanctuary; the event is recorded in several chronicles, which recount that Charlemagne attacked the fortified site of Eresburg, and destroyed the idol called *Irminsul*.[10] Rudolf of Fulda, writing around 863–5, talks of the worship of *Irminsul* (*Translatio Sancti Alexandri*, 676):

> Frondosis arboribus fontibusque venerationem exhibebant. Truncum quoque ligni non parvae magnitudinis in altum erectum sub divo colebant, patria eum lingua Irminsul appellantes, quod latine dicitur universalis columna, quasi sustinens omnia.

> They gave veneration to leafy trees and to springs. Also they worshipped a trunk of wood of no small size raised up high under the sky, calling it *Irminsul* in their own tongue, which in Latin is 'universalis columna' (universal column), as if sustaining everything.

Widukind, writing a good deal later (around 950) but recalling the oral traditions of his Saxon ancestors, gives a rather garbled account of a particular rite focused on an Irminsul (*Res Gestae Saxonicae* 19–21); an aged warrior Hathagat seizes a war standard:[11]

---

[9] In an interesting essay, Murphy (1992, 205–20) traces the evidence for this idea in the Old Saxon *Heliand*, noting for example how the word *mahtig*, 'mighty', must be understood as 'magic, having innate power', a concept derived from paganism, yet applied by the poet to the most Christian of objects, the bread at the Last Supper.

[10] The accounts are: *Annales Mosellani*, MGH SS XVI, 496; *Annales Petaviani*, MGH SS I, 16; *Annales Laurissenses Maiores*, MGH SS I, 150; *Annales Fuldenses* MGH SS I, 348; the *Annales Einhardi* have a similar account to the *Annales Laurissenses Maiores*, except, following the *Annales Fuldenses*, they call *Irminsul* an *idolum* rather than a *fanum* (MGH SS I, 151); *Annales Laurissenses Minores*, MGH SS I, 117; *Annales Iuvavenses Minores*, MGH SS I, 88.

[11] Leaving aside weaknesses in Widukind's language, the account may be described as garbled in that it is not clear what *sacra sua* refers to exactly—I take it to be the Irminsul itself, which Widukind immediately goes on to describe, without, however, naming it directly: the name is to be inferred from

Hic arripiens signum, quod apud eos habebatur sacrum, leonis atque draconis et desuper aquilae volantis insignitum effigie, quo ostentaret fortitudinis atque prudentiae et earum rerum efficatiam, et motu corporis animi constantiam declarans ait [...]

Seizing a standard, which was held sacred among them, marked with an image of a lion and a dragon and of an eagle flying down from above to show the effect of strength and wisdom and such matters, and demonstrating by the movement of his body the constancy of his mind, he said [...]

He then gives a speech which stirs the Saxons into action, and after a bloody night battle they celebrate:

Mane autem facto ad orientalem portam ponunt aquilam, aramque victoriae construentes secundum errorem paternum sacra sua propria veneratione venerati sunt: nomine Martem, effigie columpnarum imitantes Herculem, loco Solem, quem Graeci appellant Apollinem. Ex hoc apparet aestimationem illorum utcumque probabilem, qui Saxones originem duxisse putant de Graecis, quia Hirmin vel Hermis Graece Mars dicitur; quo vocabulo ad laudem vel ad vituperationem usque hodie etiam ignorantes utimur.

When morning came they placed the eagle-standard at the eastern gate, and constructing an altar to victory they worshipped their own holy things with due veneration, following the error of their fathers: they imitate Mars by the name they give it, Hercules by the pillar form it has, and the sun, whom the Greeks call Apollo, by its location. From this it is clear that the supposition is likely of those who trace the origin of the Saxons to the Greeks, since Hirmin or Hermes is the name of Mars in Greek; in our ignorance we use this word to this day for praising or cursing.

From these accounts it is to be inferred that *Irminsul* was the name of a sacred column, in the form of a large trunk of wood. *Sul* is a column, but *Irmin* has both a general and a particular meaning. It meant 'great', probably in the sense of endowed with magic power (see Tolley 2009, I, 277–8), whence Rudolf

the incorrect identification of Hirmin with Hermes (which is followed by the further incorrect identification of Hermes with Mars—an identification which, however, probably indicates that a Germanic war god was worshipped in this case). Widukind also fails to clarify the relationship between the eagle-standard and the Irminsul.

inferred the meaning 'universalis columna', which was viewed as 'sustaining everything', an understanding paralleled in Sámi analogues (see below). However, the sense of the word could also have been 'column of Irmin': Irmin—or an earlier form of the word—was one of the three sons of Mannus, 'Man', the ancestral founders of the Germanic peoples; this is to be inferred from the name *Herminones*, assigned by Tacitus to one of these three divisions (*Germania*, ch. 2). Thus the Saxons may have looked upon the *Irminsul* not merely as the 'universal column', but also as the embodiment of their demi-god ancestor; compare how the first man in Norse is called *Askr*, 'Ash', probably to identify him as a branch/twig of the world ash tree, with which Irminsul, as representing the 'world pillar', is to be associated. Compare also Jordanes' statement (*De Origine Actibusque Getarum*, ch. 13) that the Goths worshipped their ancestors and called them *Ansis* (cognate with Old Norse *æsir*, 'gods'), a word that, even if perhaps not formally derived from **ansaz*, 'beam' (Lorenz 1984, 95; see de Vries 1977, *s.v.* 'áss' for the etymologies), would nonetheless have evoked such a connection.

It is probable that the image of the Irminsul as a support of the cosmos is related to the supporting post of the ancient German house: thus the house-post constitutes a microcosm of the world tree/pillar. Hertlein (1910, 75) comments:[12]

> I believe the architecture of the Germanic house has had an influence on the concept of the *Irminsul*. Just as the house commonly had one central column, called *firstsul* ['roof column'] in the *Lex Baiuvariorum* 10:6–7 [*MGH Leges* III, 308], and by Notker, Boethius 5 called *magansul* ['powerful column'], so too one imagined a similar column in the middle of the world [seen as a] home, supporting the roof of heaven.

The house post as a microcosm of the world pillar appears to be widespread: for example, the notion is found as far afield as among the Inuit and in India (where the house post was

---

[12] Original: 'Auf die Vorstellung von der Irminsul hat, glaube ich, die Bauart des germanischen Hauses Einfluß gehabt. Wie dieses vielfach eine Mittelsäule hatte, firstsul in der *Lex Baiuvariorum* 10:6–7, bei Notker, Boetius 5, magansul genannt, so stellte man sich auch in der Mitte des Weltgebäudes und das Himmelsdach stützent eine solche Säule vor.' Graff (1834–42, s.vv.) glosses *first-* or *furstsul* as 'Hauptsäule' and *magansul* as 'Kraftsäule'; *first* is 'culmen, summitas montis', the top, ridge, roof, ceiling of a chamber.

called the 'kingpost') (Eliade 1972, 261; Coomaraswamy 1940, 58–9); also comparable is the Norse *barnstokkr*, 'child stock', a tree growing in the midst of (and it seems supporting) the hall of the Vǫlsungar (*Vǫlsunga saga*, ch. 2). A coincidence of something akin to house pillars and pillars dedicated to the thunder god occurs in Norse in the form of the *ǫndvegissúlur*, 'high-seat posts'. These were carved wooden posts forming the supports of the high seats; tradition relating to the time of the Icelandic settlement asserts that the Norsemen took them from their homes when they moved, and, as they neared the land they were to settle, they threw the posts overboard. The new house would be built where the pillars were found. The most extensive account occurs in *Eyrbyggja saga*, ch. 4, which claims that the posts were also used in temples: on one of the posts an image of Þórr was carved, and *reginnaglar*, 'divine nails', were also found in the posts. The area of the temple marked by the posts was sanctuary, indicating a protective role of the god manifested through the pillars.

The implication is that house pillars—and the *Irminsul* based upon them—were hypostatised (see de Vries 1956–7, §499); de Vries suggests that Old Norse *áss*, 'god' < **ansu* derives from the Indo-European root meaning 'breath' (de Vries 1977, *s.v.* 'áss 1'): Coomaraswamy (1940, 58–9) notes how in India breath is equated with the 'kingpost': this suggests that the Germanic evidence relates to an ancient Indo-European heritage of belief.

In terms of its setting, the site of the only locatable Irminsul on a hilltop (Eresburg) suggests a linked concept of the world mountain, or, as noted above, more generally somewhere distinctive and visible.[13] An *ad hoc* Irminsul might also be raised after a battle.[14]

[13] The site of this *Irminsul* is known relatively accurately: Löwe (1941, 3) locates it at Peterskirche on the Obermansberg; Müller (1975, 93 n. 14) adduces evidence that there was once an *Irminsul* near Hildesheim at the village Irmenseul.

[14] Also to be linked with the *Irminsul* are the Jupiter pillars, erected in the first couple of centuries ad in the Roman occupied area of Germany. Hertlein (1910, 70) considered these to represent Germanic beliefs in their carvings, but Müller (1975, esp. 49) has shown that they are in fact Gallic, and are to be regarded as honouring the god Tarannis, the god of thunder (cf. the association of Þórr, the god of thunder, with the 'high-seat pillars'; see below). Whilst a Germanic origin is not now accepted, the Germanic tribes living in this border

In the animals depicted on it (with the exception of the lion), the *aquila* seized by the warriors before battle, and set up in the east afterwards, parallels the Norse world tree as described in *Grímnismál*, st. 32, where an eagle sits on its top, and a dragon Níðhǫggr lurks at its base. The Anglo-Saxon standard from Sutton Hoo is endowed with a stag at its top, another animal associated in *Grímnismál* with the world tree. The representations of the world tree from Siberia, such as the Dolgan 'pillars', adorned with eagles on their top (Harva 1922, 16), are sometimes staffs rather than full-scale trees. In view of the features of the *aquila* which link it with the world support represented also by the Irminsul, it is conceivable that the standard was set up as part of the column itself, and that it constitutes one of the *sacra* worshipped on this occasion (it is described as *sacrum* on its first appearance).

Is there any evidence from Anglo-Saxon England for an equivalent to the Irminsul? We have little direct testimony in literary sources, but excavations at Yeavering in Bernicia have unveiled a series of holes which housed enormous posts, and these have been persuasively linked with the general notion of the world tree by Bintley (2015, 28–43). Yeavering was a royal gathering place, abandoned after Eadwine's demise in 633/634, so its structure and workings would have been familiar to many of Oswald's Northumbrian followers. It appears to have been a successor to an earlier, British, cult site, and the wooden pillars replaced earlier ones, possibly of stone: we see here the sort of appropriation of earlier native traditions by the Germanic settlers that I am suggesting took place under Oswald's aegis (with the additional involvement of imbuing these traditions with Christian understandings). The posts at Yeavering were external to the halls; one hall appears to have been dedicated to use as a church, which resulted in the removal of the post, suggesting a reuse of a specific cult site for the new religion (*ibid.*, 41). Bintley argues that the later free-standing crosses of Anglo-Saxon England were a Christian version of the earlier

area between Celts and Germans are likely to have been influenced by these cult objects. The Jupiter pillars were all demolished by the fifth century, as a result of Christian reaction against pagan worship; the Irminsul was destroyed three centuries later, but was doubtless of ancient origin.

cult pillars, which would represent an act of acculturation rather than replacement.

The purpose of the pillars and the religious attitude towards them are not wholly clear. That they had some cult significance is, however, likely, especially given evidence such as the laws of the Northumbrian priests, from *c.* 1020, which forbid any enclosure 'abutan stan oððe treow oððe wille' ('around a tree, stone or well'), suggesting that pagan practices focused on a *trēow* still continued centuries after the conversion (Bintley 2015, 122). Bintley (*ibid.*, 38–9) cites an example from the Rhineland *Lex Ribuaria*, from the 620s, where legal disputes could be resolved at the king's *staffolus*, a post beside a dais. One of the most notable features at Yeavering is the theatre, a raised seating area focused on the king's throne, behind which stood a large *stapol* or pillar (diagram *ibid.*, 38). Clearly, the *stapol* was associated with decision-making and authority (we might compare how the gods *dœma*—adjudicate—at the world tree in Norse), and it is difficult to avoid the conclusion that a pillar stretching up to the heavens acted as a manifestation of the cosmic support that imposed order on the world. The post therefore acted as a concrete symbol of royal order and authority, and the king was a personification of the cosmic order represented in the *stapol*. The post was therefore a form of sceptre, and sceptres such as that of Sutton Hoo may have been seen as small versions of such pillars (though we can make no direct link between them in terms of archaeological or literary evidence).

When Penda raised the head and arms of Oswald on stakes, he was making a statement of his own authority: the stakes were surely comparable with those at Yeavering, and symbolised the king's cosmic rule, overthrowing his enemies. We may find a similar act described in *Beowulf*, lines 925–7, where the monstrous enemy Grendel's arm and shoulder are hung under the roof of Heorot, and Hrothgar addresses the assembly from the *stapol*, a word which appears to indicate the combined dais and post; Bintley (*ibid.*, 39) suggests that the limb was in fact attached to the top of the *stapol*, in line with Penda's act. The *stapol* would therefore reach up to the top of the hall; as the hall could symbolically act as a microcosm of the world, this would mean the *stapol* acted as a world pillar, as it no doubt did when placed outside as at Yeavering, and it thus becomes comparable with the Norse high-seat pillars (the high seat being a focus of authority in the way the dais was).[15] Attaching Grendel's body parts high on the *stapol* would indicate the imposition of regal cosmic order, through the king's agent Beowulf, on the monstrous and chaotic world. Like the Irminsul, therefore, the royal *stapol* acted as a symbol of victory.

The tree as universal sustainer

In that Irminsul 'sustained everything' it clearly represented the world support, and the same is implicit in the posts of Yeavering; we may compare the pillars of the Sámi, described in the eighteenth century, for example in the following account by Jens Kildal (Reuterskiöld 1910, 94):[16]

> Annually, every autumn, there is sacrificed by pagan Lapps a reindeer ox, or another animal, to Maylmenradien [World Ruler], so that, since he is the Lapps' highest god, he should not let the world collapse, and so that he should give them luck with the reindeer; and at the sacrificial altar was set up in his honour a stick with a cleft in the end, called Maylmen stytto [world prop], with which he is to support the world. This stick is to be smeared over with the blood of the reindeer ox that is sacrificed to him.

Other accounts speak of a tree rather than a pillar as being involved in the sacrifice to the same world-supporting god (for example, Kildal 1807, 473), indicating that world pillar and world tree were largely interchangeable manifestations of the mythological world support. This is clear too from the way the world support is represented: for example, the Altaic shaman ascended to heaven via a notched birch tree from which

---

[15] Bintley (2015, 31 n. 20) also notes the huge door posts of a hall excavated at Lyminge, and contemporary with Yeavering; door posts also hold up a hall (in this case on the north and south sides), and may be seen as a variant of the *stapol* or the high-seat pillars, but with the additional symbolism of the threshold, the passage from one world to another horizontally.

[16] Original: 'Der offres af afgudiske lapper, aarlig, hvert höst, en oxe af reyn, eller andet fæe, til *Maylmenradien* fordj, at saasom hand er lappernes överste gud, hand da ikke skal lode verden nedfalde, og at hand skal give dem lykke til reyn; og ved ofre alteret settes ham til ære en stytte med en klift i enden, kaldet *Maylmen stytto*, som hand skal opstytte verden med, hvilken stytte skal være over-smurt med den oxes blod, som bliver ham ofret.'

the lower branches had been removed, making it resemble a pillar (Harva 1922, 31); the Dolgans used a pillar in their rituals, but this pillar was sometimes represented by a branched tree (Harva 1922, 33; 1933, 30–2): the cosmic aspects of the pillar are clear—it was called *tüspät turū*, 'the never-collapsing pillar', and its prototype stood before the dwelling of the High God; it culminated in a covering, representing the sky (Harva 1922, 15), and on the covering sat an eagle.

The Khanty set up a pillar, representative of the world pillar, in their villages, and prayed to it thus (Harva 1933, 30; text and German translation Karjalainen 1975, 127–8):[17]

> Seven-notched elevated man, highest god, my father, my three-sides-protecting man-father, my three-sides-watching man-[dear]-father; on the earth inhabited by my iron-pillar father, on the unsullied earth, at the foot of the holy tree I place a bloody animal as an animal sacrifice, I place a bloody animal [as] an animal sacrifice [...]

Another aspect of the pillar, as a watchful guardian, is apparent here: it assumes the same role as the guardian tree (*vårdträd*) of Scandinavian folk tradition, which protected the welfare of the farm or house where it grew (Olrik and Ellekilde 1926, 229–41); in some areas nearly every house had its *vårdträd*, usually ash, elm or linden. It was regarded as animate and in control of the welfare of the household, and offerings of milk or ale would be made to it (*ibid.* 231):[18]

> 'O God's spirit' they said on the farm Helle in Undalen, Vestagder, when they held out a bowl of ale to the farm's guardian tree. 'I grant you this, I give you this, my sister' they said in Sætesdalen, when they held out the cow's first drops of milk to the guardian tree after calving.

---

[17] My translation is from the German; I omit the Khanty original; the German reads: 'Siebenkerbiger erhabener Mann, höchster Gott, mein Vater, mein drei Seiten schützender Mann-Vater, mein drei Seiten bewachender Mann-[lieber-]Vater; auf die von meinem Eisensäulen-Vater bewohnte heilige Erde, auf die unbefleckte Erde, zum Fuss des heiligen Baumes stelle ich blutiges Tier als Tieropfer, stelle ich blutendes Tier [als] Tieropfer [...]'

[18] Original: '"O du Guds vætt" sagde man på gården Helle i Undalen, Vestagder, når man hældte en skål øl ud ved gårdens vættetræ. "Jeg under dig det, jeg giver dig, søster min" sagde de i Sætesdalen, når de hældte koens förste mælkedråber ud på vættetræet efter kælvingen.'

To fell the tree brought calamity; thus a man who did so heard the tree sing one night how he too would suffer, and his whole establishment burnt down.

De Vries (1956–7, §249) gives some instances of tree-worship among Germanic peoples, notably the oak of the Saxons of Geismar. However, it is the temple complex at Uppsala in Sweden, overlooked by a great tree which no doubt symbolised the world tree, that provides perhaps the most striking instance in Germanic paganism of sacrifice focused on a tree. Adam of Bremen, writing in the eleventh century, describes in his *Descriptio Insularum Aquilonis* (ch. 27) how in the course of a nine-day festival seventy-two animals and nine men were hanged as sacrifices in the trees of the grove at the site. The purpose of the sacrifices was clearly to maintain the might and well-being (the *ár*, good seasons) of the realm whose cult centre was the Uppsala temple.

As a world *vårdträd* guarding the life of the cosmos, the world tree is associated with fate: thus it was at the ash tree Yggdrasill that the gods gathered each day to *dœma*, to adjudicate on the affairs of the world. Bede (*Historia Ecclesiastica* ii.2, pp. 134–5) tells how the meeting between Augustine and the British bishops took place at 'Augustinæs ac' ('Augustine's oak'),[19] suggesting that the idea of counsel, judgement being associated with trees was familiar to the English of Oswald's time; in later Anglo-Saxon sources trees are frequently found as sites of gatherings, for example hundred moots, where decisions are made (see Bintley 2015, 70–8). Fate is associated with the Norse tree in particular through the presence at its foot of the spring (*brunnr*) of the maiden Urðr, 'Fate', responsible for assigning men's fates (*Vǫluspá*, st. 19–20). Near to Heavenfield was *Denisesburna*, where the battle actually took place; *burna* in English place names generally means 'stream', but it is cognate with, and originally of the same meaning, as Norse *brunnr*. Bede makes much of the fatefulness of the name Heavenfield, as presaging events that were fulfilled in the battle there; a pagan understanding

[19] The site of this was on the border of the land of the Hwicce: hence the tree is associated with boundaries, a feature noted also with reference to Heavenfield, set beside the Wall. Wallace-Hadrill (1988, 218–19) shows that Bede's information on the meeting derived from early-seventh-century Canterbury written sources.

might also naturally associate the name of the battle site with fate, if the English shared the Norse understanding of springs, especially when somehow associated with the world tree, as bestowers of fate.

In the seventeenth century Strelow recorded traditions of an evergreen ash (compare the evergreenness of the world ash tree Yggdrasill), purportedly historical, in his edition of Gotlandish Chronicles (Strelow 1633, 215):[20]

> The year 1452: Lord Ivar Axelsøn had the ash tree moved which stood on Bahrebierg ['Needle Hill', presumably named after the *Bare Aske*], green just as well in winter as in summer, called to this day the Needle Ash, so that it should stand at Visborg castle, but it withered straight after. And in the same place where there is deemed to be great sanctity, a great oak cross was raised on the hill, to which they made their sacrifices when their sheep or cattle got lost, and they would come straight back to them again.

This account illustrates how a pagan cult around what appears to have been a representative world tree could be replaced by one centring on the cross—as appears to have been engineered at Heavenfield. The tree appears as a guardian (of flocks), and is thus to be compared with the *vårdträd*. The cross clearly replaces the tree as the object of offerings. This is comparable with the offerings made to the guardian tree, and perhaps alluded to in the complex punning epithet *heiðvanr* ('used to honour') applied to Yggdrasill in *Vǫluspá*, st. 27. The word also appears to bear the meanings 'used to the bright sky' and 'used to the bright mead' (with reference to the spring of mead at its foot) (Dronke 1997, comm. to *Vǫluspá*, st. 27/3, 22/1).

---

[20] Original: 'Aar 1452, lod Herr Ifuer Axelsøn flytte it Esketræ, som stod paa Bahrebierg grønt, saa vel om Vinter som om Sommer, kaldis endnu denne Dag Bare Asken, at det skulde staa paa Viszborrig Slot, men er strax efter visznet. Oc paa samme sted formeentis stor Helligdom at være, bleff opreist et stort Ege Kors paa Bierget, til huilcket de gjorde deris Offer, naar deris Faaer eller Fæ var bortkommen, oc strax skulde være kommet dennem tilhænde igien.'

Oswald's trēow at Heavenfield

If Oswald's English followers, then, shared any of the religious traditions of their Saxon or Norse cousins, and had an understanding of the royal *stapol* such as was found at Yeavering, what might they have seen in the cross-*trēow* raised at Heavenfield? The support of the cosmos could be represented as either a living tree or as a timber post, no doubt with somewhat different emphases in the varying circumstances of use. The support was a focus of offerings: hence the cross, on which Christ was sacrificed, and before which Oswald dedicated himself, would have seemed natural in pagan terms. The Christian notion of this sacrifice being for salvation, however, would have been meaningless to the pagan mind: the offerings were to achieve practical goals such as successful harvests (*ár* in Norse terms), which might be realised on a higher level as successful rule by a king, which is precisely what Oswald wished to obtain (even if, by doing so, his greater aim was to bring salvation to his people). The world support was a watchful guardian, on a macrocosmic level, of the guardian tree of the homestead; thus Oswald's followers may have seen the cross as guarding them in the coming contest. Most traditions where world trees are found personify the tree to some degree; this appears to have been the case in Norse, where Heimdallr probably represents a personified *vårdträd* writ large. We do not see this directly in the case of Oswald, yet *The Dream of the Rood*, an early form of which was carved into the eighth-century Ruthwell Cross, shows a sensibility to such thinking, for the cross is very much personified and indeed takes on the persona of the hero who is crucified on it: Oswald, grasping his life-giving symbol of victory, may have seemed to his followers an embodiment of the cosmic support he raised before them, just as the king, visible to all in front of the *stapol* at Yeavering, was a personfication or channel of the cosmic power symbolised in the *stapol*. The *trēow*—whether living or in the form of a *stapol*—was a place of fate: it was where gods (and men in royal assembly) gathered to pass judgement, and it was the source of men's fortunes. Oswald's raising of the cross would surely have seemed a fateful act, invoking the power of the divine symbol to secure success.

The timber column, which the cross would have been seen as, partakes in the wider symbolism just outlined, but it particularly emphasises victory, as something set up for the occasion, which realises the principle of cosmic support in action through battle: to secure victory is to effect the maintenance of this cosmic order. It may be inferred from Widukind's account that an Irminsul (or a sacred symbol of it) would be raised after a victory. In raising the cross *before* battle and venerating its sanctity *propria veneratione*, Oswald proclaims his faith in victory (through the power of the cross) even when it looks least likely, being accompanied, as Bede says, by only a small force of men: in other words, he is deliberately instilling confidence in his men by anticipating an act that their pagan understanding would lead them to expect should be carried out only after victory, at least if we infer the evidence relating to the Irminsul to have had wider relevance. This mirrors the account of Adomnán, where sure victory is revealed to Oswald before the battle. The Norse and Saxon pillars were clearly channels of divine power, and this is what Oswald made of his cross, a sort of Christian metamorphosis of the Irminsul, raised in the open on an elevated plain, that would bring about the order of his divinely sanctioned rule. The Irminsul was also implicitly associated with ancestry, as were the Norse pillars, which marked a family's continuity of ownership and right to control over land, and the Irish *bile*: hence raising the pillar was to declare one's ancestral right to the rule of the land, as Oswald was doing against the usurping invader Cadwallon.

Eagles do not enter the scene of the cross at Heavenfield, yet tradition brought in an ambivalent raven/eagle in association with the antithesis of the Heavenfield cross, the Oswestry stake: a raven-like bird seeking carrion takes fleshly booty from the stake, and the stake is replaced with a wizened tree; the bird is intimated to be really some sort of eagle, a nobler species (and one which, in Latin at least, has an implicit connection with victory through the *aquila* as a war standard), and the wizened tree is transformed, burgeoning into youthful growth. A subtle interplay of motifs is at work, by which traditional mythemes of the pillar and tree, the raven and eagle, are manipulated to emphasise an essentially Christian message of Oswald's life-giving sanctity.

The imagery of the cross as a tree (in particular the Tree of Life—through Christ's death *vita redditur mundo*, as the Jarrow cross proclaims) has been a commonplace in Christian tradition from the earliest days (see for example *Reallexicon für Antike und Christentum*, II, *s.v.* 'Baum'): it is certainly one that Oswald could have exploited, revealing the cross as a victorious new form of the traditional Tree of Life, known both from pagan and biblical tradition. In the centuries following Oswald's victory Northumbria blossomed with carved crosses, many stone examples of which survive; one of them, the Ruthwell Cross, is, as noted, inscribed with a version of the great poem *The Dream of the Rood*, in which a personified cross recounts its biography—and clearly identifies itself as a *trēow*. Cramp (1965, 9) comments on the limited iconography of the Northumbrian crosses: the mostpart by far of the decoration shows a propensity to present the cross as the Tree of Life (see Collingwood 1927, ch. 6, on the development of the Tree of Life motif in the carved crosses). The Christian background is undeniable: and yet the particular focus surely illustrates a predisposition derived from the pagan past, a fruitful manipulation and joining of traditions that may have begun with Oswald himself.[21]

Adomnán's account agrees with Bede's in emphasising how something of an almost supernatural nature, from Oswald's perspective, took place on the eve of battle, which assured him of victory, but it contrasts with Bede's in the absence of the cross, and hence the wider, associated imagery of the *trēow*. Yet it is striking how Columba is described as an angelic figure towering up like a pillar to heaven, protecting all with his mantle, and bestowing victory: although the connotations are primarily Christian, both the image and the action are comparable to aspects of the traditional protective Germanic world tree, which it has been suggested in part lay behind the imagery of the Heavenfield cross. It is probably impossible to reconcile the different traditions of the eve of battle, but they appear to have played with variant motifs of a powerful conduit of divine power reaching between heaven and earth and focused on Oswald.

---

[21] The postulated development of originally pagan cult pillars into carved crosses is discussed by Bintley (2015, 44–9), who regards the typical foliate design of stone crosses as indicating that they were in origin a form of *trēow*.

The trēow as níðstǫng

Oswald seems to have been content to confine his offering to a bloodless sacrifice of prayer before battle: not so the obdurate pagan Penda. As Penda had been in alliance with Cadwallon, whom Oswald defeated at Heavenfield, he may be assumed to have known of Oswald's act of raising a cross. At Oswestry, Penda celebrated his victory over the Christian king by excising his hands and head, and raising them on stakes ('in stipitibus': Bede, *Historia Ecclesiastica* III.12, pp. 252–3)—a sort of mock crucifixion. The display of animal or human parts on stakes, the *heafod stocc*, 'head stake', is found in Anglo-Saxon sources (surveyed briefly in Bintley 2015, 37), but this appears to be an act of the most spiteful contumely on the part of the pagan king: in Norse tradition, raising a pole with someone's features on it—a *níðstǫng*, 'pole of disgrace'—was the greatest form of insult; two notable examples of the raising of the *níðstǫng* are found in *Egils saga*, ch. 57, and *Vatnsdœla saga*, ch. 34, which reads:

> Jǫkull skar karlshǫfuð á súluendanum ok reist á rúnar með ǫllum þeim formála, sem fyrr var sagðr. Síðan drap Jǫkull meri eina, ok opnuðu hana hjá brjóstinu ok fœrðu á súluna ok létu horfa heim á Borg.

> Jǫkull carved a man's head on the end of the pole and inscribed it with runes with all the spell spoken of before. Then Jǫkull killed a mare, and they opened it at the breast and placed it on the post and had it turned towards home at Borg.

Penda raises a pole with not merely Oswald's features but his actual head on it, signifying the disgrace in which he wished to cast his memory, as well as mocking his Christian beliefs. Bede does not specify, but we may well believe that Oswald's features were turned towards his own realm of Northumbria, to direct the 'divine power' his name conveyed against his own realm, in the way Jǫkull did against Borg.[22]

---

[22] Kings were regarded as being endowed with superior powers, which encapsulated the strength of their realm; this was no doubt a universal feature, but examples from Scandinavia are numerous. Chaney (1970, 113–16) gathers a number of cases where a dire emergency, such as failure of the crops or famine, resulted in the sacrifice of the king: we might mention for example Dómaldi, sacrificed for good harvests (*ár*) by his people (*Ynglinga*

Chaney (1970, 119) argues that by mounting his remains on stakes Penda was offering Oswald as a sacrifice to Óðinn, and opines that 'No more plausible explanation has [...] been offered'. The *níðstǫng*, however, does seem more plausible: Penda's point is to insult Oswald, and (probably) to turn his power through ritual means against his own kingdom; there is no need to view it as a sacrifice as such, and the point (admitted by Chaney) that sacrifices call for a living victim speaks against this interpretation.

However, this is not to exclude the possibility of an *allusion* to Óðinnic sacrifice, whether intended by Penda or discerned within folk tradition. The raising on stakes mocks the sacrifice of Christ on the cross, as noted, but the deathly stakes (trees with their life removed) also mock the life-giving, sustaining world tree that was found represented in cult, for example at Uppsala, and on which sacrifices were made, in commemoration in particular of the self-sacrifice of Óðinn himself on the mythical tree of *Hávamál*, st. 138. The Christian king had, perhaps, attempted to arrogate some of the symbolism or power of the pagan sacrificial but power-enhancing world tree by ascribing it to the cross of Christ, but now Penda had turned this power against him through symbolically converting his cross of victory into a *níðstǫng*.

The eagle

The bird that, according to Reginald of Durham, seized Oswald's remains is described as a type of *corvinus*, yet as resembling an eagle. The type of *corvinus* in question was probably a raven: this was the archetypal carrion bird of battle, and would be expected to appear to feast on the corpses. The raven has a significant role as a messenger and servant to Oswald in twelfth-century Bavarian bridal-quest tales of the king (discussed by Jansen 1995). The relationship between these tales and Reginald of Durham's

saga, ch. 15), Óláfr trételgja, burnt in his hall as a sacrifice to Óðinn because of bad harvests (*Ynglinga saga*, ch. 43), or Vikarr, sacrificed to Óðinn for fair winds (*Gautreks saga*, ch. 7). However, it is not clear that Oswald's supposed sacrifice was intended to achieve anything of this sort, and defeat in battle against an enemy is different from sacrifice of a king by his own people.

contemporary account is unclear (Jansen 1995, 235). However, Jansen concludes (*ibid.*, 239) that the raven was a survival of the cult of Woden—in Norse, Óðinn had two ravens that acted as gatherers of news, and hence intermediaries between earth and the realm of the gods (*Grímnismál*, st. 20; Tolley 2009, I, 316–17, 336, 340), a notion developed into the ravens as intermediaries between the lovers in the German tale. Something like a dove might be expected in this role; the presence of the raven implies continuity from earlier traditions where Oswald was viewed as a Woden-like figure.[23]

Yet Reginald's *corvinus* is verbally transformed into an eagle, a more noble bird that is associated particularly with the world tree in Old Norse (*Grímnismál*, st. 32; cf. Tolley 2009, I, 340, on eagles more widely in world trees), as well as with Óðinn, who flees as an eagle to bear away the sacred mead of poetry (Snorri, *Skáldskaparmál*, ch. G58; cf. Tolley 2009, I, 443, comparing Indian parallels). Óðinn's assumption of eagle form in the myth of the mead of poetry equates him with the eagle atop the world tree: the all-important mead is equivalent to the tree itself as a symbol of cosmic vitality and order (Tolley 2009, I, 445), and of course a spring of mead is found below the tree, as discussed below, further reinforcing the symbolic equivalence. Just as the mead and tree are symbolically (though not, it should be said, figuratively) equivalent, so too, it might be said, is the eagle: the bird represents the power of the tree in action, fighting off the destructive serpent at its roots, and retrieving the mead in which its power is encapsulated (taking the mead spring to bear the same significance as the mead Óðinn retrieves from the giants). There is no eagle at Heavenfield: yet, to a degree, Oswald himself might be seen as taking the role of the eagle as the personification of the active and defensive force of the world tree. Once Oswald as an active person is removed by his death, a place emerges in the legend for a sort of eagle, taking a very active part in the development of the saint's cult.

---

[23] There was a strong continental cult of St Oswald from early days (as outlined by Clemoes 1983); it is likely that the recorded English cult, as witnessed in particular by Reginald, was in part a result of interchange with its continental counterparts, but this is too complex a topic to enter into here.

Fig. 21. Eagle and waterfowl from the early-seventh-century Sutton Hoo purse lid (British Museum, approx. 3:1).

Reginald's rather comic presentation of the *corvinus* struggling with Oswald's arm and having to take a rest in the tree, then dropping its prize, such that Reginald thinks it must rather have been more like an eagle to have managed even this, in fact serves to transform Oswald from a mere fallen warrior, his corpse consumed by a crow or raven, into a king with divine power, implicitly associated with the support of the cosmos in the form of the world tree, of which the stakes form a travesty, an inversion that nonetheless finds symbolic restitution in the form of the newly envigorated ash.

That the king could be symbolised by the eagle, or at least some form of raptor, is indicated in the Sutton Hoo burial finds; the burial is almost precisely contemporary with Oswald's accession. Symbols of royalty are rife in the burial, and take many forms (the stag on top of the sceptre, recalling the royal hall Hart (Heorot) in *Beowulf*, along with a whetstone, whetting swords but also warriors, might be mentioned): it is within this context that the eagle symbols have to be interpreted. On the purse we find an eagle seizing a waterfowl (Fig. 21), a demonstration of royal power; on the shield we find separate depictions of an eagle and a dragon, recalling the archetypal enmity between these beasts, such as is found in association with the world tree in Norse; the great buckle has a series of intertwined birds and beasts, with the eagle clearly depicted at the top, then with further somewhat ambiguous animal representations below, along with serpents and what is probably a dragon at the bottom. There can be little doubt that the king buried at Sutton Hoo symbolised his rule over the chaotic world in the form of the (elevated) eagle (or perhaps raven); he is hardly likely to have been alone in espousing this imagery at this time.

The divine king

Thacker (1995, 100) notes that 'There is, perhaps, more than a grain of truth in the traditional view that the origins of devotion to Oswald lie as much in Germanic attitudes to kings and to heroic deaths in battle as in the teachings of the church'. He notes, for example, that the division of the king's body and the separate interment of parts (the head at Lindisfarne, the hands and arms at Bamburgh, the rest at Bardney monastery and thence to Gloucester) was against current Catholic practice (*ibid.*, 101); the interment of his head at Lindisfarne, the spiritual capital of Northumbria close to the royal court at Bamburgh, established a perpetual presence of divinely blessed kingship at the centre of the realm (*ibid.*, 102). Plenty of evidence for reverence of the head among Celtic peoples could be adduced (see Ross 1959 for a survey), but this is a notion that can also be paralleled from Scandinavia, notably, as Chaney (1970, 119) points out, in the case of Hálfdan the Black (*Hálfdanar saga ins svarta*, ch. 9), who was described as *ársælstr*, 'most blessed in affording good seasons', and whose body was divided up and sent to the four quarters of his realm to provide good seasons (*ár*) to the kingdom he had ruled. We find in this, as in other aspects of the cult of Oswald, a feature that reflected the concerns and cult interests of both the indigenous population of Britain and the Anglo-Saxons as culturally Germanic.

The sacred spring and the king's head

Thacker (1995, 102) notes the widespread association of Oswald with holy wells, for example at Oswestry, Elvet, Winwick, Warton, Astbury, Kirkoswald, Grasmere, Burneside, possibly Cathcart, and Heavenfield (near turret 25b). Holy wells might be thought of as 'Celtic', but to avoid begging the question, it would be more appropriate to say that holy wells are found prolifically in Britain, and are often associated with heads: for example, a common motif is the head that rises from a spring and asks a girl to comb its hair (Simpson 1962). From this it is reasonable to infer that the cult of Oswald, in which his head plays a prominent role, was from its inception inveigled in traditional folk belief.

Again, however, we may be encountering a coincidence between indigenous belief and features of Germanic paganism, since the spring or well is intimately associated with the world tree, and with a supernaturally powerful head, in Norse myth. Thus *Vǫluspá*, st. 27–8, depicts a spring beneath the 'holy tree', in which lay Óðinn's eye, a pledge he had given, implicitly for the gaining of greater spiritual foresight. From this spring Mímir drinks mead each day (in other words, he becomes wise). In *Vǫluspá*, st. 45, Óðinn consults the head of Mímr (a variant of Mímir) for advice as the end of the world approaches. In *Vafþrúðnismál*, st. 45, a human couple, Líf and Lífþrasir, shelter in the *holt* (wood or tree — the world tree must surely be intended) of hoard-Mímir, from which they emerge to populate the new world. In *Sigrdrífumál*, st. 13–14, Óðinn 'thinks up' mind-runes from the liquid flowing from the skull of Heiðdraupnir, 'Dripper of bright [mead]', and from the horn of Hoddrofnir, 'Hoard opener'; he stands on a hill when Mímr's head first speaks wisdom. One character appears to lie behind all these descriptions: Mímr, whose head resides in the spring of mead at the world tree and utters wisdom; the spring, like the tree itself, represents spiritual power and rejuvenation, reflected in Mímr's tree offering shelter for the rejuvenating couple of the new world. The uttering of fate from the spring of the world tree is also affirmed in *Vǫluspá*, st. 19–20, where three maidens emerge from it and lay down men's fortunes. (For further discussion of these myths see Tolley 2009, I, 381–3.)

Although Bede's account lacks the spring of wisdom at Heavenfield, Oswald receives spiritual guidance at his *trēow* that determines his fate, as does Óðinn. It is not spoken by a detached head (in Adomnán's version, a spirit being utters it, however), yet tradition fills this gap by ascribing supernatural powers to Oswald's own head after his martyrdom. Oswald stands on the rise of Heavenfield as he first hears (following Adomnán—though he does not specify the place) or proclaims this spiritual guidance, as did Óðinn when he first heard Mímr's head speak (and, we are to understand, proclaims what he heard). Oswald and his small band of followers (in Christian terms, implicitly a metatype of the Apostles with Christ) huddle at the *trēow* he raises in the midst of his shattered kingdom, before marching forth to bring about a new world order, now filled with the message of the Gospel, a sort of Christian version of the myth of Líf and Lífþrasir sheltering in hoard-Mímir's tree, from which they set forth to people the new world.

Exploiting the mythological landscape

I have attempted to illustrate some of the possible interplay between traditional pagan ideas and the Christianity that Oswald and some of his followers were committed to. Bede writes a hundred years after the events, at a time when Christianity was far more deeply established and when, it seems, paganism could more readily simply be ignored. But the interweaving of paganism and Christianity in the early days of the conversion must have been more complex than Bede indicates; I have tried to trace some of the ways of thought of those brought up in paganism that Oswald may have exploited in his moves to bring Christianity into the hearts of his people. Other aspects of the legend certainly represent the development of the cult of the saint, but they nonetheless build on a symbolism reflecting a conflation of Christian and folk (originally pagan) elements.

It appears, then, that the setting, on the 'heavenly field', for Oswald's declaration of faith in the cross, assuring his subsequent victory in battle, mirrors a mythological landscape focused on the world tree/pillar, a symbol of support, sustenance and guardianship which he deliberately replaces with the cross—a Christian symbol with a very similar symbolism. The site is associated—by Bede, but also probably in pagan tradition—with a *praesagium*, fateful foretellings, which finds its fulfilment in this divinely ordained victory: in Norse tradition fate is associated specifically with a spring of Urðr, and Oswald won his battle at the stream of Denisesburna near to Heavenfield, while a sacred spring takes on a prominent role in the cult of his place of martyrdom at Oswestry. Oswald's *trēow* features in the legend in a protean array of forms: as the cross he raises, echoing the great ash tree of Norse myth as well as the Saxon victory pillar, the Irminsul, and the Irish *bile*; as the stakes on which his *disiecta membra* are suspended; as the ash tree which springs up where the remains of his body drop, and possibly as the ash tree commemorating the site of the Heavenfield cross (inferred from Leland's account). Oswald himself appears infused with the power of the tree, and acts almost as a personification of this power, achieving the victory inherent in the tree's nature and becoming the guardian of his land, its *vårdträd* as it were, in person. His martyrdom results in an inversion of the flow of power: the cosmic symbols of tree and spring are infused with vigour and sanctity through their association with the saint— and thus an essentially Christian world view is promulgated using traditional, originally pagan, symbols.

Oswald in many ways emerges as a mediator and transitional being. He was the channel for divine power, in the form of the Christian faith, to spread among his people; raising a cross manifests the vertical channel of this power coming down from heaven, just as the pagan Germanic tree or pillar acted as a connection between the realms of the cosmos. Chronologically he stands at the point of transition between paganism and Christianity in Northumbria, and his victory marked the passing of any hope the British may have had of maintaining control of the Hen Gogledd, their realms in the North. Oswald's liminality is expressed in several ways in the legend. He operated on geographical boundaries: Hadrian's Wall, where Heavenfield is situated, while no longer significant as a political border, marked the ancient boundary, perhaps still of symbolic significance, between the civilised *imperium Romanum*, now being replaced by the *imperium Christianum* (which Oswald's victory achieved for Northumbria), and barbarism; Heavenfield was also roughly on a meaningful contemporary boundary between Anglo-Saxon realms to the east (particularly Bernicia) and British kingdoms to the west (particularly Rheged). His last battle, at Oswestry, was similarly in the Marches, then as now the division between Anglo-Saxon and British cultural areas.

Liminality, which ironically enhances the focal importance of its object, was also a characteristic of the world tree, and the divine beings associated with it, in some of its aspects. Heimdallr, the personal realisation of the tree, lives at Himinbjǫrg 'á himins enda' ('at the edge of heaven'), as Snorri puts it (*Gylfaginning*, ch. 27). The siting reflects Úlfr Uggason's characterisation of the god as 'ragna reinvári', 'guardian of the boundary strip of the divine powers', in *Húsdrápa*, st. 2 (*Skjaldedigtning* B1 128): this is no doubt a traditional view of the god, guarding the *heimr*, 'world/home', of the gods against ingress (see Tolley 2009, I, 375–6; I discuss *Húsdrápa*, st. 2, *ibid.* 393–402). The ingress of the giants into the world of the gods marks the beginning of the apocalyptic era of destruction and rebirth. Oswald himself, or at least the tradition that grew up around him, may have exploited these apocalyptic overtones of the mythological landscape; the battle, as a fulfilment of *praesagia* — recalling Heimdallr's preternatural foresight (*Þrymskviða*, st. 14–16), and his being 'ready with counsel' ('ráðgegninn, *Húsdrápa*, st. 2), just as Oswald was through the raising of his *trēow* — may be compared with the contest at the end of the world which forms the fulfilment of the *rǫk* (effectively the 'unravelling fate') of the gods in Norse, and which results, at least according to *Vǫluspá*, in the rising of a new, purified world, realised for Oswald in the establishment of his Christian realm, cleansed of the ruinous 'giants' led by Cadwallon. The same may be said of the Christian hero Oswald as the dreamer of *The Dream of the Rood* declares of Christ at the conclusion of his poem: it was through the cross that 'heora wealdend cwom, ælmihtig god, þær his eðel wæs' ('their ruler came, Almighty God, to where his homeland lay').

Oswald's Tree

APPENDIX

The conflagration of the hall

In the original published version of this essay I discussed a miracle reported as taking place following Oswald's death (Bede, *Historia Ecclesiastica* III.10, pp. 244–5): a Briton retrieved some earth from the spot where Oswald fell, and hung it on the post of the house he was visiting; the house burnt down, but the post was preserved. I argued that a link might exist with the Norse high-seat pillars, the *ǫndvegissúlur*, associated particularly with Þórr. The pillars were studded with *reginnaglar*, 'divine nails' (*Eyrbyggja saga*, ch. 4; Þórarinn loftunga's *Glælognskviða*, st. 10, composed *c.* 1032: *Skjaldedigtning* B1 300–1), a counterpart to which is found in the Sámi practice recorded by Schefferus (1673, 105), who describes an image of 'Thor': this refers to the Sámi god of thunder Horagalles, whose name derives, no doubt along with associated cult practices, from Old Norse *Þórr karl*: 'they strike into the idol's head a striking nail or spike and a piece of flint, so that Thor shall strike fire with it' ('i afgudabelætens hufrud [sic] slao the en slaonagel eller spiic och itt styke flintsten, thermed Tor skall slao eld'). The *reginnaglar* are most convincingly to be connected within Norse myth with the sliver of whetstone which Þórr bore in his forehead, a chip from the weapon of the giant Hrungnir, which shattered in combat with the god (*Haustlǫng*, st. 19–20: *Skjaldedigtning* B1 18, where the whetstone is described as 'red', suggesting a link with fire; the myth is also recounted in Snorri's *Skáldskaparmál*, ch. 17). Fire—connected with lightning (and hence with the god of thunder)—originating in a spike in the head of the Sámi Thor suggests that the spike in Þórr's forehead may be identifiable mythologically with the North Star (called the 'north nail' in Sámi) at the tip of the world pillar, itself hypostatised in the god Þórr.[24] In Eilífr's *Þórs-drápa*, st. 9 (*Skjaldedigtning* B1 141) Þórr is named *himinsjóli*, usually taken as 'heaven prince' (for example by de Vries 1977, *s.v.* 'sjóli'), but 'heaven pillar' is perhaps a more plausible interpretation;[25] Þórr, addressing a

[24] The north star is called in Sámi *bohinavlle* 'north nail'; other names include *veralden tšuold*, 'world pillar' or *almetšuolda*, 'heaven pillar'; *tšuold* is defined by Lindahl and Öhrling (1780, *s.v.* 'tjuold') thus: '*tjuold, tjuolda*, pole, pole. Polar star, cynosura, North Star. So called, because it remains immobile and fixed. *Wäralden tjuold*, pole or axis of the world.' Similarly, in Estonian, the north star is called 'nail of the north' (*põhja nael*); Harva (1922, 10) notes that the same nomenclature must previously have existed among the Finns, since Lappish *bohinavlle* is borrowed from Finnish; he also notes the Sámi belief that if this nail gave way the sky would collapse. A similar concept is revealed in the names of the North Star found elsewhere in Siberia. The Samoyeds called it 'nail of heaven'; the Koryaks 'nail star'; the Chukchi 'nail star' or 'pole-stuck star'.

[25] *Sjóli* could be an e-grade ablaut form of the root that appears in the o-grade in Gothic *sauls*, 'pillar', and also in Old Norse *súl*, 'pillar' (Davidson 1983, 605; for the ablaut, see Noreen 1970, §166), where the term *himinsjóli* is related to Þórr's role as guardian of the *ǫndvegissúlur*.

219

swelling torrent, declares that 'veiztu ef þú vex, at þá vex mér ásmegin jafnhátt upp sem himinn' ('you know that if you swell, then my *ásmegin* (divine power) will swell up as high as heaven', *Skáldskaparmál*, ch. 18). In a contest with giants recounted in *Þórsdrápa*, st. 18 (*Skjaldedigtning* Bı 143) Þórr makes use of 'fire' (in the form of molten metal) already present in a hall, casting it down through the house-post and on through the hall's master Geirrøðr. It seems reasonable to conclude that Þórr was viewed as personifying the world pillar, from the summit of which fire was struck (lightning strikes), and that the North Star was envisaged as a piece of whetstone in his forehead (see the more detailed discussion in Tolley 2009, I, 283–5). Yet I am now more sanguine about inferring any connection with this mythological complex in the case of Bede's house post: the house is not struck by lightning (nor is fire otherwise said to be struck within it), but burns down as a result of carelessness when a feast takes place in it; nothing particular is made of the post other than as a place for the blessed soil to reside.

There may be somewhat more force to the other parallel drawn in the original paper. The survival of the house-post in the conflagration described by Bede is paralleled by the survival of the world tree in Norse when the world is consumed by flames; the branches of the tree shelter a human couple, who go on to people the new world. The couple are said in *Vafþrúðnismál*, st. 45, to conceal themselves in 'hoard-Mímir's *holt* (tree/ wood)', and live there on morning dew. The survival in the tree takes place, according to *Vafþrúðnismál*, over the *fimbulvetr*, 'mighty winter', at the end of the world, but the poem goes on to mention Surtr's fire as marking the end of the world (cf. *Vǫluspá*, st. 50, where Surtr comes from the south with fire, and st. 54 'leikr hár hiti við himin siálfan', 'heat tosses high against heaven itself'); the couple must therefore survive this conflagration too in their tree. The hall could act as a metonym of the whole world: this is implicit in the imagery of Heorot in *Beowulf*, which is the stage upon which the heroes strut and fret their hour, signifying what is important to all mankind, and also in the name Heimdallr, both home-tree and world-tree guardian; in Bede, the image of the hall as the world is most graphically evident in the debate about adopting Christianity undertaken in Eadwine's hall (*Historia Ecclesiastica* ii.13, pp. 182–7). The fire-consumed hall may therefore allude to the apocalyptic conflagration of the world, salvation from which is represented in myth by the Adam and Eve figures of the new world, as well as by the earth rising up, with renewed vigour ('iðjagrœn'), out of the ocean again (*Vǫluspá*, st. 56), but in the English legend by the salvific soil of Oswald's martyrdom, bringing the new kingdom of Christ to his people.

Nonetheless, the predominant symbolism is clearly Christian: material objects show the sanctity of Oswald by remaining intact. Thus the house post that remains intact through contact with earth from the site of Oswald's fall parallels the stakes on which his intact remains hung for a year at the site of the battle.

Conclusion

THE DECADES COVERING THE REIGNS of the three main Northumbrian kings of the early seventh century, Æthelfrith, Eadwine and Oswald, marked transitions of many sorts. The English emerged from being warlord-dominated masters of small areas on the east coast, following traditional pagan beliefs with limited, local horizons, to become rulers of all of what was to become England, the Welsh kings having finally been defeated in most of this area, particularly in the North. The pagan horizons expanded, encompassing the broad realm of what had once been the Roman Empire, and was now an interlinked area of Christian belief and practice. The Christian realm of Northumbria appears to have been one of the most ardent supporters of the new faith, and this led to the establishment of a Church that could foster the learning and endeavour that gave us Bede and works like the Lindisfarne Gospels.

We are largely reliant on Bede as our primary source for what went on during these decisive decades. My approach has been to ask how we can widen our perspective on what Bede tells us in two ways. We can consider the motivations of the agents of history from a broader set of precepts than those of Church history, in particular politics and the play of power. This has largely been the approach in the first of each of my pairs of essays. Yet we would be wrong to think that the actors in the historical scenes discussed here were proceeding in a 'modern', rational way in all they did: although they were not Church exegetes and historians in the way Bede was, religious motivations would have played a greater part in their actions than they would for many modern Western politicians. Hence it is appropriate to try to understand Bede's typological understanding of history better, bearing in mind that he represents part of a wider and ongoing tradition of interpretation. It makes no rational sense, for example, for a group of monks to have faced an enemy of marauding savages, but an understanding of how religion, and the religious interpretation of history, operated at this period can offer plausible reasons for why such an event should have taken place (and why it need not simply have been Bede's invention).

Bede is concerned to show the self-evident superiority of Christianity over paganism, and he spends no time whatever in attempting to see historical developments from the spiritual point of view of those who were yet to adopt the new faith. Yet behind several of his accounts we may glimpse the likelihood that the process of conversion was not as straightforward as he intimates. True conversion (as opposed to mere expediency, which must in truth have been a characteristic of much conversion at this period) can only take place through conviction: someone has to understand what was right and inspiring in the beliefs they have always held, not merely what is wrong with them, before they can make that journey. I have tried to show how in both Eadwine's and Oswald's cases we may discern a play on existing pagan beliefs, either in terms of adherents seeking an explanation for the overthrow of their long-held beliefs in terms of the belief system itself, or a seeking out of ways in which the new faith reflected, complemented and fulfilled what they already believed.

References

Abbreviations
ASPR   *The Anglo-Saxon Poetic Records: A Collective Edition,*
        ed. George P. Krapp and Elliot van Kirk Dobbie, 6 vols.
        New York: Columbia University Press, 1931–42.
ÍF   Íslenzk fornrit, Hið íslenzka fornritafélag, Reykjavík
MGH   Monumenta Germaniae Historica, Hanover/Berlin
        (SS = Scriptores)

Primary Sources

Adam of Bremen, *Descriptio Insularum Aquilonis,* in *Hamburgische Kirchen-geschichte,* 3rd edn, ed. B. Schmeidler. Scriptores Rerum Germanicarum in usum scholarum ex Monumentis Germaniae Historicis separatim editi. Hanover and Leipzig, 1917.

Adomnán, *Adomnan's Life of Columba,* ed. Alan Orr Anderson and Marjorie Ogilivie Anderson. London: Nelson, 1961.

Anglo-Saxon Chronicle: Charles Plummer and John Earle, ed., *Two of the Saxon Chronicles Parallel,* vol. I. Oxford: Clarendon Press, 1892.

Annales Cambriae in Nennius, *Historia Brittonum: British History and the Welsh Annals,* ed. John Morris. Arthurian Period Sources 8. London: Phillimore, 1980.

Annales Einhardi, in MGH SS I, 135–218.

Annales Fuldenses, in MGH SS I, 337–415.

Annales Iuvavenses Minores, in MGH SS I, 88–9.

Annales Laurissenses Maiores, in MGH SS I, 134–218.

Annales Laurissenses Minores, in MGH SS I, 112–23.

Annales Mosellani, ed. Johann Martin Lappenberg, in MGH SS XVI, 491–9.

Annales Petaviani, in MGH SS I, 7–16.

Annals of Tigernach: Whitley Stokes, ed. and trans., 'The Annals of Tigernach', *Revue celtique* 16 (1895), 374–419. Available at CELT: http://www.ucc.ie/celt/published/G100002/ and /T100002A/

Annals of Ulster: Seán Mac Airt and Gearóid Mac Niocaill, ed. and tr., *The Annals of Ulster (to AD 1131).* Dublin: DIAS, 1983. Available at CELT: http://www.ucc.ie/celt/published/G100001A/

Bartrum, Peter Clement, *Early Welsh Genealogical Tracts.* Cardiff: University of Wales Press, 1966.

Bede, *The Ecclesiastical History of the English People,* ed. Bertram Colgrave and R. A. B. Mynors. Oxford: Clarendon Press, 1992 [1969].

Beowulf: Klaeber's Beowulf, 4th edn, ed. Robert D. Fulk, Robert E. Bjork and John D. Niles. Toronto: Toronto University Press, 2008.

Böhtlingk, Otto, *Über die Sprache der Jakuten*. St Petersburg: Kaiserliche Akademie der Wissenschaften, 1851.

Bradley, S. A. J., trans., *Anglo-Saxon Poetry*. London: J. M. Dent, 1982.

Breatnach, L., ed., 'The Cauldron of Poesy', *Ériu* 32 (1981), 45–93.

Bromwich, Rachel, ed. and trans., *Trioedd Ynys Prydein. The Triads of the Island of Britain*, 4th edn. Cardiff: University of Wales Press, 2014 [1961].

Cambrai Homily, trans. in Davies 1999, pp. 369–70.

The Cauldron of Poesy: see Breatnach 1981.

Charles-Edwards, T. M., ed. and trans., *The Chronicle of Ireland*. Liverpool: Liverpool University Press, 2006.

Davies, Oliver, with Thomas O'Loughlin, *Celtic Spirituality*. The Classics of Western Spirituality. New York: Paulist Press, 1999.

The Dream of the Rood, in *ASPR* II. Trans. in Bradley 1982, pp. 158–63.

Dronke, Ursula, ed. and trans., *The Poetic Edda II. Mythological Poems*. Oxford: Oxford University Press, 1997.

—— ed. and trans., *The Poetic Edda III. Mythological Poems II*. Oxford: Oxford University Press, 2011.

Edda: die Lieder des Codex Regius, 5th edn. Text, ed. G. Neckel, rev. H. Kuhn. Heidelberg: Carl Winter, 1983.

Eddius Stephanus, *Vita Wilfridi*, in Eddius, *Life of Bishop Wilfrid*, ed. Bertram Colgrave. Cambridge: Cambridge University Press, 1927. Trans. James F. Webb, *The Age of Bede*, pp. 103–82. Harmondsworth: Penguin, 1965.

Egils saga Skallagrímssonar, ed. Sigurður Nordal. ÍF 2. 1933.

Eilífr Goðrúnarson, *Þórsdrápa*, in Daphne L. Davidson, ed., 'Earl Hákon and his Poets'. D.Phil. thesis. Oxford University, 1983.

Eyrbyggja saga, Eiríks saga rauða, ed. Einar Ó. Sveinsson and Matthías Þórðarson. ÍF 4. 1935.

Finnsburh Fragment, in *ASPR* VI. Trans. in Bradley 1982, pp. 507–9.

Gautreks saga, in *Fornaldarsögur norðurlanda*, ed. Guðni Jónsson and Bjarni Vilhjálmsson, III. Reykjavík: Forni, 1943. Trans. in *Gautreks Saga and Other Medieval Tales*, trans. Hermann Pálsson and Paul Edwards. London: University of London; New York: University Press, 1968.

Geoffrey of Monmouth, *The History of the Kings of Britain*, ed. and trans. L. Thorpe. Harmondsworth: Penguin, 1968.

—— *The History of the Kings of Britain. An Edition and Translation of De Gestis Britonum*, ed. Michael D. Reeve, trans. Neil Wright. Woodbridge: Boydell, 2007.

Gildas, *The Ruin of Britain and Other Documents*, ed. and trans. Michael Winterbottom. Arthurian Period Sources 7. London and Chichester: Philimore, 1978.

Giraldus Cambrensis, *Descriptio Kambriae*, ed. J. F. Dimock, in *Giraldi Cambrensis Opera*, vol. VI. Rolls Series 21. London: Longmans, 1868.

Grímnismál, in Dronke, *The Poetic Edda III*. Trans. also in Larrington 2014.

Hálfdanar saga ins svarta, in ÍF 26, *Heimskringla*, vol. 1, ed. Bjarni Aðalbjarnarson. 1941.

References

Haustlǫng: see Þjóðólfr.

Hávamál, ed. David A. H. Evans. London: Viking Society for Northern Research, 1986. Trans. also in Larrington 2014.

Haycock, Marged, ed. and trans., *Legendary Poems from the Book of Taliesin*, 2nd edn. Aberystwyth: CMCS Publications, 2015 [2007].

Helgakviða Hjörvarðssonar I, in *Edda*, ed. Neckel and Kuhn. Trans. in Larrington 2014.

Helgakviða Hundingsbana, in *Edda*, ed. Neckel and Kuhn. Trans. in Larrington 2014.

Hervarar saga ok Heiðreks: Christopher Tolkien, ed., *The Saga of King Heidrek the Wise*. Nelson Icelandic Texts. London and Edinburgh: Nelson, 1960.

Historia Brittonum: Nennius, *British History and the Welsh Annals*, ed. and trans. John Morris. Arthurian Period Sources 8. London and Chichester: Philimore, 1980.

Irenaeus, *Against Heresies*, in Alexander Roberts and W. H. Rambaut, trans., *The Writings of Irenaeus*, II. Ante-Nicene Christian Library IX. Edinburgh: T. & T. Clark, 1869.

Jordanes, *Romana et Getica*, ed. T. Mommsen. MGH Auctores Antiquissimi V, 1. Berlin, 1882.

Judith, in *ASPR* IV. Trans. in Bradley 1982, pp. 495–504.

Kildal, S., *Efterretning om Finners og Lappers Hedenske Religion*, ed. Capt. Abrahamson, 1730. Det Skandinaviske Litteraturselskabs Skrifter 1807, pt 2, pp. 446–75. Copenhagen, 1807.

Landnámabók, ed. Jakob Benediktsson. ÍF 1. 1968.

Larrington, Carolyne, trans., *The Poetic Edda*, 2nd edn. Oxford: Oxford University Press, 2014.

Leland, John, *The Itinerary of John Leland in or about the Years 1535–1543*, ed. Lucy Toulmin Smith, 5 vols. London: George Bell & Sons, 1906–10.

Life of St Beuno, trans. in Davies 1999, pp. 213–20.

Lindahl, Erik, and Johan Öhrling, *Lexicon Lapponicum*. Copenhagen: J. G. Lange, 1780.

Lokasenna, in Dronke, *The Poetic Edda II*. Trans. also in Larrington 2014.

Lorenz, Gottfried, ed., *Snorri Sturluson, Gylfaginning (Texte, Übersetzung, Kommentar)*. Darmstadt: Wissenschaftliche Buchgesellschaft, 1984.

Maximus the Confessor, *On the Cosmic Mystery of Jesus Christ*, trans. Paul M. Blowers and Robert Louis Wilken. Crestwood: St Vladmir's Seminary Press, 2003.

Monumenta Germaniae Historica, ed. G. H. Pertz. *Leges III*. Hanover, 1863.

Monumenta Germaniae Historica, ed. G. H. Pertz. *Scriptorum Tomus I*. Hanover, 1826.

Monumenta Germaniae Historica, ed. G. H. Pertz. *Scriptorum Tomus XVI*. Hanover, 1859.

Nennius: see *Historia Brittonum*.

Origen, *Commentary on the Gospel According to John: Books 1–10* and *Books 13–32*, trans. Ronald E. Heine. Fathers of the Church: A New Translation 80 and 89. Washington, DC: Catholic University of America, 1989 and 1993.

Paasonen, H., collector, *Mordwinische Volksdichtung*, vol. I, ed. P. Ravila, Suomalais-Ugrilaisen Seuran Toimituksia 77. Helsinki: Suomalais-Ugrilainen Seura, 1938.

The Phoenix, in *ASPR* III. Trans. in Bradley 1982, pp. 284–301.

Preideu Annwfyn, in Haycock 2015.

Primary Chronicle: Samuel H. Cross and Olgerd P. Sherbowitz-Wetzor, ed. and trans., *The Russian Primary Chronicle: Laurentian Text*. Cambridge, MA: The Mediaeval Academy of America, 1953.

Reginald of Durham, *Vita Sancti Oswaldi*: in *Symeonis Monachi Opera Omnia*, ed. T. Arnold, 2 vols. Rolls Series 75. London: Longmans, 1882–5, vol. I, *Historia Ecclesiae Dunelmensis*, 326–85.

Reuterskiöld, E., ed., *Källskrifter till Lapparnas Mytologi*. Bidrag till vår odlings häfder utgivna af nordiska museet. Stockholm, 1910.

Rudolf of Fulda, *Translatio Sancti Alexandri*, in *Scriptores Rerum Sangallensium. Annales, Chronica et Historiae Aevi Saxonici*, ed. Georg Heinrich Pertz. MGH SS 2. Hanover, 1829, pp. 673–81.

The Ruin, in *ASPR* III. Trans. in Bradley 1982, pp. 401–2.

Saxo Grammaticus, *Gesta Danorum*, ed. Jørgen Olrik and Hans Ræder, 2 vols. Copenhagen: Levin and Munksgaard, 1931 and 1957. Trans. as *The History of the Danes Books I–IX*, ed. Hilda R. Ellis-Davidson, trans. Peter Fisher, I: text, 1979; II, commentary, 1980. Cambridge: D. S. Brewer.

Schefferus, Johannes, *Lapponia*. Frankfurt: Christian Wolff, 1673. Translated into English as *The History of Lapland*, Oxford, 1674.

Sigrdrífumál, in *Edda*, ed. Neckel and Kuhn. Trans. in Larrington 2014.

Skjaldedigtning: *Den Norsk-Islandske Skjaldedigtning*, ed. Finnur Jónsson, 4 vols. Copenhagen: Gyldendal, 1912–15.

Snorri Sturluson, *Edda*, ed. Finnur Jónsson. Copenhagen: Kommissionen for det Arnamagnæanske Legat (Gyldendalske Boghandel), 1931. (Includes *Gylfaginning* and *Skáldskaparmál*; see also Lorenz 1984.)

—— *Edda*, trans. Anthony Faulkes. Everyman's Library. London and Melbourne: Dent, 1987.

Strabo, *The Geography of Strabo*, ed. and trans. Horace Leonard Jones, 10 vols. Loeb Classical Library. London: Heinemann, 1917–32.

Strelow, Hans Nielssøn, *Cronica Guthilandorum. Den Guthilandiske Cronica*. Copenhagen: Melchior Martzan, 1633.

Tacitus, Cornelius, *Germania*, in *Opera Minora*, ed. Michael Winterbottom and Robert Maxwell Ogilvie. Oxford: Clarendon Press, 1975. Trans. with introduction and commentary by James B. Rives. Oxford: Oxford University Press, 1999.

Trioedd Ynys Prydein: see Bromwich 2014.

Úlfr Uggason, *Húsdrápa*, in *Skjaldedigtning* B1.

Vafþrúðnismál, in *Edda*, ed. Neckel and Kuhn. Trans. in Larrington 2014.

Vatnsdœla Saga, ed. Einar Ó. Sveinsson. ÍF 8. 1939.

Vergil, *Aeneid*, in P. Vergilius Maro, *Opera*, ed. R. A. B. Mynors. Oxford Classical Texts. Oxford: Oxford University Press, 1969.

Vita Wilfridi: see Eddius Stephanus.

Vǫlsunga saga: The Saga of the Völsungs, ed. R. G. Finch. London: Nelson, 1965.

References

Vǫluspá, in Dronke, *The Poetic Edda II*. Also trans. in Larrington 2014.
The Wanderer, in *ASPR* III. Trans. in Bradley 1982, pp. 320–5.
Widukind, *Res Gestae Saxonicae*, ed. P. Hirsch and H. E. Lohmann. MGH Scriptores Rerum Germanicarum in Usum Scholarum separatim editi LX. Hanover, 1935.
Ynglinga saga, in ÍF 26, *Heimskringla*, vol. 1, ed. Bjarni Aðalbjarnarson. 1941.
Þjóðólfr of Hvinir, *Haustlǫng*, ed. Richard North. Enfield Lock: Hisarlik, 1997.
Þórarinn loftunga, *Glælognskviða*, in *Skjaldedigtning* BI.
Þrymskviða, in *Edda*, ed. Neckel and Kuhn. Trans. in Larrington 2014.

Secondary Sources

Abels, Richard Philip, *Lordship and Military Obligation in Anglo-Saxon England*. Berkeley: University of California Press, 1988.
Adams, Max, *The King in the North. The Life and Times of Oswald of Northumbria*. London: Head of Zeus, 2013.
Adderley, Mark, 'Singing to the Silent Sentinel: Preiddeu Annwn and the Oral Tradition', *The Review of English Studies*, n.s. 60/244 (2009), 175–93.
Alcock, Leslie, *Bede, Eddius, and the Forts of the North Britons*. Jarrow Lecture 1988. Jarrow: St Paul's Church.
Barrow, Julia, 'How Coifi Pierced Christ's Side: A Re-examination of Bede's *Ecclesiastical History*, II, chapter 13', *Journal of Ecclesiastical History* 62 (2011), 693–706.
Bartrum, Peter Clement, *A Welsh Classical Dictionary. People in History and Legend up to about A.D. 1000*. Aberystwyth: National Library of Wales, 1993.
Bassett, Steven, 'In Search of the Origins of Anglo-Saxon Kingdoms', in Basset 1989, pp. 3–27 (1989*a*).
——ed., *The Origins of Anglo-Saxon Kingdoms*. Leicester: Leicester University Press, 1989.
Behr, John, Andrew Louth and Dmitri Conomos, *Abba: the Tradition of Orthodoxy in the West: Festschrift for Bishop Kallistos (Ware) of Diokleia*. Crestwood: St Vladmir's Seminary Press, 2003.
Bintley, Michael D., 'The Translation of St Oswald's Relics to New Minster, Gloucester: Royal and Imperial Resonances', *Anglo-Saxon Studies in Archaeology and History* 19 (2014), 171–81.
—— *Trees in the Religions of Early Medieval England*. Woodbridge: Boydell, 2015.
Bosworth, Joseph, and T. Northcote Toller, *An Anglo-Saxon Dictionary*. Oxford: Clarendon Press, 1898. With Toller, *Supplement*, rev. Alistair Campbell. Oxford: Clarendon Press, 1921.
Brooks, Nicholas, 'The Formation of the Mercian Kingdom', in Bassett 1989, pp. 159–70.
—— *Bede and the English*. Jarrow Lecture 1999. Jarrow: St Paul's Church.
Bu'Lock, J. D., 'The Battle of Chester, AD 616', *Transactions of the Lancashire and Cheshire Antiquarian Society* 72 (1962), 47–56.

Chadwick, N. K., 'The Battle of Chester: A Study of Sources', in N. K. Chadwick, ed., *Celt and Saxon: Studies in the Early English Border*, pp. 167–85. Cambridge: Cambridge University Press, 1963.

Chaney, William A., *The Cult of Kingship in Anglo-Saxon England. The Transition from Paganism to Christianity*. Manchester: Manchester University Press, 1970.

Charles-Edwards, T. M., *Wales and the Britons 350–1064*. Oxford: Oxford University Press, 2013.

Clarkson, Tim, *The Men of the North. The Britons of Southern Scotland*. Edinburgh: John Donald, 2010.

——*Scotland's Merlin. A Medieval Legend and its Dark Age Origins*. Edinburgh: John Donald, 2016.

Clemoes, Peter, *The Cult of St Oswald on the Continent*. Jarrow Lecture 1983. Jarrow: St Paul's Church.

Clunies Ross, Margaret, 'The Role of the Horse in Nordic Mythologies', in Timothy R. Tangherlini, ed., *Nordic Mythologies. Interpretation, Intersections, and Institutions*, pp. 50–70. Berkeley and Los Angeles: North Pinehurst Press, 2014.

Collingwood, W. G., *Northumbrian Crosses of the Pre-Norman Age*. London: Faber & Faber, 1927.

Coomaraswamy, A. K., 'The Sun-Kiss', *Journal of the American Oriental Society* 60 (1940), 46–67.

Corfe, Tom, 'The Battle of Heavenfield', *Hexham Historian* 7 (1997), 65–86.

Cramp, R., *Early Northumbrian Sculpture*. Jarrow Lecture 1965. Jarrow: St Paul's Church.

Davidson, D. L., 'Earl Hákon and his Poets'. D.Phil. thesis. Oxford University, 1983.

Davies, Ceri, *Welsh Literature and the Classical Tradition*. Cardiff: University of Wales Press, 1995.

Davies, S., 'The Battle of Chester and Warfare in Post-Roman Britain', *History* 95 (2010), 143–58.

Dawson, John David, *Christian Figural Reading and the Fashioning of Identity*. Berkeley, Los Angeles, London: University of California Press, 2001.

DeGregorio, Scott, 'Bede and the Old Testament', in DeGregorio 2010, pp. 127–41 (2010*a*).

——ed., *The Cambridge Companion to Bede*. Cambridge: Cambridge University Press, 2010.

de Lubac, Henri, *Exégèse médiévale. Les quatre sens de l'Écriture*, 4 vols. Paris: Cerf/DDB, 1959–64.

Digital Atlas of the Roman Empire, at http://dare.ht.lu.se/

Dodgson, J. McN., *The Place-Names of Cheshire*, part I. English Place-Name Society 44. Cambridge: Cambridge University Press, 1970.

——*The Place-Names of Cheshire*, part V(1:1). English Place-Name Society 48. Cambridge: Cambridge University Press, 1981.

Dumville, David, 'The Origins of Northumbria: Some Aspects of the British Background', in Bassett 1989, pp. 213–22.

References

Eagles, Bruce N., *The Anglo-Saxon Settlement of Humberside*. British Archaeological Reports, British Series 68. Oxford: British Archaeological Reports, 1979.

Egeler, Matthias, *Avalon, 66° Nord. Zu Frühgeschichte und Rezeption eines Mythos*. Ergänzungsbände zum Reallexikon der Germanischen Altertumskunde 95. Berlin: De Gruyter, 2015.

Eliade, M., *Shamanism: Archaic Techniques of Ecstasy*, trans. Willard R. Trask. Bollingen Series 76. Princeton: Princeton University Press, 1972 [1951].

Evans, Stephen S., *Lords of Battle. Image and Reality of the 'Comitatus' in Dark-Age Britain*. Woodbridge: Boydell, 1997.

Faull, Margaret Lindsay, 'The Location and Relationship of the Sancton Anglo-Saxon Cemeteries', *The Antiquaries' Journal* 56 (1976), 227–33.

Furry, Thomas J., *Allegorizing History. The Venerable Bede, Figural Exegesis, and Historical Theory*. Distinguished Dissertations in Christian Theology 10. Eugene, Oregon: Pickwick Publications, 2013.

Geiriadur Prifysgol Cymru. A Dictionary of the Welsh Language, at http://welsh-dictionary.ac.uk/gpc/gpc.html

Gelling, Margaret, *The West Midlands in the Early Middle Ages*. Leicester, London and New York: Leicester University Press, 1992.

—— 'The Word Church in English Place-Names', in Quinton 2009, pp. 7–14.

Goldberg, Martin, 'Ideas and Ideologies', in David Clarke, Alice Blackwell and Martin Goldberg, ed., *Early Medieval Scotland. Individuals, Communities and Ideas*, pp. 141–204. Edinburgh: National Museums of Scotland, 2012.

Graff, E. G., *Althochdeutscher Sprachschatz oder Wörterbuch der Althochdeutschen Sprache*. Berlin : Commission der Nicolaischen Buchhandlung, 1834–42.

Griffiths, D., R. A. Philpott and G. Egan, *Meols, The Archaeology of the North Wirral Coast. Discoveries and Observations in the 19th and 20th Centuries with a Catalogue of Collections*. Oxford University School of Archaeology Monograph Series 68. Oxford: Oxford University Institute of Archaeology, 2007.

Harva, Uno, *Der Baum des Lebens*. Suomalaisen Tiedeakatemian Toimituksia B:xvi no. 3. Helsinki: Suomalainen Tiedeakatemia, 1922.

—— *Altain suvun uskonto* [The religion of the Altai race]. Porvoo: Werner Söderström, 1933.

Hertlein, F., *Die Juppitergigantensäulen*. Stuttgart: Schweizerbarth'sche Verlagsbuchhandlung, 1910.

Higham, N. J., 'King Cearl, the Battle of Chester and the Origins of the Mercian "Overkingship"', *Midland History* 17 (1992), 1–15.

—— *The Origins of Cheshire*. Manchester: Manchester University Press, 1993 (1993a).

—— *The Kingdom of Northumbria, AD 350–1100*. Dover: Alan Sutton, 1993 (1993b).

—— *An English Empire: Bede and the Early Anglo-Saxon Kings*. Manchester: Manchester University Press, 1995.

Higley, Sarah Lynn, *Between Languages. The Uncooperative Text in Early Welsh and Old English Nature Poetry*. University Park: Pennsylvania State University Press, 1993.

—— 'The Spoils of Annwn: Taliesin and Material Poetry', in Kathryn A. Klar, Eve E. Sweetser and Claire Thomas, ed., *A Celtic Florilegium. Studies in Memory of Brendan O Hehir*, pp. 43–53. Celtic Studies Publications II. Lawrence, MA: Celtic Studies Publications, 1996.

Holder, Arthur G., 'Bede and the Tradition of Patristic Exegesis', *Anglican Theological Review* 72 (1990), 399–411.

Hough, Carole, 'Eccles in English and Scottish Place-Names', in Quinton 2009, pp. 109–24.

Howe, Nicholas, *Migration and Mythmaking in Anglo-Saxon England*. New Haven and London: Yale University Press, 1989.

Ivanov, V. V., and V. N. Toporov, 'A Comparative Study of the Group of Baltic Mythological Terms from the Root *vel-'*, *Baltistica* 9 (1973), 15–27.

James, Alan G., '*Eglēs/Eclēs* and the Formation of Northumbria', in Quinton 2009, pp. 125–50.

Jankulak, Karen, *Geoffrey of Monmouth*. Cardiff: University of Wales Press, 2010.

Jansen, Annemiek, 'The Development of the St Oswald Legends on the Continent', in Stancliffe and Cambridge 1995, pp. 230–40.

Jarman, A. O. H., and Gwilym Rees Hughes, ed., *A Guide to Welsh Literature I*. Cardiff: University of Wales Press, 1992 [1976].

Johnston, Elva, 'Exiles from the Edge? The Irish Contexts of Peregrinatio', in Roy Flechner and Sven Meeder, ed., *The Irish in Early Medieval Europe. Identity, Culture and Religion*, pp. 38–52. London: Palgrave 2016.

Karjalainen, K. F., *Südostjakische Textsammlungen*, ed. E. Vértes, vol. I, Suomalais-Ugrilaisen Seuran Toimituksia 157. Helsinki, 1975.

Kayser, Johan, *Beiträge zur Geschichte und Erklärung der ältesten Kirchenhymnen*. Paderborn: Ferdinand Schöningh, 1881.

Kirby, D. P., *The Earliest English Kings*. London: Unwin Hyman, 2000 [1991].

Koch, John, ed., *Celtic Culture: A Historical Encyclopedia*, 5 vols. Santa Barbara, Oxford: ABC-Clio, 2006.

Laistner, M. L. W., 'The Library of the Venerable Bede', in A. Hamilton Thompson, ed., *Bede: His Life, Times, and Writings*, pp. 23–66. Oxford: Clarendon Press, 1935.

—— *Thought and Letters in Western Europe: AD 500 to 900*, 2nd edn. Ithaca, NY: Cornell University Press, 1957.

Lapidge, Michael, *Bede the Poet*. Jarrow Lecture 1993. Jarrow: St Paul's Church.

—— *The Anglo-Saxon Library*. Oxford: Oxford University Press, 2006.

Laurent, Donatien, 'La cime sacrée de Locronan', in Gaël Milin and Patrick Galliou, ed., *Hauts lieux du sacré en Bretagne*, pp. 357–66. Brest, Centre de recherche bretonne et celtique, 1996.

Littledale, Richard Frederick, *A Commentary on the Song of Songs from Ancient and Medieval Sources*. London: Joseph Masters, 1869.

Löwe, H., 'Die Irminsul und die Religion der Sachsen', *Deutsches Archiv für Geschichte des Mittelalters* 5 (1941), 1–22.

References

Lucas, A. T., 'The Sacred Trees of Ireland', *Journal of the Cork Historical and Archaeological Society* 68 (1963), 16–54.

McClure, Judith, 'Bede's Old Testament Kings', in *Ideal and Reality in Frankish and Anglo-Saxon Society: Studies Presented to J. M. Wallace-Hadrill*, ed. Patrick Wormald with Donald Bullough and Roger Collins, pp. 76–98. Oxford: Basil Blackwell, 1983.

McKenna, Catherine, *The Medieval Welsh Religious Lyric: Poems of the Gogynfeirdd, 1137–1282*. Belmont, MA: Ford & Bailie, 1991.

MacKillop, James, *Dictionary of Celtic Mythology*. Oxford: Oxford University Press, 1998.

Malone, E. E., 'Spiritual Martyrs and Irish Monks', *American Benedictine Reivew* 2 (1951), 393–409.

Markus, R. A., *Bede and the Tradition of Ecclesiastical Historiography*. Jarrow Lecture 1975. Jarrow: St Paul's Church.

Martens, Peter W., 'Revisiting the Allegory/Typology Distinction: The Case of Origen', *Journal of Early Christian Studies* 16 (2008), 283–316.

Mason, David, *First Interim Report on Archaeological Investigations at Heronbridge, Chester, Chehire. Excavation and Survey 2002*. Chester: Chester Archaeological Society, 2002.

—— *Second Interim Report on Archaeological Investigations at Heronbridge, Chester, Chehire. Excavation and Survey 2003*. Chester: Chester Archaeological Society, 2003.

—— *Third Interim Report on Archaeological Investigations at Heronbridge, Chester, Chehire. Excavation and Survey 2004*. Chester: Chester Archaeological Society, 2004.

—— *Chester AD 400–1066: From Roman Fortress to English Town*. Stroud: Tempus, 2007.

Mayr-Harting, Henry, *The Venerable Bede, The Rule of St Benedict, and Social Class*. Jarrow Lecture 1976. Jarrow: St Paul's Church.

—— *The Coming of Christianity to Anglo-Saxon England*, 3rd edn. University Park: Pennsylvania State University Press, 1991 [1972].

Meyvaert, Paul, 'Bede the Scholar', in Gerald Bonner, ed., *Famulus Christi: Essays in Commemoration of the Thirteenth Centenary of the Birth of the Venerable Bede*, pp. 40–69. London: SPCK, 1976.

Much, R., 'Undensakre-Untersberg', *Zeitschrift für deutsches Altertum und deutsche Literatur* 47 (1904), 70–1.

Müller, W., *Die Jupitergigantensäulen und ihre Verwandten*. Beiträge zur klassischen Philologie 66. Meisenheim am Glan: Hain, 1975.

Murphy, G. R., 'Magic in the *Heliand*', in G. R. Murphy, ed. and trans., *The Heliand. The Saxon Gospel*, pp. 205–20. New York and Oxford: Oxford University Press, 1992.

Myres, J. N. L., *The English Settlements*. Oxford: Oxford University Press, 1986.

—— and W. H. Southern, *The Anglo-Saxon Cremation Cemetery at Sancton, East Yorkshire*. Hull Museum Publication 218. Hull: Hull Museum, 1973.

Noreen, Adolf, *Altnordische Grammatik I: Altisländische und altnorwegische Grammatik*, 5th edn. Tübingen: Niemeyer, 1970.

North, Richard, *Heathen Gods in Old English Literature*. Cambridge Studies in Anglo-Saxon England 22. Cambridge: Cambridge University Press, 1997.

O'Brien, Elizabeth, *Post-Roman Britain to Anglo-Saxon England: Burial Practices Reviewed*. British Archaeological Reports, British Series 289. Oxford: British Archaeological Reports, 1999.

Ó Carragáin, Éamonn, *The City of Rome and the World of Bede*. Jarrow Lecture 1994. Jarrow: St Paul's Church.

Olrik, Axel, and Hans Ellekilde, *Nordens Gudeverden*, vol. I, 1926; vol. II, 1957. Copenhagen: Gad.

Owen, Hywel Wyn, and Richard Morgan, *Dictionary of the Place-Names of Wales*. Llandysul: Gomer, 2007.

Pace, Edwin, 'Geoffrey's "Very Old Book" and Penda of Mercia', *Arthuriana* 22 (2012), 53–74.

Pipping, H., *Eddastudier I*. Studier i Nordisk Filologi 16:2. Svenska Litteratursällskapet i Finland no. 182. Helsinki: Svenska Litteratursällskapet i Finland, 1925.

—— *Eddastudier II*. Studier i Nordisk Filologi 17:3. Svenska Litteratursällskapet i Finland no. 189. Helsinki: Svenska Litteratursällskapet i Finland, 1926.

Plummer, Charles, ed., *Venerabilis Baedae Historia Ecclesiastica Gentis Anglorum*, 2 vols. Oxford: Clarendon Press, 1896.

Powlesland, Dominic, 'Early Anglo-Saxon Settlements, Structure, Form and Layout', in John Hines, ed., *The Anglo-Saxons from the Migration Period to the Eighth Century. An Ethnographic Perspective*, pp. 101–24. Woodbridge: Boydell, 1997.

Quinton, Eleanor, ed., *The Church in English Place-Names*. English Place-Name Society, Extra Series 4. Nottingham: English Place-Name Society, 2009.

Raine, J., *The Priory of Hexham: Its Chroniclers, Endowments, and Annals*, 2 vols. Durham: Surtees Society, 1864–5.

Ray, Roger, *Bede, Rhetoric and the Creation of Christian Latin Culture*. Jarrow Lecture 1997. Jarrow: St Paul's Church.

Das Reallexicon für Antike und Christentum, vol. II. Stuttgart: Anton Hiersemann, 1954.

Rivet, A. L. F., and Colin Smith, *The Place-Names of Roman Britain*. London: Batsford, 1979.

Ross, Anne, 'The Human Head in Insular Pagan Celtic Religion', *Proceedings of the Society of Antiquaries of Scotland* 91 (1959), 10–43.

Rowland, Jenny, *Early Welsh Saga Poetry. A Study and Edition of the 'Englynion'*. Cambridge: D. S. Brewer, 1990.

Simonetti, Manlio, *Biblical Interpretation in the Early Church: An Historical Introduction to Patristic Exegesis*. Edinburgh: T. & T. Clark, 1994.

Simpson, Jacqueline, 'Mímir: Two Myths or One?', *Saga-Book of the Viking Society* 16 (1962), 41–53.

Smith, A. H., *The Place-Names of the North Riding of Yorkshire*. English Place-Name Society V. Cambridge: Cambridge University Press, 1928.

—— *English Place-Name Elements*, 2nd edn. English Place-Name Society XXV and XXVI. Cambridge: Cambridge University Press, 1970.

References

Snyder, Christopher A., *An Age of Tyrants. Britain and the Britons AD 400–600*. Stroud: Sutton, 1998.

Stancliffe, Clare, 'Red, White and Blue Martyrdom', in Dorothy Whitelock, Rosamond McKitterick and David Dumville, ed., *Ireland in Early Mediaeval Europe: Studies in Memory of Kathleen Hughes*, pp. 21–46. Cambridge: Cambridge University Press, 1982.

—— 'Oswald, "Most Holy and Most Victorious King of the Northumbrians"', in Stancliffe and Cambridge 1995, pp. 33–83 (1995*a*).

—— 'Where was Oswald killed?', in Stancliffe and Cambridge 1995, 84–96 (1995*b*).

—— 'The British Church and the Mission of Augustine', in R. Gameson, ed., *St Augustine and the Conversion of England*, pp. 107–51. Stroud: Sutton, 1999.

—— and Eric Cambridge, ed., *Oswald. Northumbrian King to European Saint*. Stamford: Paul Watkins, 1995.

Straubergs, K., 'Zur Jenseitstopographie', *Arv* 13 (1957), 56–110.

Thacker, Alan, 'Membra Disjecta: The Division of the Body and the Diffusion of the Cult', in Stancliffe and Cambridge 1995, pp. 97–127.

—— *Bede and Augustine of Hippo: History and Figure in Sacred Text*. Jarrow Lecture 2005. Jarrow: St Paul's Church.

—— 'Bede and History', in DeGregorio 2010, pp. 170–89.

Thomas, Charles, *A Provisional List of Imported Pottery in Post-Roman Western Britain and Ireland* with an appendix on Tintagel by O. J. Padel. Redruth: Institute of Cornish Studies, 1981.

Timby, Jane (with other contributors), 'Sancton I Anglo-Saxon Cemetery. Excavations carried out between 1976 and 1980', *Archaeological Journal* 150 (1993), 243–365.

Tolkien, C.: see *Hervarar Saga*.

Tolley, Clive, *Shamanism in Norse Myth and Magic*, 2 vols. Finnish Folklore Communications 296–7. Helsinki: Academia Scientiarum Fennica, 2009.

—— '"Hard it is to stir my tongue": Raiding the Otherworld for Poetic Inspiration', forthcoming in Reallexikon der Germanischen Altertumskunde Ergänzungsband. Berlin: De Gruyter.

Towill, Edwin S., 'The Isle of Youth and the Baculus Iesu', *Folklore* 90 (1979), 53–65.

Tudor, Victoria, 'Reginald's *Life of St Oswald*', in Stancliffe and Cambridge 1995, pp. 178–94.

Turville-Petre, J. E., 'Hengest and Horsa', *Saga-Book of the Viking Society* 14 (1953–7), 273–90.

Vries, Jan de, *Altgermanische Religionsgeschichte*, 2nd edn, 2 vols. Berlin: Walter de Gruyter, 1956–7.

—— *Altnordisches etymologisches Wörterbuch*, 3rd edn. Leiden: Brill, 1977.

Wallace-Hadrill, J. M., *Early Germanic Kingship in England and on the Continent*. The Ford Lectures, 1970. Oxford: Clarendon Press, 1971.

—— *Bede's 'Ecclesiastical History of the English People': A Historical Commentary*. Oxford: Oxford University Press, 1988.

Watson, W. J., *The Celtic Place-Names of Scotland*. New edition with introduction by Simon Taylor. Edinburgh: Birlin, 2011 [1926].

White, Roger, and Philip Barker, *Wroxeter. Life and Death of a Roman City*. Stroud: Tempus, 1998.

Williams, Ifor, with J. E. Caerwyn Williams, *The Poems of Taliesin*. Medieval and Modern Language Series 3. Dublin: Dublin Institute for Advanced Studies, 1968.

Wright, Neil, 'Geoffrey of Monmouth and Bede', *Arthurian Literature* 6 (1986), 27–59.

Index of Biblical References

General Index

www.ingramcontent.com/pod-product-compliance
Lightning Source LLC
Chambersburg PA
CBHW022014090426
42739CB00006BA/129